BURT FRANKLIN: BIBLIOGRAPHY AND REFERENCE SERIES 382
Selected Essays in History, Economics & Social Science 90

Volume I.

THE

COURSE OF EXCHANGE;

AND ON THE

PRESENT DEPRECIATED STATE

OF THE

CURRENCY.

Volume II.

THE EFFECTS

PRODUCED BY THE

EXPENDITURE OF GOVERNMENT*

DURING THE

RESTRICTION OF CASH PAYMENTS.

OBSERVATIONS

ON THE

PRINCIPLES WHICH REGULATE

THE

COURSE OF EXCHANGE;

AND ON THE

PRESENT DEPRECIATED STATE

OF THE

CURRENCY.

By WILLIAM BLAKE

BURT FRANKLIN
NEW YORK

Published by BURT FRANKLIN
235 East 44th St., New York, N.Y. 10017
Originally published: London, 1810
Reprinted: 1969
Printed in the U.S.A.

Library of Congress Card Catalog No.: 77-80229
Burt Franklin: Bibliography and Reference Series 382
Selected Essays in History, Economics & Social Science 90

ADVERTISEMENT.

THE first intention in writing the following pages, was to animadvert on some opinions relating to the principles of political economy, which had met with a very general circulation, through the medium of several well-written pamphlets on the depreciation of the currency.

It became irksome, however, and seemed but an invidious task, to select from works that possessed generally a very high degree of merit, a few particular passages, merely to dwell upon their errors; and the author therefore determined to arrange his own thoughts upon the subject, in an order that might admit of his incidentally commenting upon such opinions of other writers, as appeared to be in opposition to his own.

It will perhaps be but too apparent that these remarks upon the principles of exchange have been written and sent to the press, with more haste than is altogether consistent with the respect due to the public; and the author would willingly have delayed the publication till he had an opportunity of revising and correcting the style : but the circumstances of the present moment seem so peculiarly suited to a Treatise of this nature, that he has not been deterred by personal considerations, from communicating his opinions to the public, on a subject which has long occupied his attention.

In the execution of his plan, his endeavour has been, to

hold a middle course between such a conciseness as might be incompatible with perspicuity, and that degree of superfluous illustration which might appear to insult the understanding of his readers.

He is not without hopes that he may escape being classed with those " who, while they imagined that they themselves " had made important discoveries, uniformly found that " no discoveries had been made by their predecessors ;" for the author neither pretends to discoveries himself, nor denies that merit to others. If the following observations have any claim upon the public attention, it can arise solely from the attempt to discriminate, more accurately than has hitherto been done, the operation of causes that have been long known, and frequently discussed ; but which have not met with so distinct and detailed a consideration as the author deems essential to a due comprehension of the subject.

May 1810.

OBSERVATIONS,

&c. &c. &c.

INTRODUCTION.

THE principles which regulate the exchange will be investigated in the simplest manner, by an arrangement that may lead the mind gradually from the separate consideration of the individual causes by which it is influenced, to the more complicated results that arise from their combined operation.

The effects of the exchange are first practically felt, when the intercourse between foreign nations has rendered it necessary to make a remittance from one country to another.

The usual mode of making a remittance, either for the discharge of debts previously existing, or for the purpose of investing it in foreign produce, is to purchase and transmit, to the person to whom the remittance is to be made, a foreign bill of exchange.

A foreign bill of exchange is an order addressed to some person residing abroad, directing him to pay a déterminate quantity of foreign currency to the person in whose favor it is drawn. The quantity, therefore, to be paid, is fixed by the sum specified in the bill ; but the amount of British currency to be given here, for the purchase of the bill, is by no means fixed, but is continually varying, from causes which it is the object of this essay to explain.

When the market price of foreign bills is high, the exchange is said to be unfavorable, because a larger sum will be required for discharging a given amount of foreign payments. When the market price is low, the exchange is said to be favorable, because the discharge of the same amount of foreign payments will be effected by a smaller quantity of British currency. Whatever therefore affects the price of a foreign bill, will affect the state of the exchange.

Now the price of bills will depend, in the same manner as that of any other commodity, upon two causes:

First, on their abundance or scarcity in the market, compared with the demand for them; and secondly, on the value of the currency in which they are to be paid, compared with the value of that with which they are bought.

If there be a certain quantity of foreign bills in

the market, and at the same time a great demand for making foreign payments or investments, the holders of bills will soon feel the effect of the competition for their purchase, and will refuse to part with them, except an additional price be given as a premium. If, on the contrary, there be an abundant supply of bills in the market, and not much demand for foreign payment or investment, there will be more persons inclined to dispose of bills, than there are persons desirous of purchasing them; and the holders, who wish to convert them into cash, will not be able to sell, except at a discount; so that this variation in the market price might take place, though the value of the currency of the respective countries continued absolutely unchanged.

Supposing, however, the quantity of bills in the market sufficient exactly to supply the demand, and that there are no more persons wishing to sell than there are persons wanting to purchase them, so that any alteration in their price, from this cause, is precluded; yet as the currency of all countries is subject to continual fluctuations in its value, the quantity of British currency to be given for a determinate quantity of foreign currency, at any period of time, will depend upon the comparative value of each. An English guinea may be worth, sometimes, a certain number of guilders, florins, or piastres, and at others a very different number, depending either upon alterations in the value of the guinea, or of the guilder, florin, or piastre. The moment that these alterations take place, the information is communicated from one part of the mercantile community to the other, and the price of foreign bills is regulated accordingly.

The rate of the *computed* exchange, then, will vary from two causes, totally distinct from each other. The first, arising from the abundance or scarcity of bills in the market, is the foundation of what may be called the *real* exchange, which depends upon the payments a country has to make, compared with those it has to receive, and has no reference to the state of the currency.

The second, arising from alterations in the value of the currency, is the foundation of what may be called the *nominal* exchange, which has no reference whatever to the state of debt and credit of the country. And as the effects, which the *real* and *nominal* exchange have upon the general dealings and commerce of the country, are as distinct as their causes, the natural mode of investigating the subject will be to follow the order which this division points out; and after tracing the operation of the *real* and *nominal* exchange independently of each other, to consider their combined effect, in treating upon the *computed* exchange.

OF THE REAL EXCHANGE.

IN order that the consideration of the *real* Exchange may be kept perfectly distinct from that of the *nominal*, let it be supposed, during the review of this subject, that the Coin of any two countries that have intercourse with each other is in a perfect state, as to purity and weight; and that the proportion which the quantity of currency bears to the commodities to be circulated by it in the respective countries, continues unchanged, so as to exclude any alteration in its value.

In the commercial dealings which take place between any two nations, the surplus produce of the one will be exchanged for the surplus produce of the other. When neither of them imports from the other to a greater amount than it exports to the same country, the debts and credits of each will balance; and there will be no difficulty in making remittances from one to the other, without the actual transfer of Bullion or money : for as the Bills drawn *by* the merchants exporting produce would exactly equal, in amount, the Bills drawn *on* the merchants importing produce, their mutual debts and credits would be easily liquidated by the transfer of Bills of Exchange; and as the supply of Bills would be equal to the demand for them, they would neither bear a premium, nor be at a discount, and the *real* Exchange would be said to be at par.

At any particular period of time, however, it may happen that a nation may have imported to a greater amount than it has exported, and consequently have more payments to make than to receive. If at that time payment were demanded, the balance due from the debtor country could only be liquidated by the transfer of money or Bullion; and the merchant, rather than incur the expense of the freight insurance and commission attending its conveyance, will be induced to give more for a Bill of Exchange, than the sum for which it is drawn. A competition will be thereby created among the purchasers of Bills upon the creditor country, and they will bear a premium in proportion to the demand. In that country, on the contrary, there will be more persons holding, than there are persons wanting Bills, and the excess above the demand can only be converted into Coin or Bullion by sending them to the place upon which they are drawn. But this Bullion or Coin cannot be conveyed to the creditor, without his paying the expense of its transit; and the holder of a Bill in the creditor country, if he be desirous of converting it into money, will be content to receive something less than its amount. There will therefore be in the creditor country a competition to sell, and Bills will be at a discount in proportion to the supply. The premium in one country will correspond with the discount in the other.

Whatever, therefore, affects the proportion between the payments to be made, and those to be received, will alter the state of the *real* Exchange.

This proportion varies principally from the following circumstances: first, from the effects of favorable or unfavorable seasons creating a difference in the customary supply of the annual produce of the land: secondly, from the alterations which take place in the amount of the foreign expenditure of a country, arising either from the expenses of foreign establishments and expeditions, subsidies to foreign powers, or remittances to absentee proprietors.

The population of the countries that have commercial intercourse with each other, though it may vary considerably in long periods of time, is not subject to any sudden changes from year to year; the wants, therefore, for annual consumption may be considered as nearly constant; but the supply of those wants depending principally on the annual produce of the land, will vary to a very great extent. If in any particular country there should be a failure in a commodity which is also the common growth of the neighbouring countries, the deficiency will be supplied, in a greater or less degree, by an increased importation; and where the failure takes place in an article of the first necessity, as for instance, in corn, which forms the principal part of the food of the people, the importation will be augmented nearly in proportion to the extent of the deficiency. The average amount of annual imports will in these cases be exceeded, and the ordinary proportion of payments between the country and foreign nations proportionably affected; and though the effects of the failure of a corn crop, from its magnitude, and its being an article of the first necessity, are most apparent, an alteration similar in kind, but not in degree, will be induced by a failure in the produce of any commodity to the use of which a country has been long habituated. In an article of mere luxury, the deficiency of its produce, by occasioning an increase of its price, may contract the consumption, and thus cause the value of the quantity exported or imported to be in a certain degree uniform; yet it may be easily conceived that a combination of circumstances would, even in commodities of less necessity than corn, lead to an unusual export or import, and therefore materially affect the state of debt and credit of a country.

The second circumstance, which has been stated

as affecting the payments and receipts of a country, is the variation in the amount of its foreign expenditure, under which head may be included, the charge of maintaining its foreign establishments, civil and military, subsidies to foreign powers, and the remittances to absentee proprietors; the last of which it may be sufficient merely to mention, since they must bear so very small a proportion to the sum total of the foreign expenditure of a great nation, that any variations in their amount would scarcely have a perceptible effect upon the general state of its payments and receipts. On the contrary, the subsidies to foreign powers, and the expense of maintaining the civil and military establishments abroad, may vary, in times of war, to an enormous extent.

Now this expenditure may be supplied either by the export of Bullion or Specie; by purchasing foreign Bills in the home market, and sending them to the place where the money is wanted; or by authorising the agents abroad to draw Bills upon the government, and discount them at the place where they are drawn, upon the best terms that the Bill-market will allow.

By the export of Bullion or Specie the expenditure would be at once defrayed, without creating any debt against the country, and therefore without producing any effect upon the *real* Exchange; but there are various reasons why this mode has not been generally adopted. In the first place, the quantity of Bullion or Specie in a country which has no mines of its own, is exceedingly limited, and the total amount that can be spared or procured for exportation will bear a very small proportion to the foreign expenditure arising from protracted warfare. In the next place, there must always be a certain expense of insurance and freight attending its transport; and whenever, therefore, foreign Bills can be procured at a less premium than the amount of that expense, or Bills on the government abroad can be negociated at a less discount, the vehicle of Bills will necessarily be preferred to that of Specie or Bullion.

The foreign expenditure of this country, as appears by the account presented to the Committee of Secrecy by Mr. Long, in 1797, was principally paid by the draft of Bills from the Continent upon England. A debt is thus created against the country equal to the amount of the Bills drawn upon the government, which must exist, in a greater or less degree, till the whole of those Bills are liquidated by the remittance of value of some kind or other. Whatever, therefore, be the proportion between the payments to be made, and those to be received, at any period of time, arising from the ordinary commercial dealings; whatever be the quantity of Bills in the home or foreign market, which are, in fact, the evidences of that proportion; the foreign expenditure of government must derange the natural state of the balance, and produce an alteration proportional to its amount *. If the Bills be drawn from abroad, they will increase the quantity of British Bills in the foreign Bill market, and lower their value from their abundance. If the foreign Bills be purchased at home for the purpose of remittance, the competition of government will immediately raise their price, and increase their scarcity. Whether the *real* Exchange, therefore, at the time of the expenditure taking place, be favorable or unfavorable, it will always be the less favorable, or the more unfavorable, in consequence of that expenditure.

We have hitherto been considering the demand for foreign Bills, as originating wholly in the necessity of liquidating balances arising from transactions that had already taken place; but there is another cause of demand, which springs from the desire of entering upon new commercial specula-

---

* See the examination of Mr. Huskisson before the Committee for enquiry into the policy and conduct of the Expedition to the Scheldt; where he states the difficulty of making the remittances to Austria without lowering the Exchange, which was already from 18 to 20 per cent. against this country.

See also Mr. Moore's Narrative of the Campaign in Spain, and the difficulty of negociating Bills there, for the supply of the army in that country.

tions, whenever the relative prices in the home and foreign markets are such, as to afford the prospect of an adequate profit. If the current *real* prices abroad are low, compared with those in the home market, there will be an increased demand for foreign Bills, for the purpose of making foreign investments; and the extent of this demand will be in proportion to the probable amount of the profits to be derived, and the unemployed capital that will admit of being diverted into that channel. As soon as a foreign price-current is received, it is compared with the price-currents at home, and the conduct of the merchant is regulated accordingly. If commodities abroad be relatively cheap, there will be more purchasers than usual of foreign Bills; if they be relatively dear, there will be fewer purchasers than usual; and thus whatever be the *real* Exchange under any given balance of payment to be made, and payment to be received, the arrival of a foreign price-current, or an alteration in the home price-current, will have an instantaneous effect upon the foreign Bill market; and the weekly, and sometimes daily, fluctuations in the course of the *real* Exchange, are attributable principally to the variations in this species of demand.

It must not be inferred, however, that because the prices of commodities cause a fluctuation in the course of the *real* Exchange, that therefore the

real Exchange causes a fluctuation in the prices
of commodities. The prices of commodities in
the home market (upon the supposition to which
we constantly adhere, that the value of the currencies throughout the mercantile republic remains
unaltered) cannot depend upon the number of
foreign Bills in the same market, but upon the
abundance or scarcity of the commodities themselves, compared with the real demand for them,
that is, the wants of consumers; and it is essential
that this peculiar feature of the *real* Exchange
should not escape the reader's attention, since it
forms one of the leading distinctions between the
real, and the *nominal* Exchange, and is the cause
of the great difference of their effects upon the
general exports and imports of the country.

It may, then, be stated generally, that, whenever there is a balance of debt against a country,
arising, either from an excess of imports over exports, a large foreign expenditure of government,
or the remittance of foreign subsidies; whenever,
in short, there is a demand for foreign payment, or
foreign investment, the price of foreign Bills will
rise, and may bear a premium; and the price of
Bills drawn on the country from abroad will fall,
and be at a corresponding discount; and, on the
contrary, when there is a balance of debt due to
a country, and a diminution of demand for foreign
payment or foreign investment, the price of Bills

drawn from abroad will increase, and may bear a premium; and the price of foreign Bills will fall in the home market, and may be at a discount.

What effects the *real* Exchange has upon the general exports and imports of the country, it will now be proper to enquire.

The merchant is regulated in the conduct of his business, by a comparison of the prices which commodities bear in the home, and foreign market; his attention is directed to the prices current, accounts of which are constantly published, and immediately communicated by his correspondents abroad. If he finds that the price of any commodity abroad is so much higher than the price of the same commodity in the home market, that its sale abroad will pay the expences of freight and insurance, and at the same time leave him an adequate profit for his trouble, he will immediately purchase and export the commodity in question. As soon as the bill of lading has been received by his correspondent to whom the goods are consigned, he will draw his Bill upon him for the amount; and if the *real* Exchange be at par, will have no difficulty in procuring money equal to the value specified in the Bill, by negotiating it in the market at home. But if the *real* Exchange should not be at par, it is evident that his calculation upon the profit he is likely to derive from the export, must include the premium, or discount, which he will receive, or pay, in the disposal of his Bill. If the Exchange is unfavorable, or, 'in other words, if the payments to be made are greater than those to be received, foreign Bills will bear a premium; and consequently, the additional sum which he will receive on the disposal of his Bill, will enable him to export with profit, though the difference of prices of the commodity at home and abroad were such, as would not allow him to export, with the *real* Exchange at par. The more unfavorable the *real* Exchange, the less might be the difference of prices that would induce him to export; so that an unfavorable state of the real Exchange will operate as a bounty upon exportation, to the amount of the premium, which he will receive upon his foreign Bill.

The same calculation upon the state of the *real* Exchange will be necessary, if the difference of prices at home and abroad should lead him to import. But whatever be the state of the *real* Exchange, it will affect the importing merchant, and the exporting merchant, in a directly opposite manner: for the importing merchant must pay for the goods he imports, either by purchasing a foreign Bill to remit to his correspondent abroad, for which, if the *real* Exchange be unfavorable, he must pay a premium; or, if his correspondent abroad is authorised by the importing merchant to draw a Bill upon him for the payment of the goods consigned, as that Bill cannot be converted into money without a loss, he must draw for such an additional sum above the invoice price of the goods, as will counterbalance the discount to be allowed in negotiating his Bill in the foreign market.--- This additional sum, therefore, paid by the importing merchant in the premium of the foreign Bill, or drawn for by the correspondent to make up the loss on the discount, will be so much deducted from his profit. Unless, then, the difference of prices at home and abroad be such as to admit of this deduction, the merchant must cease to import; so that an unfavorable *real* Exchange will operate as a duty upon importation, in proportion to the premium on a foreign Bill, or the corresponding discount on the Bill drawn from abroad; and in the same manner it is easy to see, that a favorable *real* Exchange will operate as a duty upon exportation, and will afford a bounty upon importation.

An unfavorable *real* Exchange will, therefore, have the effect of forcing the exports of a country; because, during its unfavorable state, the merchant can afford to sell at a lower price to the foreign consumer, and this diminution of price will naturally lead to an increased consumption. It will contract imports, because the importing merchant must sell foreign produce at a higher rate to the home consumer, to draw back the duty imposed upon him by the unfavorable state of the *real* Exchange, and consequently the high price will diminish the home consumption.

It is evident that during an unfavorable state of the *real* Exchange, the bounty received by the exporting merchant does not depend upon the nature of the commodity he exports. Whatever kind of goods he sends abroad, it gives him the power of drawing upon the person to whom he consigns them, to the amount of their value; and upon this Bill he receives the premium that the market affords. He will of course select those commodities for exportation, which, besides the premium afforded by his Bill, will give him the greatest profit, by the difference of price abroad and at home. Of all the commodities, which are the objects of request among trading nations, there is none perhaps that is subject to so little variation in its *real* price, as Bullion. The annual quantity produced from the mines is very nearly constant,---its distribution, from the facility with which it is transported, is exceedingly uniform,---and its value, and consequently its real price, throughout Europe at least, must be considered as nearly the same. Unless, then, the bounty afforded by the unfavorable state of the *real* Exchange, were greater than the expenses attending the transit of Bullion, it would be of all others the commodity * least likely to be selected by the exporting merchant : but that same uniformity of value and of price, which would prevent its being exported before the premium on a foreign Bill exceeded the expenses of the transit of Bullion, would be the very cause, why, as soon as the premium had reached that point, it would immediately be chosen as one of the most eligible for exportation.

The export and import of Bullion are generally conducted by a class of the community remarkable for their shrewdness, and the small profits upon which they transact their business ; and as soon as the premium on a foreign Bill exceeds, by a very small amount, the expenses of the transit of Bullion, the certainty of the profit compensates in some degree for its smallness, and the opportunity, when it occurs, is seldom neglected. The adverse debt will then begin to be paid, by the Bullion merchants exporting to take advantage of the premium ; and the competition will be such, that the *real* exchange will be very rapidly brought down,

---

* Mr. Thornton, apparently from not being aware of the mode in which the export of ordinary produce was increased by an unfavorable *real* Exchange, seems to imagine that the greater part of the adverse balance must necessarily be paid in Bullion. (pp. 131 to 134.)

so as no longer to afford a profit upon the export of this article. The exporters of consumable produce will during this period co-operate with the Bullion merchants ; and when the latter have ceased to derive a profit, the former will still continue their operations, till the unfavorable Exchange is reduced to par, or, in other words, till the exports have been such, as to counterbalance the adverse debt, and render the quantity of foreign Bills in the market equal to the demand.

From this statement it is obvious, that the natural limit to the amount of the *real* Exchange is the expense of the transit of Bullion ; and long before it has arrived at that point, the export of ordinary produce will be forced, and its import restrained ; so that the *real* Exchange can scarcely begin to deviate from par, without calling into action a principle that will correct its deviation. It may oscillate a little on the one side, or the other, from its point of rest, but can hardly admit of remaining either permanently favorable, or permanently unfavorable, to a nation, in the ordinary course of its transactions *.

---

* This observation must be understood to apply to the general balance that subsists between any one nation, and the whole of those with which it has commercial intercourse ; it being evi-

It must not be inferred, however, because the expense of the transit of Bullion is the limit of the *real* Exchange, that it is therefore a fixed limit, and capable of being estimated at a certain percentage on the price of a foreign Bill : for when the *real* Exchange has caused a transit of Bullion to any considerable degree, it will at length create a difference in the market price of Bullion itself. This article will become scarce in the country from which it is sent, and abundant in that into which it is flowing. Its price will rise in the former, and fall in the latter. The exporter, therefore, will then have to calculate the difference of prices in the home and foreign market; and if in the first instance the profit were out just sufficient to induce him to export, it is clear that after the change has taken place, the exportation of Bullion, under the same rate of Exchange, will cease.

Mr. Boyd, in his evidence before the Secret Committee of the House of Lords, in 1797, respecting the mode of remitting the Imperial loan to Vienna, states, " that he thought the remit- " tances by Bills of Exchange were not quite " so favorable as those in Bullion ; but, if he had

---

dent that where a nation trades with more than one country, the *real* Exchange may be constantly favorable with one, provided it be constantly unfavorable with another.

" stuck exclusively to Bullion, the price of this
" article would have risen so high here, and
" probably sunk so low at Hambro', that in-
" stead of a good, it would have become a bad
" remittance." The limit therefore of the *real*
Exchange can only be fixed at a certain rate,
upon the supposition that the price of Bullion
is the same in the home and the foreign market;
for when the *real* price of Bullion abroad is less
than it is at home, the transit of Bullion will not
take place, unless the rate of Exchange be sufficiently high, not only to pay the expenses of
transit, but also to compensate for the loss attending the difference of home and foreign prices.
When, on the contrary, the price of Bullion
abroad is higher than in the home market, it is
equally evident that Bullion will be exported, when
the *real* Exchange is less than the expenses of the
transit of Bullion.

And thus it is that a very small part of the payment of an unfavorable balance is effected by the
transit of Bullion, since its transit can scarcely
begin to take place, without rendering it a more
unprofitable article of export than ordinary consumable commodities. For the former cannot,
generally speaking, be considered as a commodity
the consumption of which will be augmented by a
diminished price, its use being confined to the
wealthy few, who are not likely to encrease the

D

quantity of their plate, or indulge themselves more freely in the purchase of ornamental manufactures, from the temporary variations in the market price of Bullion: but it is not so with ordinary produce. The great mass of mankind will always endeavour to purchase their comforts at the lowest possible rate. If by means of an unfavorable Exchange our merchants can supply the nations of the Continent with British manufactures, cheaper than when the Exchange is at par, our manufactures will be bought and consumed; and in proportion to the degree in which the Exchange is unfavorable, in the same proportion, shall we be enabled to enter more easily into a competition with the manufacturers abroad, even in their own market.

A possible case may, nevertheless, be supposed, where the government may, from political causes, be induced to continue a scale of warfare, demanding a larger foreign expenditure than can be supplied by a proportional excess of exports over imports; and, consequently, if the quantity of Bullion in the country were extremely limited, the *real* Exchange might, notwithstanding the usual causes that check and prevent its fluctuations, deviate so much from par, and create so great a drain of Bullion, as to raise its market price above its mint price.

It is certain that the Bullion merchants would in that case, rather than pay the advanced market price, endeavour to collect the current Coin for the purpose of exportation. A pound of gold at the English mint is coined into forty-four guineas and a half, or 46*l*. 14*s*. 6*d*. * By exchanging, then, bank-notes at the Bank, for coin, they can always procure a pound of gold for 46*l*. 14*s*. 6*d*. in notes; and so long as they have this power of purchasing gold at the mint price, at the Bank, they will not give a higher market price elsewhere. If the paper, therefore, be convertible into Coin at the option of the holder, the Bullion merchants will be constantly pouring in their notes upon the Bank, to be exchanged for Coin, which will be exported † as fast as it can be procured; and thus a drain upon the Bank will be

---

* Throughout this pamphlet, the Author, in speaking of Bullion, has confined his observations to Gold Bullion only; first, because the Gold Coin is now the only one in which a legal payment can be made for debts above 25 *l*. in amount; and, secondly, because he has derived considerable assistance from, and had frequent occasion to refer to, Mr. Mushet's valuable Tables of the Exchange between London and Hambro', since the year 1760, in which the price of Gold Bullion only is noted.

† It is true the laws have affixed most severe penalties to the melting or exporting the current Coin of the realm; but these penalties have always been found insufficient for its protection, the Coin having uniformly disappeared, whenever either of the above practices has been attended with an adequate profit.

established, to a greater or less extent, in proportion to the amount of foreign payment that must be discharged ; before the *real* Exchange is sufficiently elevated to prevent any profit upon the export of Bullion. As long as this drain continues, the Bank will be compelled to purchase Bullion, and to coin, for the purpose of supplying the demand occasioned by the return of its notes; and as the purchase must be made at the then market price, it is evident that in whatever degree that shall exceed the mint price, the Bank must sustain a loss proportional to the difference; and that a continuance of the drain, under such circumstances, might eventually lead to its ruin.

It was upon this ground that the Directors of the Bank, in the year 1795, remonstrated in so urgent a manner against any further loans to the Emperor; lest the drains, which those loans occasioned, should prove fatal to that establishment. In a letter from the Directors to Mr. Pitt, dated October 8, 1795, after observing upon the continual drain that the loan to the Emperor had occasioned; they proceed to state, " that the present " price of gold being from 4*l.* 3*s.* to 4*l.* 4*s.* per " ounce, and our guineas being to be purchased " at 3*l.* 17*s.* 10½*d.*, clearly demonstrates the " grounds of our fears, it being only necessary to " state these facts to the Chancellor of the Ex-

" chequer *." Now those very facts ought to have
led Mr. Pitt to suspect, that the drain upon the
Bank, at that time, arose from some other cause
than the loans to the Emperor; for it has been
already shewn how impossible it is, that the Bullion merchant should for any length of time continue the export of Bullion, without increasing
the quantity abroad, and lowering its price so
much, that it would no longer afford a profitable
speculation. Mr. Pitt should have recollected,
that for the last twenty-one years from 1774,
when the reformation in the gold Coin took place,
though the *computed* Exchange between Hambro'
and London had frequently been so unfavorable to
London, as far to exceed the expenses of the
transit of Bullion, the quantity required for export had been so easily supplied, either from the
spare Bullion, or from the export of the Coin, that
the market price of bullion had never exceeded the
mint price, except only for about six months, at
the time of the peace of Versailles, in the year
1733; and then only by about 3*s*. 2½*d*. in 100*l*.,
not much more than $\frac{1}{700}$th part. Now as during a
great part of that period, the country was engaged
in active warfare, which would cause, from the
variations in the amount of the foreign expenditure, occasional demands for large foreign pay-

---

* P. 152, Secret Committee of the House of Lords, 1797.

ments, one would have expected, that such an excessive increase of the market price above the mint
price, as was asserted by the Bank Directors to
have taken place, amounting to 7*l.* 4*s.* 5½*d.* per
cent. being forty-five times greater than any variation that had occurred in the former war, would
have led him to receive their remonstrances with
considerable suspicion.

If, in addition to this, he had called to mind
that the excess of the market price above the mint
price, could be accounted for, and might have
taken place, though no loan to the Emperor had
been in a course of remittance; that the excess of
the market price of Bullion over the mint price had
existed to a very great extent, attended with a
drain upon the Bank, prior to the year 1774, when
the gold currency was degraded below its standard weight; that the drain, under such circumstances, would have equally existed, though there
had been no demand for the exportation of Bullion,
(as will be fully explained, in the Section upon the
Nominal Exchange;) it seems unaccountable that
he should so easily have yielded to the representa-
tions of the Directors; and it is the more to be
lamented, since the impressions he then received,
seem to have had considerable influence in producing the fatal measure of permanent restriction
on Bank payments, which began in the year 1797,
only fourteen months after this period.

But assuming it to be the fact, that the foreign expenditure at that period was greater than on any former occasion, and that the real cause of the drain was that assigned by the Bank Directors, still they had the means of prevention within their own power; for it will be shewn, in the next Section, on the *nominal* Exchange, that when the currency of a country consists partly of Paper, and partly of Coin, and that the former bears a large proportion to the latter, the Bank can at all times contract the issue of its notes, and produce a considerable diminution in the total amount of the currency. By this means the *nominal* prices of commodities, and amongst the rest, that of Bullion, will be lowered. As soon, therefore, as a reduction has thus been effected in the price of Bullion below its mint price, the drain upon the Bank will at once be stopped; since it will no longer be the interest of the Bullion merchant to purchase gold at the mint price, by exchanging notes at the Bank, when he can procure it at a cheaper rate in the market. The Bank Directors were so well aware of this mode of counteracting the effects of a drain upon them, that they had recourse to it at the very period of making their remonstrances; and the market price of Bullion, which had been 9*s.* 7*d.* per cent. below its mint price, in the beginning of the year 1795, and which probably might never have been raised, had not the Bank, at this period, extended its paper from 11 to 13½ millions, was, by the subsequent contraction of it to 9½ millions, again reduced, before the middle of the year 1796, to 9s. 7d. below the mint price. Unfortunately too for the country, this same counteracting principle was resorted to, when the drain took place in the beginning of the year 1797, arising, not from a demand for bullion for the purpose of exportation, nor from an excess in its market price above the mint price, neither of which existed at the time *; but solely from the alarm occasioned by the fears of invasion;---a drain that will always occur under similar circumstances, and which will be aggravated, rather than relieved, by a contraction of paper.

It should be carefully remembered, that the profit from the export of Bullion in consequence of an unfavorable *real* Exchange, does not arise from Bullion selling for a higher price in the foreign than in the home market, nor from any scarcity of Bullion abroad occasioning an extraordinary demand for it; but solely from the demand for

---

* In January 1797, the *computed* Exchange between Hambro' and London was 5l. 4s. per cent. in favour of London, and during the year rose to 13 per cent; it never being, at any part of the year, less than 3l. 2s. in favour of London. The market price of Bullion, at the same period, was never above its mint price.

foreign bills, for the purpose of making foreign payments, being so great, that the premium upon them exceeds the expenses of the transit of bullion; and, consequently, the transit will take place and afford a profit to the exporter, though the price of bullion be precisely the same abroad as it is at home.

When such a quantity of bullion has been exported as to raise its market price above the mint price, the coin being obtainable at the mint price, will be exported in preference to bullion; not in consequence of any depreciation in the value of the coin, for it will purchase the same quantity of ordinary produce after the rise of the price of bullion as before; nor because it is more valuable abroad than it is here, for it will not purchase more in the foreign than the home market; but it will be exported, for the same reason that the bullion is exported, to take advantage of the premium on foreign bills, and will be sent, though the price of bullion be precisely the same in the continental market as the English mint price.

After what has been stated, it will be sufficiently apparent, upon what a false foundation the old notions respecting the advantages of a favorable balance of trade are built, and how futile all attempts must be to procure and detain bullion, beyond the quantity that is actually wanted for consumption. The transit of bullion from a high or low *real* exchange is an unnatural transit, not arising from the wants of the country into which it flows, but depending solely on the profits which a temporary pressure for foreign payments affords to the bullion merchants on the sale of foreign bills; and as soon as the cause that has produced the temporary influx subsides, (an event that will sooner or later necessarily take place, by the import of such ordinary produce as is wanted for the purposes of consumption, and increased enjoyment of the people,) the superfluous and unused quantity of bullion that has been accumulated, will flow back from the country where its abundance has rendered its real price low, to those nations from which it had been unnaturally sent, and where its scarcity will have rendered its real price high.

Much of the confusion that attends this question would have been avoided, had the dealers in bills of exchange, and the dealers in bullion, (that is, the persons who export or import bullion for the supply of consumers,) been two distinct classes of merchants. It would then have been seen that the profits of the dealer in bills of exchange flowed through very different channels from those of the deal r in bullion. If at any time the course of exchange were such as to afford a profit to the bill merchant by the sale of foreign bills, he would export that bullion which had been imported for the use of the manufacturer, and would continue to export till it no longer afforded a profit. The bullion dealer would then begin to re-import, in consequence of the difference of prices in the home and foreign markets, the bullion that the bill merchant had sent away, in consequence of the high premium on foreign bills. Whatever derangement the bill merchants might occasion in the quantity of bullion that would be otherwise naturally distributed among the different countries according to their wants, would be remedied by the operations of the bullion merchants, who would find their advantage in restoring the equilibrium that the bill merchants had destroyed.

The dealer in bills of exchange would have employment, when there was the least difference between the prices of bullion in the home and foreign market, and the *real* exchange at the the greatest deviation from par.

The bullion dealer would be most engaged, when there was the greatest difference in these prices, and the *real* exchange at its least deviation from par.

Had this distinction been attended to by Lord King, he would never have entertained such erroneous opinions respecting the exports of silver from this country to India, nor have considered them as indications of an exchange constantly in favor of England against the Continent; for he would have seen, that the export of bullion is not regulated merely by the speculations of the dealers in bills of exchange, but is effected, like that of any other commodity, when there is such a difference in its real prices at any two places, as will afford a profit on its transit; an occurrence that will frequently take place, even with an exchange at par.

OF THE NOMINAL EXCHANGE.

THE market price of a foreign bill has been stated to depend upon two circumstances:—first, on the scarcity of bills in the market compared with the demand for them; and secondly, on the value of the coin or currency in which they are to be paid, compared with the value of the coin or currency with which they are bought.

The first of these, as connected with the *real* exchange, formed the subject of the foregoing Section; we shall now proceed to examine the nature and effects of the second, on which depend the alterations of the *nominal* exchange; and as in treating of the *real* exchange we endeavoured to keep the subject as distinct as possible from the question of the *nominal* exchange, by supposing no alteration to take place in the value of the currencies in the respective countries; so in tracing the effects of the *nominal* exchange, we shall suppose the state of the *real* exchange to remain unaltered; or the mutual dealings and intercourse between the nations composing the great mercantile republic to be such, that the price of foreign bills is not affected by any variation in their abundance or scarcity, but that the supply of them is constantly sufficient to answer the *real* demand.

In this case the variations in their price can arise only from changes in the comparative value of the currencies in which they are paid, and those with which they are bought.

It will not be necessary, therefore, to enter into any enquiry respecting those changes which have taken place from the discovery of the American mines, or which have arisen from any cause that would affect all currencies in an equal degree; since the object is not to compare the value of currencies now, with what they were at any former period, but to estimate the local alterations that have taken place in the currency of one country, without a corresponding alteration in that of others.

The currency of every nation is subject to continual fluctuations in its value, principally from three circumstances.

First, An alteration in the quality and standard purity of the metal of which the coin is formed.

Secondly, An alteration in the quantity of the metal contained in coin of the same denomination.

Thirdly, An alteration in the total amount of the currency of a country, without a corresponding alteration in the commodities to be circulated by it.

The first of these is now seldom resorted to in a civilized country, even under the most pressing necessities of the government.

The second has been frequently adopted by princes and sovereign states, who through a mistaken policy have imagined that they derived a benefit from diminishing the quantity of metal contained in their coins. The English pound contained, in the time of Edward the First, a pound of silver. The French livre contained a pound weight of silver, in the time of Charlemagne. The English pound contains, at present, only one third, and the French one 66th part of their original value *; but I believe, except in Turkey, there is no instance of this practice being countenanced by any of the modern governments. The

---

* Smith's Wealth of Nations, vol, i. p.39.

metallic currencies, however, of most nations, even where the governments have been desirous of maintaining them in a state of the utmost possible perfection, have been much diminished in value by being worn from use, and clipt or otherwise degraded by the illicit practices of the people. To avoid the confusion that would follow from the constant fluctuations in the value of currencies, merchants have adopted a mode by which they endeavour to estimate the extent of these fluctuations; and for this purpose, have ascertained with tolerable accuracy, in what quantities of coin of the mint standard in different countries, an equal weight of gold or silver of the same standard fineness is contained. Thus it has been determined, that a pound sterling of the English mint contains the same weight of silver, of a certain fineness, as 33 schillings 8 grotes * of the Hambro' banco-

---

* From the evidence before the Secret Committee of the House of Lords, in the year 1797, it appears that there is a difference in the mode of estimating the par of Exchange with Hambro'; the house of Goldsmid considering 33. 8. and Mr. Boyd's 34. 8. as the par of Exchange. The difference seems to have arisen, from the former estimating the par according to the standard of Hambro' banco money; the latter, according to the actual currency of Hambro' which appears to be more than 3 per cent. below the standard of the banco money. Upon this supposition there is less difficulty in reconciling the apparent contradiction, that 3 schillings above the par, has the same

money; and in speaking of the exchange with Hambro', 33. 8. is in the technical language of merchants said to be the par of exchange. In the same manner the par of exchange with France is fixed at 24, because 24 livres of the mint standard of France contain the same weight of silver, of a certain fineness, as the pound sterling of the English mint.

By means of this rule, the merchants of one country would never be at a loss to estimate what quantity of their own money would be equivalent to a specific sum of foreign money, so far as regarded the weight of metal, provided the coins of the respective countries contained the due weight of their respective mints. But in some countries the coins are more, in others less worn, and clipt or otherwise degraded below the mint standard. When these alterations have taken place, it would be necessary either to establish a new par of exchange,

---

effect, one way, upon the transit of gold, that 4 grotes below par has the other; a fact that was stated by Mr. Goldsmid's partner, but which he was unable satisfactorily to explain.

If the Hambro' currency were so much degraded below the banco money, that 35 schillings 4 grotes currency were worth no more than 33 schillings 8 grotes banco money, there would be a *nominal* Exchange of 1 schilling 8 grotes against Hambro', for every pound sterling; and if the par is estimated at 33. 8, 4 grotes below that sum, and 3 schillings above it, would be equally distant from the *real* par of 35 schillings 4 grotes.

to guide merchants in their money transactions,
or, as is now the general usage, not to alter the
par of exchange, but to mark the fluctuation of
the currency, by considering it as so much above
or below the established par. In King William's
time, before the reformation of the silver coin,
(silver being then the metal in which the payments
of the country were legally made,) the current coin
was rather more than 25 per cent. below its standard value. The established par, however, was not
altered, but the exchange was said to be 25 per
cent. against England *. Before the reformation
of our gold coin in 1774, the guinea contained so
much less than its standard weight, that it was degraded 2 or 3 per cent. when compared with the
French coin at the same period ; and the exchange
between England and France was then computed
to be 2 or 3 per cent. against this country ;---upon
the reformation of the gold coin, the exchange
rose to par. The Turkish government, in the
course of the last forty years, has made three great
alterations in its coin. Before these frauds were
committed, the Turkish piastre contained nearly
as much silver as the English half crown; and in
exchange, the par was estimated at 8 piastres to
the pound sterling. The consequence of these

---

* Smith's Wealth of Nations, vol. ii. p. 216.

repeated adulterations has been, the reduction of the silver in the piastre to one half, and a fall in the exchange of 100 per cent., bills on London having been bought in Turkey, in 1803, at the rate of 16 piastres for every pound sterling*. Now though it is not absolutely conclusive, that these alterations in the *computed* exchange were entirely owing to the fluctuations in the value of coin, because the *real* exchange at the time might not be constant; yet the correspondence of the difference of exchange, with the acknowledged degradation of the coin, renders it more than probable, that the fall of the *computed* exchange arose from an alteration in the *nominal* exchange only.

It is unnecessary to enter further into the detail of the consequences that arise from the degradation of the coin below its mint standard. As soon as that degradation (which never can remain long concealed) is discovered, the inconveniencies that would otherwise attend the commercial intercourse are obviated by a corresponding alteration in the *computed* exchange; and though during the continuance of the degradation, the *nominal* exchange will remain permanently unfavorable to the country in which it prevails, it will be immediately restored to par, by a reformation of the circulating

---

* Foster, on Commercial Exchange, p. 93.

medium. We will therefore, in the remaining part of this enquiry into the nature and effects of the *nominal* exchange, suppose, that the currencies are not degraded below their mint standards, and confine our observations to the third cause, which has been stated to affect the value of currencies, viz. the ratio, which the total amount of the currency in one country bears to the commodities to be circulated by it, compared with the ratio that the currencies of other countries bear to the commodities which they are respectively employed to circulate. It is the fluctuation from this cause, which at present principally affects the *nominal* exchange.

Had the currencies of commercial states been confined to the precious metals only, it is scarcely possible that any increase of currency, more than was demanded by the wants of increasing wealth, could have taken place in countries that had no mines of their own. As the metals of which the coin was composed must have been purchased at their value, no possible motive can be conceived, that would induce the holder of bullion to convert it into coin, unless there was a real demand for it. The circulating medium of modern times no longer consists of the metals only, almost all nations having adopted, on a greater or less scale, the use of paper currency, issued, generally, under the sanction of government, by corporate bodies or banks, who are responsible for the payment of it in specie on demand. As the profits of these corporate bodies or banks are in proportion to the quantity of the paper they can permanently keep in circulation, there can be no doubt, that every effort consistent with prudence, will be made to augment that quantity. But it is impossible that such an increase can take place in the quantity of any commodity that is given in exchange for others, whose quantity is not augmented in the same proportion, without affecting their comparative value. If the currency of a country is increased, while the commodities to be circulated by it remain the same, the currency will be diminished in value with respect to the commodities, and it will require a larger proportion of the former to purchase a given quantity of the latter; or, in other words, prices will rise. If we were in the habit of considering money as purchased by commodities, instead of commodities being purchased by money, the diminution in the value of money from its abundance, would be immediately apparent. " Mr. " Thornton admits, in the most explicit manner, " that if the quantity of circulating medium is " permanently augmented, without a correspond- " ing augmentation of internal trade, a rise will " unavoidably take place in the price of ex- " changeable articles. Indeed this is a principle " upon which all the writers on Commerce, both

" practical and speculative, are agreed : they have
" thought it so undeniable as to require no par-
" ticular illustration, and have rather assumed
" it as an obvious truth, than as a proposition
" that depended on inference. Upon this idea is
" founded Mr. Hume's well-known argument
" against banks, and it is equally implied in Dr.
" Smith's confutation of that objection; it forms
" the foundation of those presumptions from which
" Mr. Boyd has lately inferred an improper in-
" crease of Bank of England paper; and it is im-
" plicitly admitted, likewise, by Mr. Thornton,
" one great object of whose book is to persuade the
" public that there has been no such increase *."
Without entering, therefore, into an unnecessary
argument, I shall, for the present, assume as
admitted, that the increase of currency, while the
commodities to be circulated remain the same,
will be attended with an increase of nominal
prices, and a correspondent depreciation in the
value of money.

Now it is impossible, when the currency of a
country has been thus depreciated, that the same
amount of it should purchase the same sum of
foreign money as before its depreciation. A
foreign bill, or an order for payment of a

---

* Edinb. Review, v. i. p. 178.

given sum of foreign money abroad, will not be sold, unless for such an increased amount of the depreciated currency, as will counterbalance the dimunition of its value. Foreign bills will, therefore, bear a premium, in proportion to the depreciation.

In the same manner a bill on the country where the currency is depreciated will be bought abroad, where money retains its value, for a much less *nominal* sum than the amount for which it is drawn; or, in other words, will be at a discount. Suppose, for instance, that the coins being in the utmost state of perfection in England and France, and the *real* exchange at par, the augmentation of the total amount of the currency in England were such as to raise prices here, to double their former amount, it would require, in that case, twice the sum to purchase the same commodity in England that would be required in France. The same *nominal* sum would, therefore, be only of half the value:---24 livres in France would purchase an order for the payment of 2*l.* sterling in England, and the *nominal* exchange, would be 100 per cent. against England.

An augmentation of currency that affects prices, cannot take place without a corresponding alteration in the *nominal* exchange. Merchants, from the average sale of the produce which they receive and remit, and from the uninterrupted correspondence which they hold with each other, expressly for the communication of the prices current, have not much difficulty in distinguishing those fluctuations which are owing to the partial abundance or scarcity of a few articles, from that general increase of price which denotes a depreciation of currency;---or should they, from want of experience, be tempted to engage in commercial speculations, from a difference of prices not depending upon the *real* demand, but arising merely from an over-issue or contraction of currency, the loss upon their returns would infallibly teach them more caution in future.

After the par of exchange, therefore, has been established, an alteration in the value of currency, whether it arises from a debasement of the coin below its standard, a diminution of weight below the mint regulation, or depreciation of its value from relative over-issue, will alike affect the price of a foreign bill, and be made evident by an unfavorable *nominal* exchange.

It now remains to trace the operation of the *nominal* exchange on the several exports and imports of the country.

When foreign bills bear a premium from an unfavorable *nominal* exchange, it appears advantageous, upon a superficial view of the subject, to export produce, in consequence of the profit arising from the sale of the bill, which the merchant would be authorised to draw upon his correspondent abroad. But a very little consideration will shew that there is, in this respect a striking difference between the *real* and the *nominal* exchange.

It is true that the merchant will obtain a premium upon his bill, but it is this premium which alone enables him to export. The same cause that has given rise to this premium, has increased the *nominal* prices of the articles, which he buys, for the purpose of exportation, in the home market; whatever he gains upon the bill, he loses in the purchase of his goods. The merchant, therefore, must calculate what is the difference at home and abroad, in the real prices of commodities, by which I mean the prices at which those commodities would be bought and sold, if no depreciation of currency existed. If those prices are such, as to admit of a profit, the merchant will continue to export, whether the *nominal* exchange be favorable or unfavorable ;---that circumstance can make no difference whatever in his transactions.

Suppose, for instance, the currencies of Hambro' and London being in their due proportions, and therefore the *nominal* exchange at par, that sugar, which from its abundance in London sold at 50*l.* per hogshead, from its scarcity at Hambro' would sell at 100*l.* The merchant, in this case, would immediately export. Upon the sale of his sugar, he would draw a bill upon his correspondent abroad for 100*l.* which he could at once convert into cash, by selling it in the bill-market at home, deriving from this transaction a profit of 50*l.*, from which he would have to deduct the expenses of freight, insurance, commission, &c. Now suppose no alteration in the scarcity or abundance of sugar in London and Hambro', and that the same transaction were to take place, after the currency in England had been so much increased that the prices were doubled, and consequently, the *nominal* exchange 100 per cent. in favor of Hambro'. The hogshead of sugar would then cost 100*l.* leaving, apparently, no profit whatever to the exporter. He would, however, as before, draw his bill on his correspondent for 100*l.*; and as foreign bills would bear a premium of 100*l.* per cent. he would sell this bill in the English market for 200*l.* and thus derive a profit from the transaction amounting to 100 depreciated pounds, or 50*l.* estimated in undepreciated currency; deducting, as in the former instance, the expenses of freight, insurance, commission, &c *.

---

* The reader will observe how much the nominal income and apparent profits, of the merchant are increased by the depreciation of the currency.

The case would be precisely similar, *mutatis mutandis*, with the importing merchant. The unfavorable *nominal* exchange would appear to occasion a loss amounting to the premium on a foreign bill, which he must give in order to pay his correspondent abroad. But if the difference of *real* prices in the home and foreign markets were such as to admit of a profit upon the importation of produce, the merchant would continue to import, notwithstanding the premium; for that would be repaid to him in the advanced *nominal* price at which the imported produce would be sold in the home market.

Suppose, for instance, the currencies of Hambro' and London being in their due proportions, and therefore the *nominal* exchange at par, that linen which can be bought at Hambro' for 50*l*. will sell here at 100*l*. The importer immediately orders his correspondent abroad to send the linen, for the payment of which he purchases at 50*l*. a foreign bill in the English market, and on the sale of the consignment for 100*l*. he will derive a profit amounting to the difference between 50*l*. and the expenses attending the import.

Now, suppose the same transaction to take place, without any alteration in the scarcity or abundance of linen at Hambro' and London, but that the currency of England has been so augmented, as to be depreciated to half its value. The *no-*

minal exchange will then be 100 per cent. against England, and the importer will not be able to purchase a 50*l.* foreign bill for less than 100*l.* But as the prices of commodities here will have risen in the same proportion as the money has been depreciated, he will sell his linen to the English consumer for 200*l.* and will, as before, derive a profit amounting to the difference between 100*l.* depreciated money, or 50*l.* estimated in undepreciated money, and the expenses attending the import.

The same instances might be put in the case of a favorable exchange; and it would be seen in the same manner, that *nominal* prices and the *nominal* exchange being alike dependent upon the depreciation of currency, whatever apparent advantage might be derived from the former, would be counterbalanced by a loss on the latter, and *vice versâ.*

For the very same reasons that the *nominal* exchange produces no alteration in the imports or the exports of ordinary produce, it can have no effect on the export or import of bullion. Nothing can be more evident, than that bullion must be subject to the same variation in its prices from an alteration in the value of currency as any other commodity. If the value of currency is diminished, the prices of all commodities must advance,

and that of bullion among the rest *. How then is
the profit of the merchant, from the export of
bullion, to arise? Is it not evident that upon an
unfavorable *nominal* exchange, whatever premium
he may gain upon his bill, as much will be lost in
the advanced price which he must pay for the
bullion?---Yet all writers upon the subject of political œconomy, that I have met with, seem to be
persuaded, that when the rate of exchange has
deviated from par beyond the expenses of the
transit of bullion, bullion will immediately pass;
and the error has arisen, from not sufficiently distinguishing the effects of a *real*, and a *nominal* exchange. This false opinion seems to have been
strongly impressed upon all the merchants and Bank
Directors who were examined before the Secret
Committee of the Houses of Lords and Commons,
in the year 1797; nor does Mr. Pitt himself appear to have been exempt from its influence. Mr.
Bosanquet expressly declares his opinion " that the
" favorable state of the exchange afforded a pros-

---

* " Bullion is a commodity, and nothing but a commodity,
" and it rises and falls on the same principle as all other com-
" modities. It becomes, like them, dear in proportion as the
" circulating medium for which it is exchanged is rendered
" cheap; and cheap in proportion as the circulating medium
" is rendered dear."---(Thornton, Paper Credit, p. 202.)

" pect of purchasing foreign gold, and setting the
" mint at work," (p. 32. Com. H. of Lords, &
passim.) Now it is absolutely impossible that an
exchange, arising from depreciation of currency,
can have any effect upon the export or import of
bullion. For supposing the *nominal* exchange at
par, and the *real* prices of bullion in London and
Hambro' precisely the same, it is clear there could
be no motive to export bullion, but that, on the
contrary, it would be attended with the certain
loss of the expenses of transit. Every thing else,
then, remaining the same, let the currency in
England be augmented so that the prices of commodities shall rise 4 per cent. and bullion of course
among the rest; the depreciation of the currency
will immediately be indicated by an unfavorable
nominal exchange of 4 per cent. Is it possible
that the bullion merchant can be deluded with
the idea, that he can derive any benefit from a
premium of 4 per cent. upon his bill, when he
purchases bullion here at an advanced price, and
sells it at Hambro' 4 per cent. lower? Does he not
lose as much from the difference of prices, occasioned by the depreciation, as he gains by the
premium on his bill, occasioned by the same depreciation; and consequently subject himself to all
the expenses attending the transit, in the same
manner as when the *nominal* exchange is at par?

For the same reason, there would be no advantage derived from the import of bullion if the *nominal* exchange were favorable. Suppose it were 4 per cent. in favor of this country;---it is evident that money here would be 4 per cent. more valuable than at Hambro'; prices, therefore, would be 4 per cent. lower, and foreign bills in the English market would be at 4 per cent. discount. Under those circumstances, if foreign bills were purchased to be invested in bullion at Hambro', and the bullion were sent here, would it not be sold in the English market at 4 per cent. less than was given for it at Hambro'? thus destroying every advantage derived from the *nominal* exchange, and subjecting the importer to the same loss, as in the former instances. Is it then to be wondered at, that with such opinions as the Bank Directors seem to have entertained, they should be so totally at a loss to reconcile the facts with their false theory respecting the export and import of bullion? During the course of the year 1796, for eleven months previous to the Bank restriction, the exchange had been, with only two exceptions, favorable; and at the end of February 1797, was so high as considerably to exceed the expenses of the transit of bullion; yet when Mr. Raikes, on the 13th March, was examined before the Secret Committee of the House of Com-

---

* Secret Committee of the House of Commons, p. 23

mons, he acknowledged, that measures had been taken by the Bank to procure a supply of bullion, but without effect, as it could not be imported except at a considerable loss. On the 14th, Mr. Bosanquet stated to the same Committee, that the influx of bullion is occasioned by a favorable exchange; that the exchange had not been unfavorable for many months; and, when asked whether the importation had been such as it ought to have been, considering the state of the exchange, replied *, " I am not able " to answer these kind of questions." The fact is, that the *nominal* exchange might for years continue in favour of a country, and not cause a single ounce of bullion to flow into it, or have any effect upon the general state of exports and imports, which would proceed in their usual course, regulated only by the wants of consumers, and the supply of commodities †.

It is in vain therefore to look for any remedy for a high *nominal* exchange from any alteration in the

---

* Secret Commiitee of the House of Commons, p. 28.

† It is not to be inferred, that because the *nominal* exchange has no effect on the general exports and imports, that therefore the country sustains no injury ; the contrary of which will be shewn, in treating of the foreign expenditure of government, and the unequal pressure that the depreciation occasions on the different classes of the community.

exports and imports of a country. When it arises from a degraded state of the coin, a new coinage immediately restores it to par;---when it arises from the augmentation or contraction of currency, the restoration of the currency to a due proportion with the commodities to be circulated by it, will be the true and only remedy.

In what manner this restoration of the currency to its level is effected, it will now be proper to enquire.

In all countries the weight of bullion contained in any specific quantity of coin issued at the mint is determined by law. At the English mint, a pound weight of gold is coined into 44½ guineas, which, at 21s. the guinea, is equal to 46l. 14s. 6d. or 3l. 17s. 10½d. per ounce. This is said to be the mint price of gold in England, or the quantity of coin which the mint returns for standard gold bullion. An ounce of gold, therefore, so long as it remains in the shape of coin, can never be worth more than 3l. 17s. 10½d. because while it retains that form, it cannot be legally tendered in payment for more than that sum. As soon therefore as an over-issue of currency has raised the prices of all commodities, and that of bullion among the rest, the weight of gold contained in any specific quantity of coin will sell for a higher *nominal* value in bullion, than it will pass for in the form of coin, or, as it is usually expressed, the market price of bullion will exceed the mint price, and there will be a profit attending the conversion of coin into bullion proportionate to the difference of the *nominal* value. Accordingly, the conversion immediately takes place, requiring very little greater excess of the market price above the mint price, than will pay for the fire that is to melt the coin. The operation is so simple, and requires so little apparatus, that it may be performed with the utmost secresy, and no penalties of the law, or vigilance of the officers of the Mint or Bank, have ever been found adequate to its prevention.

To account for this, there is no necessity for supposing a demand for bullion abroad. It is the conversion, that prevents the currency from ever exceeding the due proportion that is wanted for the purposes of circulation: for it can * never exceed that proportion, without augmenting the *nominal* price of bullion, and affording, as long as there is a superfluous quantity, a profit to the melter.

It is true that the same conversion may take

---

* The reader will apply the proper limitation to this general assertion, which is not meant to convey the idea that the effect will be instantaneous, or that it may not be counteracted by other causes, but that the over-issue of currency will have this tend ency, and that ultimately the *nominal* price of bullion will be raised above its natural price, in proportion to the over-issue.

place, by exporting the coin to any foreign country, where it will be estimated according to its
weight in bullion, and pass for its intrinsic value;
and probably this circumstance has led so many
writers to assign the capability of the transit of
coin, as the reason why currency convertible into
coin can never be depreciated by excess. But it
is evident that, of the two modes of conversion,
that by melting will be preferred, since it will be
unattended by any expenses of transit. If the
market price of bullion in London were 4 per cent.
above its mint price, in consequence of the depreciation of currency, while at Hambro' there was
no depreciation whatever, 100 guineas conveyed
to the latter place would purchase the same value
in commodities that 104 guineas would do in London; but as the expense of sending them would
amount to 3 per cent. *, there would be a profit
to the exporter of one guinea only; whereas the
100 guineas, melted in London, would immediately sell in the market for 109l. 4s., leaving a
clear profit of four guineas by the operation. It
is absurd, then, to suppose that any man would
expose himself to the penalties of the law, by exporting coin for a profit of 1 per cent., when with-

* The expense, as stated by Mr. Eliason, is 3l. 12s. 11d. per
cent..---Evidence Secret Committee House of Lords, 1797, p. 96.

out subjecting himself to severer penalties, he might, by melting it, secure a profit of 4 per cent.

It is the melting, therefore, in consequence of the high market price at home, and not the export in consequence of a high *nominal* exchange, that will cause the disappearance of the coin. It is true, that after the melting has proceeded for some length of time, (unless indeed the melted coin be purchased for the purpose of being re-coined,) there will be a gradual accumulation of bullion beyond what may be wanted for consumption; and this abundance may render the commodity so cheap, that the bullion merchant may find his advantage in exporting it, in consequence of the difference of the *real* prices in the home and foreign markets. But this exportation is the effect of the melting, and not the cause of it. It is not a demand for the exportation of bullion that has caused the melting of the coin; but the coin being melted, to take advantage of the high *nominal* price of bullion, has lowered its real price so much, as to afford a profit upon its exportation. It is by no means necessary, however, that the bullion produced by the melting should be exported, since there may be a greater demand for bullion at home, for the purposes of manufacture, than there is abroad. The melter will always derive his profit by selling the melted coin at the high market price, which the bullion merchant

will be equally ready to give, whether he sell to
the home manufacturer, or the foreign---whether,
at the time, he be effecting the import or the export of bullion.

A want of attention to this distinction, so essentially necessary towards a just conception of the
principle, which regulates the quantity of currency and the increase of prices, has led to some
very erroneous opinions respecting what is called
the universal level of currency : for it has been
maintained by many writers upon political economy, and implied by almost all, that specie
leaves the country where it is depreciated in consequence of the inferiority of its value to the currency of other countries * ; that if the currencies of

---

* This error pervades Mr. Wheatley's Work on the Theory of
Money and Principles of Commerce. He was well aware of the
fact, that specie is frequently exported in consequence of an unfavorable exchange ; but as he does not admit of any alteration
in the exchange, from the abundance or scarcity of foreign bills,
(which is the real cause of the export of specie, when it does
take place,) he attributed the effect, to the difference in the value of currencies ; and thence inferred, that the export of coin
was the remedy for its depreciation---a principle, that leads at
once to the conclusion, that prices might be indefinitely augmented, if the currencies of all nations were proportionally
increased.

Mr. Ricardo and Mr. Mushet have fallen into the same error,
respecting the export of specie, and do not seem to be aware,
that the alteration in prices, from over-issue or contraction of

other nations were depreciated in an equal proportion, there would be no advantage attending the export; and that upon the supposition of the currency being proportionally increased throughout the world, prices might be universally and indefinitely augmented; whereas the export has no relation whatever to the value of currencies in other countries, but arises entirely from the relative value of gold in the form of coin, and in the form of bullion.

The coin of this country, when sent abroad, passes only for its intrinsic value, according to its weight, and it will not be sent abroad from an unfavorable *nominal* exchange, unless its value in the shape of bullion is greater than its value in the form of coin. But the real value of bullion on the Continent is no more affected by the depreciation of the currency there, than it is here. If there be a profit upon the export of coin from this country at a time when the currency is depreciated here, and is not depreciated upon the Continent, there would be the same profit, if the currency of the Continent were depreciated also; for the market

---

currency, has no effect upon the exports and imports of ordinary produce; since they uniformly describe commodities as flowing from the nominally cheap, to the nominally dear market, without adverting to the counteracting effects of the *nominal* exchange.

price of bullion, at which our exported coin would then be sold abroad, would be so much higher in proportion to the depreciation of the foreign currency. Suppose that the currency at London and Hambro' being in their due proportions, and the *nominal* exchange at par, the *real* price of bullion corresponds in both places with the English mint price. Let the currency at London be depreciated by over-issue 4 per cent. ; the market price of bullion at London would then exceed the mint price 4 per cent., and the nominal exchange would be unfavorable to the same amount. Under those circumstances, a merchant exporting 100*l.*'s worth of specie to Hambro', and drawing a bill upon his correspondent, would gain 1 per cent. by the transaction : for the specie, on its arrival at Hambro' where the market price of bullion, according to the hypothesis, corresponds with the English mint price, would sell in the bullion market for 100*l.* The English merchant would therefore draw for 100*l.* ; and, foreign bills bearing a premium, would sell his bill in the English bill market for 104*l.*, which, after deducting 3 per cent. for the expenses of transit, would leave him a profit of 1*l.* per cent. Now suppose the currency at Hambro' to be also depreciated to the amount of 4 per cent.; the nominal exchange will then be at par, but the market price of bullion at Hambro' will exceed the English mint price 4 per cent. The 100*l.*'s worth of

specie will sell at Hambro' for 104*l*.; the merchant will therefore draw upon his correspondent
for 104*l*., and the exchange being at par, will
procure 104*l*. for his bill in the English bill market;
and deducting 3 per cent. for the expenses of
transit, he will obtain a profit of 1*l*. per cent. as
before.

It has been already demonstrated that bullion
will not be exported under an unfavorable *nominal*
exchange, merely in consequence of that exchange; and the reason why specie is exported
under the same circumstances, is, that the coin,
while it remains here, passes for less than its worth,
and that abroad it passes for its real value;---in this
country it forms a part of the currency, and partakes
of the depreciation,---abroad, it passes as bullion,
and is relieved from the depreciation. But it is
quite clear that even in the export of specie, there
would be no profit whatever, unless its depreciation were greater than the expenses attending its
export; and therefore were there no other remedy
for a depreciated currency than the export of specie, the *nominal* exchange might for any length of
time continue unfavorable, to an extent somewhat
less than the expenses of the transit of bullion.
But the fact is, that no such continuance of an
unfavorable exchange, even to that extent, can
take place, so long as the currency is capable of
being converted into bullion: for as soon as the

depreciation is evinced by an elevation of the market price of bullion above the mint price, that moment the conversion of the superfluous currency commences ; and it depends upon the comparative demand for bullion, in this country, and the demand upon the continent, whether the melted specie be exported or not.

It must be admitted, that, as soon as the depreciation has exceeded the expenses of the transit of specie, and thus afforded an option as to the mode of converting it into bullion, the foreign merchant, by buying abroad the bills upon England, which will necessarily be at a discount, and ordering his correspondent to whom he sends the bills, to invest them in English specie, will be enabled to procure bullion at the English mint price. So that as long as he can dispose of the bullion at that price abroad, he will derive a profit equal to the excess of the discount at which he has bought the English bills, above the expenses of the transit of specie. But it having been already shewn, that the profit on melting always exceeds the profit on exporting, by the amount of the expenses attending the export, it can never be believed that a merchant would collect the current coin, and by exporting it, subject himself to the penalties of the law, for the sake of obliging his foreign correspondent, and enabling him to acquire a profit of 1 per cent., when by melting the same coin, he might himself, with less risk, obtain a profit of 4 per cent.

Again, if the *nominal* exchange were rendered favorable, 4 per cent. by a forced contraction of the currency, and the price of bullion were lowered with that of other commodities, so as to be 4 per cent. below the mint price; would any merchant purchase foreign bills at a discount of 4 per cent., and send them to Hambro' to be invested in foreign coin, for the sake of gaining 1 per cent. upon its import, when, by employing the same capital in the purchase of bullion in the home market, and converting it into coin at the mint, he would derive a profit of 4 per cent.?

The only case in which a superior advantage would be obtained from the export of specie, rather than from the conversion of coin into bullion, or from the import of specie rather than the conversion of bullion into coin, would be, when the over-issue or contraction of the currency had created a premium or discount of 4 per cent. on foreign bills, without producing an alteration of 1 per cent. in the market price of bullion. But it has been already shewn, that the nominal price of bullion is raised or lowered in the same manner as that of other commodities, to which it would otherwise no longer bear its natural relative value. Such an occurrence, therefore, if possible, can be but temporary, and does not affect the general argument.

Where the currency consists partly of coin, and partly of paper convertible at option into coin, it is for the same reason absolutely impossible that it can continue permanently in a state of depreciation : for should the Bank be so imprudent as to issue notes beyond the demands of increasing wealth, as soon as the augmentation of prices, and a consequent unfavorable *nominal* exchange, denoted the depreciation of the currency, the market price of bullion would exceed its mint price, and all that portion of the circulating medium which could be converted into bullion would begin to disappear. The paper of the Bank would be returned to be exchanged for coin, which would be immediately melted, and sold in the form of bullion, for notes, at the advanced nominal price. These, in their turn, would be sent to the Bank to be in the same manner exchanged for coin, which would be melted and sold as soon as procured.

Now this process might be going forward, and continue to drain the Bank of its gold, without the slightest demand for bullion abroad, or without any demand for foreign payments. It would equally take place, though the country were receiving payments instead of making them---though it were importing bullion instead of exporting it. Should the Bank persist in its over-issue, and still endeavour to throw the same quantity of notes into circulation, the Directors would be compelled to purchase bullion, and coin it into guineas, in order to supply the drain occasioned by the return of their notes; and as Mr. Thornton states, "they "will have to do this at the very moment when "many are privately melting what is coined. "The one party might be melting and selling, "while the other is buying and coining; and each "of these two contending businesses will be car-"ried on, not on account of an actual exportation "of each melted guinea to Hambro'; but the ope-"ration, or at least a great part of it, will be con-"fined to London---the coiners and melters living "on the same spot, and giving constant employ-"ment to each other *."

Mr. Winthorp, in the evidence he gave before the Secret Committee of the House of Commons in 1797, (p. 46 and 47,) concluded that because there was a drain upon the Bank, there must necessarily be a drain upon the country; and stated "his belief that the coffers of the Bank ge-"nerally shew whether money is coming into or "going out of the country." I should hope it would be unnecessary, after what has been already

---

* Thornton on Paper Credit, p. 125.

Mr. Thornton admits that the melting is not always connected with the export of bullion; but as the object of his Book was to shew that the currency was not depreciated, it was impossible for him to give even a plausible explanation of this part of his subject, without attributing the effect to an unfavorable *real* exchange.

observed, to offer any thing further in refutation of such opinions. The drain upon the Bank will begin under any circumstances, whenever the depreciation of currency from over-issue has raised the market price of bullion above its mint price; and it will continue, till the loss which the Bank must suffer by the purchase of bullion to supply the drain, shall compel the Directors to diminish the number of their notes, so as to bring back the currency to its natural level. The price of bullion will then fall to its mint price, and no longer afford a profit on being melted; the *nominal* exchange will invariably mark the amount of the depreciation during its continuance; and when the depreciation ceases, the *nominal* exchange will rise to par.

The adoption of a paper currency, therefore, can never be injurious to a country, so long as it is convertible at option into specie. The temptation to its over-issue will always be sufficiently checked by the principle that has been just explained; and, independently of the convenience of making the larger payments, it will certainly be advantageous to carry on the circulation of a country by a cheap, rather than a costly, machinery.

It is obvious, that as the nominal prices of commodities will be increased by the over-issue of currency, so, for the same reasons, the contraction of it below the natural wants of circulation, will diminish the *nominal* prices in the same proportion. A smaller quantity of currency will then measure the same value, and the nominal exchange will be favorable to the country where the value of the currency is increased. This is an event that does not often occur; for as the profits of a bank that issues paper-money depend upon the quantity it can circulate, the directors of the establishment will generally take care that the supply shall not be less than the demand. When the market price of bullion, however, has from any cause been elevated above the mint price, the Bank has always the power of giving the currency an artifical value by a diminution of its total amount; and it is evident that by such a diminution, the price of bullion will be lowered in the same proportion as that of any other commodity. Bullion will then be of less value in the market than in the form of coin, and the merchant will carry it to the mint, to obtain the profit attending its conversion into specie. If, under such circumstances, there should be a demand for bullion for the purpose of exportation, this would evidently occasion no drain upon the Bank, while it could be procured at a cheaper rate in the market; and should the demand for exportation continue so long as to raise the price of this commodity, in consequence of its scarcity* the

---

* The scarcity here spoken of refers only to the partial-scarcity

Bank would always have the power by a greater contraction of its currency, to lower its *nominal* price, and thus preserve the superiority of its value in the form of coin over its value in the shape of bullion.

It is thus that the value of the currency is made to correspond with that of the precious metals of which it is composed, or into which it is convertible; and as long as they continue to be the standard by which the value of other commodities is estimated, the circulating medium of the whole mercantile republic will suffer no permanent alterations, but what arise from the variation in the intrinsic value of the precious metals themselves.

It is some proof of the truth of these positions respecting the uniformity of the value of currency, that from the period of the reformation of the gold coin in 1774, to the year 1797, the *computed* exchange between London and Hambro' was generally in favor of the former, arising, probably, from the superiority of our coin; and that it seldom varied, except in 1793, more than 5 per cent. on the one side or the other of par. In

---

arising in particular countries from the temporary unequal distribution of bullion, and not an actual scarcity arising from a permanent diminution of the usual quantity produced at the mines.

that year the *computed* exchange rose to 10 and
11 per cent. in favor of this country, owing to
the sudden contraction of currency that took
place in consequence of the run upon and failue
of the country banks, at the breaking out of the
French revolutionary war, which had the effect
of raising the *nominal* value of the currency here
to the degree indicated by the favorable exchange. During the whole of this period the
market price of bullion never exceeded its mint
price, except in the year 1783, by the very trifling
amount that has been already specified; and in
the year 1795, when the Bank had extended its
paper from less than 11 to upwards of 13 millions
and a half.

After this review of the subject, and the strong
evidence which presents itself that the currency
of a kingdom, whether consisting of coin only, or
partly of coin and partly of paper, can never be
augmented beyond its due proportion, so long as
the paper is convertible at pleasure into specie---
can any one for a moment doubt of the result,
should this salutary check be removed, and at the
same time the paper currency be made a legal
tender for the payment of debts*?

---

* By the Restriction Act, bank notes are not absolutely a legal tender; but if a tender be made in notes, the debtor cannot
be arrested.

Without this latter provision, motives of prudence might induce the Bank so to restrain its issues, as not to create an open discount upon its notes, and thus introduce a paper and a money price for commodities; but under the protection now afforded by the Restriction Act, there is no reason why it should not push the issue of this currency to the utmost possible limit, and particularly if there be a confidence in the public, that sooner or later the notes will be convertible into gold. There is no doubt, that with respect to the Bank of England this confidence is strongly felt by the public, and with good reason. Bank of England notes are never issued but for a valuable consideration, being principally advanced either upon Exchequer bills or in discounting the bills of merchants. Unless, therefore, the government is unable to redeem the former, or the merchants should be incapable of paying the latter when they become due, there must always be sufficient funds in the Bank to answer the demands upon it*. The depreciation from over-issue is therefore by no means necessarily connected with any want of confidence in the resources of the Bank, but rests upon an en-

---

* There must in fact be more than sufficient, since the value of the outstanding notes must be less than that of the bills upon which they were issued, by the amount of the interest deducted at the time they were discounted.

tirely different foundation, and might equally take place, whether the currency consisted partly of coin and partly of paper, or was composed entirely of the former: for it is not the paper only, but the whole currency, both the paper and the coin, so long as it remains in the form of coin, that is depreciated by over-issue. But as the latter is convertible into bullion by melting, it will be consigned to the crucible, for the purpose of removing the depreciation that it suffers, while it constitutes a part of the currency.

The advocates for the Bank restriction triumphantly ask, how it is possible that the notes can be depreciated, if 100*l*. in bank notes will purchase as much as 100*l*. in specie: but the question, as applied to the depreciation of the currency, is absurd; for the notes and the coin are alike depreciated *, and therefore exchange, as before, for the

---

* This opinion is controverted in the Edinbro' Review, No. 25, p. 54, apparently, under an idea that, as the price of gold and silver is nearly the same in all the countries of the world, a depreciation of the current specie in this country must necessarily be accompanied by a corresponding depreciation of the currency of all nations upon the face of the earth. But there is a material distinction between the depreciation of the specie, and the depreciation of the gold and silver that forms the specie. The first may be effected by the over-issue of the Bank, but that can have no influence on the *real* value of the bullion, which the specie contains. As an *argumentum ad hominem* against Mr. Thorn-

K

same quantity of produce in the market. But their intrinsic value is not the same, because guineas being convertible into bullion, the one may be relieved from its depreciation by a change in its form ; whereas the other cannot *. This conversion is constantly going on, and must continue till not a piece of coin is left in circulation,

---

ton, it is indeed conclusive, because he imagines the remedy for a depreciated currency consists in the exportation of coin to other countries, where it is not so depreciated. It would be impossible, therefore, for the specie to continue permanently degraded, upon his principles, unless the value of the currency of every other nation were equally so. But it has been shewn that the remedy for depreciated currency from over-issue depends on its conversion into bullion, and not upon its exportation.

The gold and silver currency may therefore fall in value below the level of the currency of neighbouring states, but this cannot be the case with the gold and silver of which it is composed.

* As long as the bank note for a guinea is convertible into gold bullion, at the option of the holder, its intrinsic value may be said to be the same as a guinea. Take away the convertibility, and the intrinsic value of the note is the value of the ink and paper of which it is composed. No banking operation, nor legislative provision, can ever alter the real value of the gold bullion in a guinea; but the number of nominal pounds to be given for that quantity of gold bullion, may be increased in the proportion that the total number of pounds in the currency is increased beyond what is wanted.

unless its weight be so much reduced below the
standard as not to be worth the melting. The
disappearance of the coin is the proof of its depreciation. The reason why the ordinary shop-
keeper does not make a distinction between the
payments made to him in gold, and those which
he receives in paper, is, the confidence he feels
that at some time or other the notes will be paid
in specie, and that he is in the meantime deterred
by the penalties of the law from melting the
guineas---the only mode by which he can derive
a superior profit, from a payment in coin. But
the occupation of melting the specie is nevertheless
followed by a less scrupulous class of the community, who have not hesitated to give a premium for
guineas, whenever an opportunity offered of purchasing them, and of profiting by their conversion,
without danger of detection *. But the difference
in the intrinsic value of the notes and the guineas
is not the less real, because it cannot openly be
avowed. If the coin were allowed by law to be
melted, if the penalties for this offence were less
severe, or if guineas could be collected without
exciting the suspicion of the officers of the Bank

---

* An instance of this has recently come before the public,
in consequence of an information against a person charged
with selling guineas for more than they are allowed to pass for
by law.

and the Mint, neither the Restriction Bill, nor the provision that bank notes may be tendered as legal payment, would prevent a paper and a money price for commodities, and consequently an open discount upon bank paper.

The drain upon the Bank, in the year 1797, is allowed by all the Directors to have arisen from the alarm of invasion. The market price of bullion was, at the time, below its mint price; the exchange with the Continent was in favor of London; and therefore all the causes, that are usually assigned, as creating a drain upon the Bank, were operating in a contrary direction. The alarm originated, according to the evidence given by Mr. Burdon, one of the proprietors of the Newcastle bank, before the Secret Committee in 1797, from the orders that had been issued for taking an account of the stock of the farms of Northumberland, for the purpose of regulating the mode in which the county was to be driven, in case of invasion. The farmers immediately sold their produce at very low prices, and the notes which they received from the purchasers were poured in upon the persons by whom they were issued, to be exchanged for specie; in consequence of which, the banks at Newcastle were obliged to stop payment, and their failure was followed by a similar run upon the country banks throughout the kingdom, many of which were in like manner obliged to stop.

The alarm was communicated to the metropolis, and occasioned a drain upon the Bank, which had already been called upon for considerable advances, in consequence of the run upon the country banks. The distress of the mercantile class, from the great extent of the failures, and the general distrust they occasioned, aggravated by a violent, and therefore improvident, contraction of the usual quantity of bank paper, combined to produce that crisis which terminated in the restriction of cash payments at the Bank. It is unnecessary now to enquire how far this restriction at the time was politic or otherwise. It probably was a measure of prudence; but as the evil was temporary, so also ought to have been the remedy. It might have been expected, that the complete relief of the merchants, and the returning confidence of the people, would have been considered as the signal for discontinuing a law, which has given the Bank Directors a power of permanently altering the value of the circulating medium of the country. It has, however, been decided otherwise; and the consequence has been, that as the fears of the Bank Directors have been dispelled, the quantity of currency has been gradually increased, and has produced all those symptoms, which any person acquainted with the theory of money and exchange would easily have anticipated;---an augmentation in the price of commodities, an increase of the market price of bullion over the mint price, and an unfavourable *nominal* exchange.

The effect of the over-issue of bank-notes upon the *computed* exchange may be visible from comparing the amount of the notes in circulation in the years 1795 and 1797, with the *computed* exchange at the same periods. The amount was augmented in February 1795, to 13½ millions *, and the exchange between Hambro' and London, which was then 6 per cent. above par, fell, before September, to 3½ per cent. against England. In February 1797, the paper in circulation was reduced to 8½ millions, and the exchange between Hambro and London rose to 6*l*. 18*s*. per cent. in favor of England. By the last returns presented to Parliament, it appears that the bank notes now in circulation amount to 21 millions, the market price of gold in November was 15*l*. 8*s*. 2*d*. per cent. above the mint price, and the exchange between Hambro and London 16*l*. 18*s*. per cent. against England.

Should any one still be sceptical on the subject, a short survey of the mode in which the business of the Bank is conducted will probably remove his doubt. It has been already shewn, that so long as its notes are convertible at option into specie, a bank can never permanently keep in circulation more paper than the wants of the country require. But it is not perhaps, quite so clear, in what manner the over-issues of a bank that is

* Secret Committee of the H ouse of Lords in 1797, p.176.

not liable to be called upon for cash payments, will augment the *nominal* prices of all commodities.

The notes of the Bank of England are issued to the merchants who are in want of money, on the security of bills of exchange of not more than 60 days date, which are brought to the Bank for discount.

On the receipt of the bill, the Bank gives to the merchant an equal amount in notes, deducting the interest at the rate of 5 per cent. When the bill is due, the Bank presents it for payment, and receives the amount in full, deriving a profit from the transaction equal to the interest of the notes for the time. The oftener this process can be repeated, and the greater the amount of the notes it lends, the greater will be its profits.--- Now it is evident, that if the purchases of the merchants could be effected by their own bills, it would be unnecessary for them to apply to the Bank for discounts; this application, then, is of itself a decisive proof that the bills of private merchants will not pass in the market with the same facility as the bills of a national Banking Company. The conversion, therefore, of the bills into notes is an increase of currency, which could not take place without the assistance which a bank affords.

Now the merchant regulates the scale of his

transactions by the amount of the capital he can command. The greater the extent of this capital, the larger the profits he will expect to derive from its employment. If he can make a profit of 10 per cent. by his business, he will always be willing to extend it by borrowing capital, for which he is to pay an interest of only 5 per cent. Here then are two parties exactly suited to the supply of each others wants, and co-operating from mutual interest towards the same object. The profits of the Bank are in proportion to the paper currency it can lend, and the expected profits of the merchant are in proportion to the paper currency he can borrow. Under such circumstances it is idle to talk of the Bank Directors having the power to contract their discounts when they perceive there has been an over-issue, unless a motive can be shewn for the exercise of that power. While the Restriction Act is in force, the only rule of their conduct will be the validity of the bills that are offered for discount, and they are bound by the duty they owe to the Bank Proprietors who appoint them, to profit by the facilities thus imprudently granted by the government, and to employ to the greatest possible advantage the funds of which they have the disposal.

It is equally idle to say that the merchant will not employ all the capital he can command, or

that his credit will enable him to borrow *. By
the facilities that are now given to discounts, the
merchants can always, either by immediate application to the Bank by means of their bankers,
or, if in the country, by the intervention of the
country banks, coin their credit into currency,
which will operate upon the markets wherever it
makes its appearance: for the prices of any
given supply of produce will depend upon the
number of purchasers, and the extent of the
capital they can command. The more easily
capital can be procured, the greater will be
the competition in the market. Whenever
the prospect of a profitable speculation offers,
merchants will be eager to embark in it, and
the demand, which, under ordinary circumstances,
would be regulated by the amount of *real* capital
capable of being diverted into that channel, will
now be augmented in proportion to the *fictitious*
capital, called into existence by the facilities

---

* See a whimsical pamphlet published by Mr. Smith on the
Theory of Money. He asks, would bankers and merchants apply
to have good bills discounted at the Bank, if bank notes were
depreciated? The answer to which is obvious. The depreciation
in no way affects the dealings of the merchants; who buy and
sell at the high *nominal* prices, and whose profits are nominally
increased in the same proportion as money is depreciated.

T

afforded from the Bank discounts; and thus an over-issue of notes will immediately take place, creating an additional number of purchasers, or increasing their powers of purchasing in proportion to the over-issue. If the increased currency be employed in a foreign speculation, it immediately acts upon the foreign bill-market, and creating there a fictitious demand, it affects the *nominal* exchange; if it be employed by the bullion-merchant, it raises the market price of that article; if by the home dealer, it augments the prices of native commodities. No sooner has it left the merchants by whose means it was called into existence, than it passes to the wholesale dealers and master manufacturers, who, in their turn, will raise the prices in their respective markets by a competition which is called into action merely by the over-issue.

If the evil were confined to the increased quantity of currency thus thrown into circulation by the Bank of England, it might not be attended with injurious consequences of such magnitude as are now experienced : but the misfortune is, that the same law which protects the National Bank, and enables it thus to derange the natural state of the circulating medium, confers the same power on all the country banks throughout the kingdom, which are now relieved from the fears and inconvenience to which under ordinary circumstances they would be subject, should they at any time be tempted to issue their notes beyond the amount which the wants of their respective districts might require.

The country banks are, in the same manner as the Bank of England, enabled to supply their respective connexions with funds for speculation. If the excess of their paper should at any time excite doubts of their solvency, and create a run, they may be supplied by their correspondents in London with notes from the great central paper mint; and thus are all the lesser establishments throughout the kingdom absolved from every difficulty. They issue their notes almost without limit, and by these means enable the country dealers to enter into speculations and purchases, which, without their assistance, could never have been effected. Can any one then be surprised that prices should rise, when every addition of currency is attended with profit to the Bank by which it is issued; and that there can never be an additional issue of currency without creating additional purchasers to the same amount?

An objection has been urged against this view of the subject, which deserves to be noticed. It has been stated, that if only such bills are discounted at the Bank, as have been drawn in consequence of *bonâ fide* commercial transactions, no additional currency is thrown into circulation, more than the

wants of the mercantile community require; that th
bills so discounted are the representatives of the property, by the transfer of which they are created; and
thus a distinction has been attempted to be drawn
between real and fictitious bills; or, as the latter are
more generally termed, bills of accommodation. But
it will not require much consideration to perceive
that this, as far at least as concerns the over-issue
of currency, is a distinction with little, if any, difference. Mr. Thornton has well observed, that
" notes given in consequence of a real sale of
" goods cannot be considered as on that account
" certainly representing any actual property.----
" Suppose that *A*. sells 100*l*. worth of goods to *B*.
" at six months credit, and takes a bill at six
" months for it; and that *B*. within a month after,
" sells the same goods to *C*. at a like credit, tak-
" ing a like bill; that *C*. after another month,
" sells them to *D*.; and so on: there may, at the
" end of six months, be six bills of 100*l*. each,
" existing at the same time, and every one of
" them may possibly have been discounted. Of all
" these bills, then, one only represents any actual
" property. If the credit given be a credit of twelve
" months instead of six, 1200*l*. instead of 600*l*.
" would have been the amount of the bills drawn
" on the occasion of the sale of goods, and 1100*l*.
" would have been the amount of those that repre-
" sented no property. In order to justify the sup-

" position that a real bill represents actual pro-
" perty, there ought to be some power in the bill-
" holder to prevent the property which the bill
" represents from being turned to other purposes
" than that of paying the bill in question.* "

Now had these bills never been discounted, their
circulation would have been confined to those persons only, with whom the parties, whose names appear on the bill, had credit; and their effect
upon the general currency of the country would in
such case have been exceedingly limited, compared with that which they have in the more negoti-
able form of the notes of a Banking Company.

" One of the motives of the seller who desires to
" have a note for goods sold, is, that he may engraft
" on the transaction of the sale the convenient con-
" dition of receiving from the buyer a discountable
" note of the same amount with the value of the
" goods. A fictitious note, or note of accommoda-
" tion, is a note drawn for the same purpose of being
" discounted, though it is not sanctioned by the cir-
" cumstance of its having originated in an actual
" sale of goods †." The Bank of England professes
to refuse the discounting of any bills except those
drawn for *bonâ fide* mercantile considerations; and
so far as their own interests are concerned, it may

---

* Thornton on Paper Credit, p. 30.   † Ibid.

be a very proper and highly prudent regulation: but to the public, it is of little moment upon what degree of security the Bank may think right to lend its notes; nor can the Directors, with all their vigilance, discriminate between real and fictitious bills. Whether real or fictitious, their conversion into notes will alike augment the currency of the country, which, without the check that has been pointed out in the foregoing pages, may be increased in an unlimited degree. In the case of the real bill, a *bonâ fide* transaction takes place prior to its being converted into currency, in consequence of a credit subsisting between the drawer of the bill and the seller of the goods. In the fictitious bill, for want of that credit between the drawer and the seller, the conversion of the bill into currency takes place in the first instance, and the *bonâ fide* transaction follows.

From what has been stated, the distinction between the *real* and the *nominal* exchange will be sufficiently apparent;---they have been found to differ most essentially, both in their causes and effects.

The *real* exchange has been proved to depend upon the proportion between the foreign payments which a country has to make, and the payments it has to receive.

The *nominal* exchange depends upon the comparative value of currencies.

The *real* exchange has an immediate effect upon the exports and imports.

The *nominal* exchange, whether favorable or unfavorable, has no effect whatever upon exports and imports.

An unfavorable *real* exchange. if its rate be sufficiently high, will cause an export of bullion, and may, under peculiar circumstances, lead to a drain upon the Bank.

An unfavorable *nominal* exchange, whatever be its rate, will not necessarily lead to any export of bullion, but will immediately cause a drain upon the Bank. for the conversion of coin into bullion,

When the market price of bullion exceeds the mint price, in consequence of its export from an unfavorable *real* exchange, the currency is not depreciated. for it bears the same relative value to all other commodities; it is the *real* price of bullion that is raised, from a temporary scarcity.

When there is an excess of the market price of bullion above the mint price, together with an unfavorable *nominal* exchange, the *real* price of bullion is not altered, for it bears the same relative value to all other commodities; it is the currency that is depreciated, from a temporary abundance.

The *real* exchange cannot be permanently favorable or unfavorable, whatever be the state of the currency.

The *nominal* exchange may continue for any

88

length of time favorable or unfavorable, provided
the value of the currency continues to be depreciated.

Now the *computed* exchange depends upon the
combined operations of the *real* and *nominal* exchange, and unless the distinctions just pointed
out are kept constantly in view, it will be impossible to reconcile the contradictory results to which
it appears to give rise.

OF THE COMPUTED EXCHANGE.

THE *computed* exchange is determined by the
fluctuations of the price which a foreign bill bears
in the market, but affords no criterion by which
to distinguish whether those fluctuations arise
from variations in the state of the *real*, or of the *nominal* exchange. As these are perfectly independent
of each other, it is evident that if both are favorable,
or both unfavorable, the *computed* exchange will
denote their sum; but if the one is favorable, while
the other is unfavorable, it will express their difference, and may be at par, though neither the

real or *nominal* exchange are so, provided the un-favorable state of the one be counteracted by the favorable state of the other. Now let any one for a moment consider, what different phœnomena would present themselves under an apparently similar state of the exchange, according to the mode in which that similarity was produced. For the *computed* exchange would be at par, if the *real* and *nominal* exchange were so; that is, if the supply of foreign bills were equal to the demand, and the currencies of other countries of the same value with our own, in which case the exports and imports would proceed in their ordinary course.

It would be at par, though the *real* exchange were unfavorable in any degree, if the *nominal* exchange were favorable in the same degree; that is, if the high price of foreign bills, arising from their scarcity, were counteracted by the superior value of our currency over that of other countries. In this case the unfavorable *real* exchange would induce an increased exportation and diminished importation;—it would occasion a demand for bullion for exportation, without creating any drain upon the Bank; because from the contraction of the currency, the market price of bullion would be below the mint price. Ordinary produce would be cheap, the *real* exchange would be gradually restored to par by the operation of the exports and imports; and the *nominal* exchange would be raised to par by the conversion of bullion into coin.

The *computed* exchange would also be at par, though the *real* exchange were favorable, provided the *nominal* exchange were unfavorable in a similar degree; or, in other words, provided the low price of foreign bills, arising from their abundance, were counterbalanced by the depreciation of our currency compared with that of foreign countries. In this case there would be a diminished export and increased import, arising from the favorable state of the *real* exchange, attended with an influx of bullion; but there would at the same time be a drain upon the Bank, in consequence of the market price of bullion exceeding the mint price, from the over-issue of currency. Ordinary produce would be dear; the operation of the exports and imports would gradually restore the *real* exchange to par; and the *nominal* exchange would return to the same level by the conversion of the superfluous currency into bullion.

Again, the *computed* exchange might be in favor of a country, under very opposite states of the *real* and *nominal* exchange. Thus it would be 2 per cent. in favor of this country, if the *real* exchange were 3 per cent. above, and the *nominal* exchange 1 per cent. below par. It would also be two per cent. in favor of this country, with a favorable *nominal* exchange to the amount of 3 per

cent. and an adverse *real* exchange of 1 per cent.
In the same manner, an adverse *computed* exchange
might be shewn to arise from very opposite states of
the *real* and *nominal* exchange*; and it would be
easy to point out, under any given circumstances,
in what manner the merchant would derive his
profit from the produce he was engaged either in
exporting or importing. Suppose, for instance,
the *computed* exchange between Hambro' and
London to be 1 per cent. against this country, and
that this arises from a *real* exchange which is
favorable to the amount of 4 per cent. and a *nominal* exchange unfavorable to the extent of 5 per
cent.; let the *real* price of bullion at Hambro' and

---

* Mr. Wheatley, who assigns the relative values of currencies as
the exclusive cause of the fluctuations in the *computed* exchange,
has endeavoured to prove, that the rate of exchange has constantly corresponded with the relative issues of currency. But
the tables published by Lord King and Mr. Mushet furnish abundant proof of fluctuations in the exchange, without a corresponding alteration in the currency. Since the year 1797, when
the correcting principle of the *nominal* exchange was removed
in consequence of the Bank Restriction Act, there is, as might
be expected, a general coincidence between the increase of bank
notes in circulation and the adverse *computed* exchange; yet
even within that period, there have been considerable intervals
when the *computed* exchange between Hambro' and London has
been in favor of the latter, and that too at the time when the
greatest issues of currency recorded in Mr. Mushet's tables took
place, viz. in May 1804, and January 1805.

London be precisely the same, and consequently the *nominal* prices different by the amount of the *nominal* exchange or 5 per cent. Now if the expences of freight, insurance, &c. on the transit of bullion from Hambro' are 3 per cent. it is evident that a profit would be derived from the import of that article, notwithstanding the *computed* exchange was 1 per cent. against us. In this case the merchant must give a premium of 1 per cent. for the foreign bill to pay for the bullion;---100*l.* worth of bullion at Hambro' would therefore cost him 101*l.* and the charges of importation would increase this sum to 104*l.* Upon the subsequent sale, then, for 105*l.* of depreciated currency in the home market he would derive from the transaction a profit of 1*l.* This sum is precisely the difference between the *real* exchange and the expenses of transit, that part of the *computed* exchange which depends upon the *nominal*, producing no effect; since whatever is lost by its unfavorable state, is counterbalanced by a corresponding inequality of *nominal* prices.

In the same manner it might be shewn, that with a favorable *computed* exchange, bullion might be flowing out of the country; but it would be tedious to multiply instances, which, as the intelligent reader will easily conceive, may be infinitely varied. Those which have been now adduced are sufficient to shew, what contradictory conclusions may be drawn from any given rate of the *computed* exchange, and how impossible it is, from that alone, to determine either the relative value of currencies, or whether, what is usually called the balance of trade, be favorable or unfavorable to a nation *.

---

* A singular instance of the confusion arising from a want of attention to these distinctions occurs in the following passage from the fifth Number of the Quarterly Review: " Mr .Thornton " having used the following expression---' If at any time the ' exchanges of the country become so unfavorable as to pro-' duce a material excess of the market over the mint price of " gold.'---' Mr. Ricardo comments on this representation by "; concisely saying, ' Here the cause is mistaken for the effect.' " Mr. Thornton seems to us indisputably correct; not but that " the unfavorableness of the exchange, and the rise in the bullion " price of gold, alternately act as cause and effect; but the " former may, in some cases, not improperly be said to precede " the latter, and it certainly does so in the case of a bad harvest, " of which Mr. Thornton is speaking in this case." P. 157.--- Here it is evident that Mr. Thornton's observation, if confined to the *real* exchange is correct. Mr. Ricardo's comment, if limited to the *nominal* exchange, may also be considered as correct, though it would have been more accurate to have stated, the unfavorableness of the exchange, and the excess of the market over the mint price of gold, both, as effects of the depreciation of the currency; and the Reviewer may be correct, if his observations are intended to apply to the *computed* exchange. The apparent contradictions arise from confounding the *real*, the *nominal*, and the *computed* exchange, under the general, unqualified term, exchange.

The merchant, by knowing the *computed* exchange, and the current prices in the home and foreign market, and without any acquaintance with the theory of exchange, or the principles which regulate it, will always have sufficient practical data to guide him in his commercial transactions ; but the statesman should beware in making general legislative provisions, that he is not misled by the partial statements of men, whose individual interests are frequently in direct opposition to the general welfare of the country.--- This remark is not meant to convey any illiberal insinuations against a most useful and respectable class of the community ; but experience sufficiently proves that self-interest gives a bias to the mind, which, without its being conscious of the influence, will mislead and pervert the judgment.---- Perhaps a more than ordinary degree of caution is requisite, in this commercial country, where there seems to be a prevailing opinion, that the riches of the merchants are evidence of the benefits that the nation derives from its foreign trade ; it being forgotten, or unnoticed, that the profits of that class of persons are derived from the pockets of their countrymen: and that the advantages of foreign commerce consist in the stimulus it gives to the increase of the produce of the land and labour of the country; and to the opportunity which it affords, of exchanging the suplus produce thus called into existence for an equivalent, and only an equivalent produce, collected from every climate, and materially contributing to the enjoyments and the comforts of the community.

Of the Effects of the Depreciation of the Currency on the Expenditure of Government, and on the Interests of the different Classes of the Community.

The foreign expenditure of government being principally discharged by the remittance or the draft of bills, must be subject to the premium or discount in proportion to the *computed* exchange. Whatever be the amount of that expenditure, it will always be effected with greater or less advantage, according as the computed exchange is favorable or otherwise. It is of no consequence, so far as the disbursements of the Treasury are concerned, in what way the foreign expenditure is ultimately discharged by the country: for as long as bills are made use of, as the immediate mode of payment by the government, so long must the government, whenever the *computed* exchange is unfavorable, pay the premium for foreign bills, or submit to the discount upon its own;

and so long, on the other hand, will it derive the advantage of the discount on foreign, and the premium on its own bills, whenever the state of the *computed* exchange is in favor of the country. It is therefore most essential to the interests of government, that the *computed* exchange should at all times be as favorable as possible. Now this can only be produced by a careful attention to the state of the currency, and its effects upon the *nominal* exchange; for the circumstances that affect the *real* exchange are not, at all times, within its controul.

Bad harvests and deficient crops will always create an encreased and unusual importation; and in the same degree, a demand for foreign payment. This will eventually, indeed, be discharged by an increased exportation; but in the mean time, and during the continuance of the pressure, the *real* exchange will become unfavorable, and will continue so till the consequent bounty upon all exported, and the duty upon all imported, commodities, shall restore it to par.

The *nominal* exchange, on the contrary, is completely within the controul of government, and can never be either permanently favorable or unfavorable, so long as the legislature exercises a due degree of vigilance over the state of the circulating medium. If the coin, in which the legal payments of the country are made, is not degraded, and the paper is convertible at option into specie, it is impossible that the currency can ever be reduced below the almost uniform value, which the precious metals preserve among the different nations of the earth; because the depreciation of the currency will always be prevented, by the conversion of any superfluous quantity of it into bullion.

Should the legislature be induced by temporary circumstances to interfere with this regulating principle, and restrict the issuers of notes from the obligation of paying in specie, the consequences are easily foreen, and must soon be felt. There will be no longer any limit to the depreciation of the currency; the *nominal* exchange will continue permanently unfavorable, and will render the *computed* exchange so much the less favorable, or so much the more unfavorable, in proportion to the extent to which the currency may have been augmented beyond its natural amount.

The government, under these circumstances, will be utterly unable to relieve itself from the loss which must be incurred upon the total amount of its foreign expenditure, in whatever mode it is discharged; for the *nominal* exchange has a very different effect on the foreign payments of the state, and those of merchants in the course of their commercial transactions. The exporting merchant gains a premium on his bill equivalent to the *nominal* exchange, and by that advantage is repaid,

N

what would be otherwise lost in the high price he must give for his goods here, and the low price at which he must sell them abroad;---he derives no profit, and he suffers no loss. The importing merchant gives a premium for the foreign bill with which he pays for the produce he imports, but is repaid by the high *nominal* price at which he sells the produce at home. He also derives no profit. and sustains no loss.

But the government has no means of repaying itself for the loss occasioned by the *nominal* exchange. The equivalent is received abroad, and consumed there, and the bill for which the premium has been given will purchase precisely the same quantity of produce, whatever may have been paid for it here. Neither would the situation of government be altered, if, under an idea of saving the *nominal* exchange, it were induced to export commodities for the immediate supply of its armies, or its foreign establishments ; for independently of the expenses of the transit, it would lose the whole amount of the *nominal* exchange, in the high prices at which the commodities would be bought in the home market. If bullion could be procured, there would still be the same loss; first, in the expenses of the transit; and secondly, in the high market price at which it must be bought here, while abroad it would pass for no more than its intrinsic value.

Without access to the documents and vouchers of government, there is no very accurate mode of estimating the amount of the foreign expenditure; but some approximation to it may be made, by a comparison of the exports and imports. It has been already observed, that the foreign expenditure of a country can only be discharged by the export of commodities to an equal amount; and as the equivalent is received and consumed abroad, it follows, that in every country where there is a foreign expenditure, the exports must exceed the imports to that extent:---the larger the expenditure, the greater will be the excess of exports over imports. From this acknowledged truth, the inference seems very obvious, or at least there is strong presumptive evidence to lead to this conclusion, that if a foreign expenditure cause an excess of exports over imports, an excess of exports over imports will denote a foreign expenditure.--- Yet even at this day there are not wanting men in the Cabinet, in the Senate, and among the best-informed classes of society, who still adduce as a proof of the gains, that are made by foreign commerce, this same excess, which indicates expenditure, and not receipt *. Mr. Pitt was continually

---

* The same inference has been drawn, from the excess of exports, by the present Chancellor of the Exchequer, while these

vaunting of the resources of the nation, as evinced
by this circumstance; and Mr. Rose, in his " Brief

---

sheets have been passing through the press. See his speech upon
opening the budget.

The gradual increase, both of the annual imports, and exports,
has been frequently adduced as a decisive proof of the flourish-
ing state of our commerce—a conclusion that may be exceedingly
fallacious. The *nominal* value of the exports and imports will
in some degree keep pace with the increase in the *nominal*
price of commodities, and will swell the apparent amount of
merchandize exported and imported, without any material addition to the actual quantity. That the present increase arises
principally from this cause. is rendered more than probable. by
a comparison of the relative amount of tonnage employed for
the transport of that merchandize, in the years 1807 and 1809
The following table is drawn up from the returns made to the
House of Commons, January 30th and March 24th, 1810 :

Tonnage of Vessels, British and Foreign, including their repeated Voyages, in the several Ports of Great Britain, from and to all Parts of Europe.		
Year ended 5th Jan..	Inwards. Tons.	Outwards. Tons.
1808	944.282	811.255
1810	882.255	814.811
Official Value of the Imports and Exports for three Quarters, ending the 10th of October.		
Year.	Imports.	Exports.
1807	19.717.396	22.464.875
1809	29.000.782	39.824.104

As the nature of the commodities is specified in the returns,

Examination," states, with the same view, the annual balance of trade in favour of this country at 14,800,000*l.* Mr. Necker, acting upon similar principles, estimated the annual balance in favor of France at 3,000,000*l.*; and all other countries have in like manner prepared official statements of exports and imports, and boasted of a favorable balance *. Those, who have entered into the spirit of the observations upon the *real* exchange, will think it unnecessary that I should dwell upon these absurd opinions respecting a balance of trade, either favorable or unfavorable to a nation; it being evident, that, though at any particular mo-

---

and does not appear to vary materially, as to the proportions of value and bulk in the respective years, the equality in the amount of tonnage employed is conclusive, that the apparent increase of trade is in a great measure *nominal.*

* " There is no mine, however productive, that could supply
" the necessary stores for the balances that are claimed by the
" different nations of the world. One country claims a balance
" of 14,800,000*l.* and another of 5,000,000*l.* another of 3,
" and others of 2 and 1, to the aggregate amount of nearly
" 40,000,000*l.* annually; and as all assert their commerce to be
" favorable, it is obvious that their collective balances must be
" paid by a continual influx of bullion from the mines corre-
" spondent with their amount; but the annual produce of the
" mines of the world does not exceed 7,000,000*l.*" (Wheatley,
on the Theory of Money, p. 139.)

ment there may have been more produce sent from
a country than has been received in return for it,
and that bullion does occasionally pass to liquidate the balance, this happens merely in consequence of a derangement of the usual commercial
exchanges, and the bullion must eventually again
leave the country into which it flows, unless de-
tained there by the wants of the people, either for
the purpose of ornamental manufacture, or an
extended currency, in consequence of increased
wealth.

All trade, whether foreign or domestic, consists
in an exchange of equivalents. Gold and silver
will be sent as the equivalent, when gold and silver
are wanted for use. The hardware and woollens of
England are exchanged for the silks and the wines
of France, because these are more desired than
the bullion of France. If it were the taste of the
people of England to use gold and silver for their
ordinary utensils, the bullion of France would be
demanded as the equivalent. But they prefer the
wines and silks, and rather than forego these luxuries, are content with utensils formed of coarser
materials. When the exports exceed the imports,
(as they must do, when there is a foreign expenditure, the equivalents for the excess are received
" abroad in as full and ample a manner, as if the
" produce which they purchased were actually im-
" ported and entered in the Custom-house books,

" and afterwards sent to the seat of war for
" consumption. But from the circumstance of
" its not being inserted in the Custom-house
" entries as value received against the produce
" exported for its payment, the latter is deemed
" to constitute a favorable balance, when it is in
" reality exported to liquidate a balance against
" us *."

Notwithstanding, therefore, the inaccuracy of
the Custom-house returns, and the difficulty of
ascertaining the actual value of the imports and
exports,---notwithstanding that the imports from
the East and West Indies are confounded with the
imports arising from trade, when in fact they are
merely remittances; the one, of territorial revenue
invested in produce; the other, of rents and profits
remitted to absentee planters resident in this country;---notwithstanding also, that the contraband
trade introduces an immense quantity of commodities, which do not appear in the Custom-house
returns; yet as the inaccuracies of one period are
probably neither much greater nor less than those
of another, if the ratio of the excess of exports to
the foreign expenditure in one year, is known, it
is fair to conclude, that the excess of any other

* See Wheatley on the Theory of Money, p. 219.

year will be nearly in the same proportion to the foreign expenditure of that year.

It appears from the accounts presented by Mr. Long to the Secret Committee of the House of Lords, in 1797, that the foreign expenditure in the year 1796, the fourth year of the French revolutionary war, amounted to 10,649,000*l.*; and the excess of exports above the imports, for the same year, taken from the Custom-house books, is 7,331,494*l.*; so that the foreign expenditure is to this excess in the ratio nearly of 10 to 7*. The excess of exports over imports for three quarters of the year 1809, is 17,359,229*l.* or above 23 millions for the year, as appears by the returns from the Custom-house presented to parliament the 10th of January 1810; but as these returns are exclusive of the imports from India, the amount of those imports must be deducted, to make the calculation correspond with the returns for 1796, in which those imports are included. The sale of the East India Company's goods, from March 1, 1809, to March 1, 1810, amounted to 8,237,035*l.*

---

* The excess of exports over imports appears to be actually less than the foreign expenditure, in consequence of the produce remitted from the East and West Indies being entered in the Custom-house returns as imports.

the excess of exports over imports for the year
1809, after deducting this sum, would be about
15 millions, which, according to the ratio obtained for the year 1796, would give a foreign expenditure of 21 millions; and considering the enlarged scale of our military operations, together
with the establishments in Sicily and Malta, it will
perhaps be thought not much beyond the truth.
During the whole of the year 1809, the exchange
between London and Hambro' was never less than
7 per cent. in favor of the latter; and, increasing
gradually towards the end of the year, it rose in
the month of November to 16 per cent. Mr.
Huskisson, in his examination before the Committee for enquiring into the policy and conduct
of the expedition to the Scheldt, states the difficulties of negotiating bills in Spain, and in the
Mediterranean, as much greater than at Hambro';
so that it is not improbable an additional expenditure of some millions has been incurred in consequence of the unfavorable state of the exchange,
occasioning a correspondent loss to this country,
which might have been entirely avoided, had the
currency been sufficiently contracted to reduce
the *computed* exchange to par.

Without, however, placing too much reliance
upon an estimate, which at best can only be considered as an approximation, it must be evident,

that whatever may be the loss of government from this cause, it can only be supplied by laying additional burthens on the people. But this is not the only injury sustained in consequence of the depreciation of the currency; the same evil pervades the whole expenditure of government.--- Whatever purchases are made must be at an increased cost in proportion to the *nominal* high prices that an excessive currency produces. It will be felt through all the departments of the state, and the enlarged scale of expense must be balanced by an encreased scale of taxation. It is a matter of general notoriety, that money within these few years has been considerably reduced in value. The depreciation has been visibly going forwards since the time of the Bank restriction; and as long as it continues, the interests of the Bank are in direct opposition to those of the government and the public.

If the evils of an excessive currency affected all classes of the community equally, there might be less reason for complaint; but the misfortune is, that one class suffers no injury whatever, while another is subjected to the whole pressure, without the possibility of relief. It is of no consequence to the merchant whether he purchase with guineas the commodities which were formerly bought with shillings. His exports and his imports are in no degree affected; he is, in a great measure, relieved from the fear of pecuniary embarrassment; and in the same degree that the value of money is lowered, his *nominal* profits are increased. Without possessing greater means than before, of commanding the comforts and the luxuries of life, he feels himself relatively raised in the scale of society, as far at least as property has the power of raising him, in proportion to the *nominal* thousands he receives.

The landed proprietor is subject to all the evils of a depreciated circulating medium during the continuance of his current leases. As they expire, an opportunity is afforded him of profiting from the high *nominal* prices of produce, by raising his rents, and thus, to a certain degree, of preserving his relative station in life; but the uncertainty of seasons, and the consequent excessive variations in the prices of agricultural produce, will prevent him from increasing the amount of his income in the same proportion that its value is diminished; and as the depreciation proceeds, he must suffer from its effects, in proportion to the length of time for which his leases are renewed.

But it is upon that class of the community, which receives a *nominal* income, that the depreciation of the currency acts with the greatest severity. The public creditor, the annuitant, the clergyman, the physician, the lawyer, the soldier, and the sailor---all the civil officers of government ---all persons receiving salaries only,---in short, all those who have no produce to dispose of, by the high price of which they might have the opportunity of remunerating themselves for the losses which the depreciation induces. They not only bear the increased burthens which the government is compelled to impose in consequence of the depreciation, but the remainder of their income no longer possesses the same power of procuring the necessaries and comforts of life.

Let this view of the injury sustained by the class receiving a *nominal* income be contrasted with the advantages which the Restriction Act has conferred on the Bank proprietors.---Since the year 1797, the proprietors of Bank Stock have received,

In 1799, a bonus of 10 per cent. Loyalty.

In 1801, - - - 5 per cent. Navy 5 per cent.

In 1802, - - - 2½ per cent. Ditto.

In 1804, - - - 5 per cent. Cash.

In 1805, - - - 5 per cent. Ditto.

In 1806, - - - 5 per cent. Ditto.

In 1807, the dividend was raised from 7 to 10 per cent which, with the payment of the Property Tax, makes more than 11 per cent regular interest; and 100*l.* stock has increased from 127½*l.*

its price in 1797, to 280l. its price in 1809*.
Besides which, there is generally understood to be
a very large surplus, which has not yet been divided
amongst the proprietors; and, if the vast sums of
money that have been expended during this period
upon the buildings of the Bank, be considered,
some idea may be formed of the immoderate profits that have been acquired by this establishment.

The question therefore is simply this, whether
the interests of so large a part of the community
are to be sacrificed for the benefit of the proprietors of bank stock, and the different banking part-
nerships throughout the kingdom; and it is yet to
be explained on what grounds the continuance of
a system can be justified, which, if it were wise at
the time of its adoption, has long ceased to be either
equitable or politic. It might be called for by im-
perious necessity, during the moment of alarm, and
may be again resorted to, should similar circumstances demand it; but in the mean time, it seems
no more than right, that the Bank should be content
with the profits that are to be acquired in a pursuit,
which has at all times afforded an adequate remuneration to those who have embarked in it, without
the assistance of a legislative provision, that has

---

* Reflections on the Abundance of Paper, &c. by Sir Philip
Francis.

deranged, and will continue to derange, so long as it exists, the circulating medium of the country.

Applications are continually making to parliament for an increase of salary to those who are unable to meet the pressure of the times, and to keep up appearances suitable to their stations in life. Instances of this have recently occurred, as well in the case of the inferior clergy, as of the officers of the army and navy. The salaries in all public offices, and public trading companies, are obliged to be raised, to enable the persons who are employed in them to purchase the necessaries of life *. Those who sell as well as buy, have the means of transferring the weight from their own shoulders; but the possessor of a *nominal* income receives the same number of pounds, whatever be their value;-- he is a buyer only, and must submit to his fate. The effects of *ordinary* taxation are the depression of the same class, and a tendency, as it proceeds to confound the different ranks of society. It is the more incumbent therefore upon the legislature to be careful, that this depressed class be not overwhelmed by that *extraordinary* taxation, which

---

* Mr. Rose, in his pamplet on the Public Expenditure, in speaking of the increase of the expense of collecting the Excise revenue, observes, " The increase in the Excise is nearly altogether for the augmentation of the salaries of the officers on " the establishment, to enable them to exist." p. 54.

arises from the necessity of increasing the *nominal* revenue of government, in proportion to the depreciation of its value.

The mode in which these evils are to be remedied, it is unnecessary, after what has been already said, for me to point out. When the cause that has produced the mischief is removed, the evils will subside of themselves. Lord King very justly observes, " Had parliament been called upon to " authorize any of those direct frauds upon the " currency, which have often disgraced arbitrary " governments; had it been recommended to " tnem to raise the denomination of the current " coin. there can be no doubt that such a pro- " posal would have been rejected with indigna- " tion. Yet an abuse of the same nature has " been established by law in this country. The " power of reducing the value of the currency by " a silent and gradual depreciation, is more dan- " gerous, from the very circumstance of its being " less direct, and less exposed to observation.* "

The difficulty that now presents itself is, in what manner to revert to the former system, without injury to the Bank, or to the merchants, who have so long been indulged with the accommodation of

---

* Thoughts on the Restriction of Cash Payments at the Bank, p. 121.

procuring the discount of their bills;—and this difficulty is the more embarrassing, from the very peculiar and unprecedented combination of circumstances that exists at the present moment.

In consequence of the large army now maintained by this country on the Continent of Europe, and in the Mediterranean, our foreign expenditure is unusually great; and the export trade, which under the ordinary facilities of commercial intercourse, would enable us to defray this expenditure, is subjected to impediments from the controul exercised by the enemy over the commerce of the Continent, which it is difficult to overcome. Our merchants are compelled to find secret and circuitous modes of introducing their merchandize into foreign countries, which, even after its introduction, is liable to immediate confiscation *.—

---

* It has been said, that, in the countries more immediately under the controul of the French, the merchants refuse to take our produce in exchange, and demand specie or bullion in payment for what we import from them. Should this be the fact, it is a strong proof that the French decrees have produced their effect, and that the risk of confiscation has to a certain extent prevented British merchandize from being introduced into those countries. It will be impossible, under these circumstances, much longer to continue such a commercial intercourse, unless the means be found of procuring a very unusual supply of bullion from the American mines : and it will become a question, whether the South American market can take such a quantity of British pro-

This must operate as a very powerful check upon the export of the staple produce of the country; and great as the comparative excess of exports appears to be, from the last returns of the Custom-house that have been laid before Parliament, it is probable that the foreign expenditure would have demanded and produced a much greater excess, but for the restrictions that the French decrees have imposed upon our commerce. It is said, too, that the deficiency in the last year's harvest has occasioned an increased and unusual importation of foreign grain; so that the *real* exchange has been acted upon by the combined influence of all the causes that can render it unfavorable;---a large foreign expenditure, demanding an excess of exports which the restrictions on commerce obstruct; and an increased importation, to supply the failure of an article of the first necessity, counteracting the effect of the export trade, and diminishing its excess. If the market price of

---

duce as will be sufficient to supply the bullion that will be wanted for effecting the usual imports from Holland and France, and that part of the Continent, where the French decrees can be enforced. Independently of this, the accumulation of bullion on the Continent will by degrees render its real price so low, that the quantity to be given in exchange for commodities imported from thence, must be continually augmenting, and of course the price of continental produce so much enhanced to the consumer here, as at length to stop the consumption altogether.

bullion, therefore, were ever raised above the mint price by an unfavorable *real* exchange, it might be expected under the circumstances now enumerated; and should this be the case, and the Bank be immediately rendered liable to the payment of its notes in specie, there would be no possibility of its withstanding the drain that would immediately commence, without such a sudden contraction of paper as would endanger the stability of the merchants. For the *nominal* and the *real* exchange being both unfavorable in a great degree, the process of melting the coin, and the export of bullion, would be carried on at the same time;— the first, to take advantage of the difference between the market and the mint price of gold; the second, on account of the excess of the premium upon foreign bills above the expenses of the transit of bullion; and this drain would continue till the issues of bank paper were sufficiently contracted, to lower the market price of bullion below its mint price.

It is not easy to ascertain what degree of contraction might be requisite to produce this effect, for the issues of the country banks are probably to the full as much above their due proportion, as those of the Bank of England. In the year 1795, before the drain took place which became the subject of such serious complaints to Mr. Pitt, the usual amount of bank notes in circulation was about 11 millions; at the time of the drain, the

issue had been increased to 13 millions, and from
the 25th of February 1795, to the 25th of February 1797, had been violently contracted to 8½ millions. At that time bank notes were in common
circulation in all parts of the kingdom, and had
not been so completely displaced as they have
since been, by the country notes. The paper circulating medium, therefore, required for the capital, and parts immediately adjacent, would probably not exceed 10 millions. The quantity of
coin at the same period may be estimated by the
proportion between the cash and paper payments
at the Bank, as given in evidence by Mr. Abraham Newland, before the Secret Committee of the
House of Lords *. He states, that previously to
the restriction, if the dividends to the public creditor amounted to 14,000,000l., not more than
from 1,300,000l. to 1,400,000l. would be paid in
cash. If in so large a payment, where cash in
any quantity might be demanded, and where
there must have been many fractional sums, one
tenth only were paid in specie, it is fair to conclude that not more than one tenth would be given
in the other money transactions of the metropolis.
He adds, that 100,000l. would be sufficient for all
the cash payments of the Treasury;---that in the

* p. 63.

the gross produce of the Customs, which then
amounted to 3,000,000*l*., the Bank did not receive above 3000*l*. in specie;---in the produce of
the Excise, stated at 7,000,000*l*., not more than
60,000*l*. ;---and in the instalments of a loan, consisting of much larger sums, not above 1 per cent.
upon the whole *. So that taking 1 to 10 as the
probable proportion of the specie to the notes,
there would be about one million of the former in
circulation, making, together with the paper, 11
millions for the total amount of the currency of the
metropolis. By the last returns of the House of
Commons, the bank notes in circulation on the 12th
of Jan. in the present year, exclusive of the Bank
post bills, amounted to 20,522,810*l*.; and as the
quantity of these notes that circulate in the country
is very trifling, it is not improbable that the currency
of the capital has been nearly doubled in the course
of the last thirteen years. The general opinion is,
that the country banks have made a still more extensive use of the privileges which the Restriction
Bill has afforded, and have multiplied their paper
to an enormous amount. There seems every reason, therefore, to conclude, that the circulating
medium would be under-rated at double its amount,
in the year 1797: and consequently that if the

---

* See Wheatley on the Theory of Money, p. 142.

country does not require a greater quantity of currency now, than it did at that time, the Bank must contract its paper one half, or to about 11 millions, before commodities could be brought back to their natural prices *.

Those who have attended to the distress in which the merchants were involved at the period to which we have referred, by a reduction of bank paper from $13\frac{1}{2}$ to $8\frac{1}{2}$ millions in two years, may conceive how infinitely more they must suffer by a sudden diminution of it from 21 to 11 millions. But this circumstance, which is a cogent reason against the immediate repeal of the Bank Restriction Bill, is also the strongest proof of the effect which the contraction of currency has upon prices; for whence could the distress of the merchants arise, but from their being compelled to dispose of their stock at reduced prices? They have now been so long habituated to the enhanced rates, that their purchases have been made with reference to this system, and under an expectation of deriving their present high *nominal* profits from its continuance. The number of purchasers in the

---

* The increase of prices, arising from the gradual progress of taxation, will probably require a larger circulating medium than might be wanted in 1797.

market, occasioned by the increased issues of paper, will be withdrawn, when the paper is again contracted, and consequently the holders of produce that has been bought upon credit, and for which bills are outstanding, must sell in the falling markets, in order to meet their acceptances when they become due. The Bank also, in consequence of the drain, will be compelled to reduce its paper, which it cannot effect, without refusing its usual discounts. The merchant, no longer possessing the means as before, of coining his credit into currency, must either sell, or be unable to make good his payments. In the same proportion as an increase of buyers was created by the over-issue, the contraction will create an increase of sellers; and thus it appears evident, that so sudden a diminution of currency, as would be necessary to protect the Bank, if the restriction were immediately withdrawn, would inevitably occasion great pecuniary distress, and be attended with the most injurious consequences to the credit and commerce of the nation.

But there is no necessity for such violence. The Bank may gradually diminish the amount of its paper, in the same manner in which it has for the last thirteen years been gradually increased. It is true such a proceeding will not be so popular with the merchants, but it will not be attended with

any real injury to their interests, whilst it will
confer a substantial benefit on the possessor of a
nominal income, a benefit to which he is upon
every principle of justice entitled.

It is only necessary for parliament to determine
the amount of the annual dimunition of the issues
of the Bank, and to enforce the continuance of
the measure, till it is found that the market price
of bullion is permanently reduced, in a trifling degree, below its mint price. The currency will
then be of the same value as if it consisted entirely
of the precious metals, and the restriction may be
removed without the slightest injury to the Bank,
or any real injury to the merchant. This experiment may be made with the utmost safety, both
to the Bank and the country; because parliament
will at any time have the power of increasing or
diminishing the annual contraction, should it be
found that, in the first instance, too low or too
high a limit had been assigned *.

---

* The Bank has been indulged so long in the exercise of the
extraordinary privileges conferred upon it by the legislature, and
has, by its extensive advances, acquired such a controul over the
finances of individuals, and of government, that it may, perhaps, have become questionable, whether the Directors of that
establishment have not, at this moment, the power of dictating
their own terms ; and whether the legislature may not be under
the necessity of receiving, rather than of proposing conditions.

It will require, however, much caution and some firmness, lest the legislature should be misled by the clamours of those who will first feel the effects of the remedy; for as the Bank will immediately experience a diminution of its profits, and probably be at length compelled to lower the interest to the proprietors; as the issues of the country banker will be restrained within their natural limits; and as the merchant, under the first alarm which the falling prices will excite, and without forming a just conception of its cause, will not fail to exclaim against a system apparently so adverse to his interests; there can be little doubt but that the public, during its progress, will be assailed with the most gloomy predictions of the decline of the general wealth, and the ruin of the commercial prosperity of the nation. But a full and accurate acquaintance with this most important subject, will lead the government and the people to disregard and despise such idle and interested clamours,----to consider these effects not as symptoms of decay, but as evidences of the efficacy of a measure tending to restore the energies of the country. It will teach them the necessity of perseverance, not

---

Should these conjectures have any foundation in truth, they furnish the most cogent reasons for the immediate extinction of a power, whose existence is incompatible with the independence and the supremacy of government.

merely for the purpose of obviating those mischiefs
which have hitherto been experienced, but in order to prevent the still greater evils, which must
infallibly result from an adherence to the same
system. Above all, it will induce them to submit
with cheerfulness to those trifling and partial inconveniencies, which may occasionally be experienced during the progress of the remedy, while
they look forward with confidence to the re-esta-
blishment of the ancient scale and order of things,
and the consequent increase, not only of the comforts of the great mass of the community, but of
the resources, the powers, and the independence
of the government.

In the following Tables, the figures indicating the per centage in favor of, and against London, denote pounds and the decimal parts of pounds, which are not carried beyond one decimal place.

		Hamburgh.	in favor of London.	against London.	Standard Gold per oz.	above its Mint Price.	below its Mint Price.
1760	Jan. 1	36 4	7 .9		3 18 6	0 16 0 2	
	March 4	36 1	7 .1		3 18 9	1 2 5 2	
	May 2	35 6	5 .4		3 19 1	1 11 1 0	
	July 1	32 6		3 .5	3 19 0	1 8 10 2	
	Sept. 2	32 2		4 .5	4 0 1	2 16 8 2	
	Nov. 4	31 8		6	3 19 4	1 17 5 1	
1761	Jan. 2	32		5	3 18 10	1 4 7 1	
	March 3	32 5		4 .3	3 19 8	1 6 0	
	May 1	32 2		4 .5	4 0 0	2 14 6 3	
	July 3	31 11		5 .2	4 0 6	3 7 5	
	Sept. 1	32 5		3 .8	4 0 6	3 7 5	
	Nov. 3	33		2	3 19 4	1 17 5 1	
1762	Jan. 1	32 11		2 .3	3 19 0	1 8 10 2	
	March 2	33 9	0 .2		3 18 9	1 2 5 2	
	May 4	34 3	1 .7		3 19 3	1 15 3 3	
	July 2	34 8	2 .9		3 19 10	2 10 3 2	
	Sept. 3	35 1	3 .9		3 19 4	1 17 5 1	
	Nov. 4	35 2	4 .2		3 18 10	1 4 7 1	
1763	Jan. 1	34 2	1 .4		4 0 0	2 14 6 3	
	March 1	33 11	0 .7		4 0 6	3 7 5	
	May 3	34 2	1 .4		4 1 3	4 6 8	
	July 1	34 3	1 .7		4 1 6	4 7 5	
	Sept. 2	34 7	2 .7		4 1 6	4 13 1 3	
	Nov. 3	34 11	3 .7		3 18 9	1 2 5 2	
1764	Jan. 3	34 5	2 .2		3 18 3	0 9 7 2	
	March 2	35 2	4 .4		3 18 3	0 9 7 2	
	May 1	34 11	3 .7		3 18 3	0 9 7 2	
	July 3	35 1	4 .2		3 18	0 3 2 2	
	Sept. 4	35	3 .9		3 18	0 3 2 2	
	Nov. 2	35 1	4 .2		3 18	0 3 2 2	

		Hamburgh.	Per centage in favor of London.	Per centage against London.	Price of Standard Gold per oz.	Per centage above its Mint Price.	Per centage below its Mint Price.
1765	Jan. 1	35 1	4 .9		3 18 0	0 3 2.1	
	March 1	34 10	3 .4		3 18 0	0 3 2.2	
	May 3	34 11	3 .7		3 18 0	0 3 2.2	
	July 3	34 9	3 .2		3 18 8	0 3 2.2	
	Sept. 3	34 4	1 .9		3 18 2	1 0 3.3	
	Nov. 3	34 4	1 .9		3 18 7	0 7 5.3	
1766	Jan. 3	34 6	2 .4		3 18 8	0 18 2.1	
	March 4	34 9	3 .2		3 18 8	1 13 3.3	
	May 2	34 11	3 .7		3 19 0	2 10 3.2	
	July 1	35 1	4 .9		3 19 10	1 8 10.2	
	Sept. 2	35 3	3 .7		3 19 0	1 8 10.2	
	Nov. 4	35 8	5 .4		3 19 0	1 15 3.3	
1767	Jan. 2	35 6	5 .9		3 19 4	1 17 5.1	
	March 3	35 8	6 .4		3 19 10	2 10 3.2	
	May 1	35 8	5 .9		3 19 8	2 6 0	
	July 3	35 11	6 .6		3 19 5	1 19 7	
	Sept. 1	35 6	5 .4		3 19 5	1 19 7	
	Nov. 3	34 11			3 18 8	1 0 3.5	
1768	Jan. 1	34 4	1 .9		3 18 9	1 2 5.5	
	March 4	34 8	2 .9		3 19 1	1 11 0.1	
	May 3	34 7	2 .7		3 19 6	2 1 8.3	
	July 1	34 5	2 .2		3 19 5	1 19.7	
	Sept. 2	33 6		6 .5	3 19 7	2 3 10.1	
	Nov. 1	33 2		1 .5	3 19 9	2 8 1.3	
1769	Jan. 3	33 4		1	4 0 3	3 11 8.1	
	March 3	33 8			4 0 8	3 11 8.1	
	May 2	33 8		.5			
	July 4	33 6					

Year	Month	Hamburgh	in favor of London	against London	Standard Gold per oz.	above its Mint Price	below its Mint Price
1770	Jan. 2	33 2		1 .5	4 0 6	3 7 2	
	March 2	33 5		1 .5	4 0 4	3 3 5	
	May 1	33 3		1 .3	4 0 4	3 3 1	
	July 3	33 4		1	4 0 2	2 18 10	
	Sept. 4	33 2		1 .5	4 0 0	2 14 6	
	Nov. 2	33 5		0 .8	4 0 0	2 14 8	
1771	Jan. 1	33 8	0 0 .2		3 19 6	2 1 3	
	March 1	33 9		0 .5	3 18 9	1 4 2	
	May 3	33 6		2	3 18 10	1 13 5	
	July 2	33		2 .3	3 19 2	2 8 7	
	Sept. 3	32 11		2 .8	3 19 9	2 11 1	
	Nov. 1	32 7		3 .3	3 19 0	3 9 6	
1772	Jan. 3	32 11		2 .3	3 19 8	3 0 3	
	March 3	32 10		2 .5	4 0 7	4 0 3	
	May 1	32 1			4 0 0	3 13 10	
	July 3	33 5		1	4 0 9	2 14 6	
	Sept. 1	33 8		1 .3	4 0 0	1 8 10	
	Nov. 3	34			4 0 0	0 3 2	
1773	Jan. 5	35	0 9		3 19 0	0 3 2	
	March 2	34 11	3 9		3 18 0	0 3 2	
	May 4	34 8	3 9		3 18 0	0 1	
	July 2	34 9	3 7		3 17 11		
	Sept. 3	34 9	2 9		3 17 9		0 3 3 2
	Nov. 2	34 10	3 9		3 17 9		0 3 3 2
1774	Jan. 4	34 7	3 2		3 17 9		0 3 3 2
	March 3	34 9	3 4		3 17 9		0 3 3 2
	May 1	34 5	2 7		3 17 9		0 3 3 2
	July 2	34 2	3 2		3 17 9		0 3 3 2
	Sept. 2		2 2		3 17 9		0 3 5 7
	Nov. 1		1 4		3 17 7		0 3 5 7

		Hamburgh.		Per centage in favor of London.	Per centage against London.	Price of Standard Gold per oz.			Per centage above its Mint Price	Per centage below its Mint Price.		
1775	Jan. 3	34	3	1 .7		3	17	7		0	7	5 3
	March 3	34	5	2 .2		3	17	7		0	7	5 3
	May 2	34	4	1 .9		3	17	7		0	7	5 3
	July 4	34	5	2 .2		3	17	7		0	7	5 3
	Sept. 1	34	4	1 .0		3	17	7		0	7	5 3
	Nov. 3	34	2	1 .4		3	17	7		0	7	5 3
1776	Jan. 5	34	1	1 .2		3	17	7		0	7	5 3
	March 3	33	9	0 .2		3	17	7		0	7	5 3
	May 3	33	8		1 .3	3	17	7		0	7	5 3
	July 2	33	3		0 .8	3	17	7		0	7	5 3
	Sept. 3	33	5		1 .8	3	17	7		0	7	5 3
	Nov. 1	33	1		1 .5	3	17	7		0	7	5 3
1777	Jan. 3	33	2		2 .5	3	17	7		0	7	5 3
	March 4	33	0		2 .5	3	17	7		0	7	5 3
	May 2	32	10		3 .3	3	17	7		0	7	5 3
	July 1	32	7		4 .5	3	17	7		0	7	5 3
	Sept. 2	32	2		4 .3	3	17	7		0	7	5 3
	Nov. 4	32	1		2 .8	3	17	7		0	7	5 3
1778	Jan. 2	32	4			3	17	7		0	7	5 3
	March 3	32	9	1 .4		3	17	7		0	7	5 3
	May 1	34	2	2 .7		3	17	7		0	7	5 3
	July 3	34	7	2 .2		3	17	7		0	7	5 3
	Sept. 1	34	5	3 .4		3	17	7		0	7	5 3
	Nov. 3	34	10	4 .4		3	17	7		0	7	5 3
1779	Jan. 1	35	6	5 .9		3	17	7		0	7	5 3
	March 2	35	8	7 .4		3	17	6		0	9	7 2
	May 4	36	2	6 .4		3	17	6		0	9	7 2
	July 2	35	10	0 .2		3	17	6		0	9	7 2
	Sept 3	33	0			3	17	6		0	9	7 2

		Hamburgh.	in favor of London.	against London	Standard Gold per oz.	above its Mint Price	below its Mint Price
1780	Jan. 4	34 6	2 .4		3 17 6		2 7 9 0
	March 3	35 7	5 .6		3 17 6		2 7 9 0
	May 2	35 2	4 .4		3 17 6		2 7 9 0
	July 4	34 8	2 .9		3 17 6		2 7 9 0
	Sept. 3	34 1	1 .2		3 17 6		2 7 9 0
	Nov. 3	33 10	0 .4		3 17 6		2 7 9 0
1781	Jan. 2	34 1	1 .2		3 17 6		2 7 9 0
	March 2	33 11	0 .7		3 17 6		2 7 9 0
	May 1	33 7	0	0 .3	3 17 6		2 7 9 0
	July 3	32 1		4 .8	3 17 6		2 7 9 0
	Sept. 4	32 2		4 .5	3 17 6		2 7 9 0
	Nov. 2	31 11		5 .2	3 17 6		2 7 9 0
1782	Jan. 1	31 9		5 .7	3 17 6		2 7 9 0
	March 1	32 10		2 .5	3 17 6		2 7 9 0
	May 3	32 11		2 .3	3 17 6		2 7 9 0
	July 2	32 11		2 .3	3 17 6		2 7 9 0
	Sept. 3	32 6		3 .5	3 17 6		2 7 9 0
	Nov. 1	31 8		3 .6	3 17 9		2 7 3 0
1783	Jan. 3	32 7		3 .2	3 17 9		2 7 3 0
	March 4	32 5		3 .8	3 17 9		2 7 3 0
	May 2	31 9		5 .7	3 17 9		2 2 3 3
	July 1	31 6		6 .5	3 18 0	2 2 3 0	
	Sept. 2	31 6		6 .5	3 18 0	2 2 3 0	
	Nov. 4	32 9		6 .5	3 18 0	2 2 3 0	
1784	Jan. 2	33 6	0 .2	2 .8	3 18 0	2 2 3 0	
	March 4	33 9	1 .9	0 .5	3 18 0	2 2 3 0	
	May 2	34 4	1 .9		3 17 10 2	2 2 3 0	
	July 2	34 4	2 .7		3 17 10 2		2 9 3 3
	Sept. 3	34 7	2 .9		3 17 10 2		2 9 3 3
	Nov. 2	34 9	2 .9		3 17 10 2		2 9 3 3

		Hamburgh.	Per centage in favor of London.	Per centage against London.	Price of Standard Gold per oz.	Per centage above its Mint Price.	Per centage below its Mint Price.
1785	Jan. 7	35 4	3 .9		3 17 10 2		2 7 9 0
	March 1	35 11	4 .9		3 17 10 2		2 7 9 0
	May 3	34 11	3 .7		3 17 10 2		2 7 9 0
	July 1	35 6	5 .4		3 17 6		2 7 9 0
	Sept. 2	35 4	4 .9		3 17 6		2 7 9 0
	Nov. 1	35 3	4 .7		3 17 6		2 7 9 0
1786	Jan. 3	34 10	3 .4		3 17 6		2 7 9 0
	March 3	34 11	3 .7		3 17 6		2 7 9 0
	May 2	34 5	2 .2		3 17 6		2 7 9 0
	July 4	34 3	1 .7		3 17 6		2 7 9 0
	Sept. 1	34 3	1 .7		3 17 6		2 7 9 0
	Nov. 3	34 6	2 .4		3 17 6		2 7 9 0
1787	Jan. 2	34 5	2 .9		3 17 6		2 7 9 0
	March 2	34 7	2 .7		3 17 6		2 7 9 0
	May 1	34 7	2 .7		3 17 6		2 7 9 0
	July 3	34 8	2 .9		3 17 6		2 7 9 0
	Sept. 4	35 1	3 .9		3 17 6		2 7 9 0
	Nov. 2	35 1	4 .2		3 17 6		2 7 9 0
1788	Jan. 1	35 3	4 .7		3 17 6		2 7 9 0
	March 4	35 4	4 .9		3 17 6		2 7 9 0
	May 2	35 1	4 .2		3 17 6		2 7 9 0
	July 1	55 1	3 .9		3 17 6		2 7 9 0
	Sept. 2	35 1	3 .2		3 17 6		2 7 9 0
	Nov. 4	34 9	3 .4		3 17 6		2 7 9 0
1789	Jan. 6	34 10	3 .2		3 17 6		2 7 9 0
	March 3	35 1	4 .2		3 17 6		2 7 9 0
	May 1	35 6	5 .4		3 17 6		2 7 9 0
	July 3	35 7	5 .6		3 17 6		2 7 9 0
	Sept 1	35	5 .1		3 17 6		2 7 9 0

Year	Month	Day	London	London	London	Gold per oz.	Mint Price.	Mint Price.	Bank of England notes in Circulation.
1790	Jan.	29	35	2	3 .9	3 17 6		3 17 10½	10,245,280
	March	1	35	2	4 .4	3 17 6		3 17 10½	11,160,590
	May	4	35	4	4 .9	3 17 6		3 17 10½	11,348,700
	July	2	35	7	5 .6	3 17 6		3 17 10½	11,510,270
	Sept.	3	35	6	5 .4	3 17 6		3 17 10½	11,601,950
	Nov.	2	35	7	5 .6	3 17 6		3 17 10½	12,060,620
1791	Jan.	4	35	6	5 .4	3 17 6		3 17 10½	11,764,680
	March	1	35	11	6 .4	3 17 6		3 17 10½	11,225,840
	May	3	35	10	6 .6	3 17 6		3 17 10½	11,239,170
	July	1	35	6	6 .4	3 17 6		3 17 10½	11,765,280
	Sept.	2	35	2	5 .4	3 17 6		3 17 10½	11,316,790
	Nov.	1	35	6	4 .4	3 17 6		3 17 10½	11,157,040
1792	Jan.	3	34	6	2 .4	3 17 6		3 17 10½	11,963,820
	March	2	34	3	2 .4	3 17 6		3 17 10½	12,100,650
	May	1	34	5	1 .7	3 17 6		3 17 10½	10,938,620
	July	3	34		2 .2	3 17 6		3 17 10½	10,967,310
	Sept.	4	34	3	0 .9	3 17 6		3 17 10½	11,159,720
	Nov.	2	35	4	1 .7	3 17 6		3 17 10½	10,366,450
1793	Jan.	1	35	7	4 .9	3 17 6		3 17 10½	10,343,940
	March	1	36	6	8 .6	3 17 6		3 17 10½	10,927,970
	May	3	37	2	11 .3	3 17 6		3 17 10½	
	July	3	37		10 .3	3 17 6		3 17 10½	
	Sept.	1	36	3	6 .9	3 17 6		3 17 10½	
	Nov.	3	35	9	4 .7	3 17 6		3 17 10½	
1794	Jan.	3	35	4	6 .1	3 17 6		3 17 10½	
	March	4	36	7	7 .9	3 17 6		3 17 10½	
	May	2	36	6	8 .6	3 17 6		3 17 10½	
	July	1	35	2	5 .4	3 17 6		3 17 10½	
	Sept.	2	35	5	3 .9	3 17 6		3 17 10½	
	Nov.	4	34		2 .2	3 17 6		3 17 10½	

Year		Hamburgh.	Per centage in favor of London.	Per centage against London	Price of Standard Gold per oz.	Per centage above its Mint Price.	Per centage below its Mint Price.	Amount of Bank of England notes in circulation.
1795	Jan. 2	34 6	2 .4		3 17 6		0 9 7 2	12,432,240
	March 3	35 10	6 .4		3 17 6		0 9 7 2	10,912,680
	May 1	34 4	1 .9		3 17 6		0 9 7 2	11,034,790
	July 3	32 6			3 17 6		0 9 7 2	11,608,670
	Sept. 1	32 10		2 .5				10,824,150
	Nov. 3	32 7		3 .5				10,770,200
1796	Jan. 1	33 2		2 .5				9,720,440
	March 3	33 2	0 .4	3 .3				9,645,710
	May 1	33 7		1 .5	3 17 6		0 9 7 2	8,640,250
	July 1	33 7		0 .3	3 17 6		0 9 7 2	11,103,880
	Sept. 2	33 7	2 .7	0 .3	3 17 6		0 9 7	10,828,880
	Nov. 1	34 7	5 .4					11,641,400
1797	Jan. 3	35 9	3 .2		3 17 6 2		0 9 7 2	13,043,480
	March 3	34 6	6 .9		3 17 6 2		0 9 7	13,234,440
	May 2	36 6	8 .4		3 17 10 2			12,115,640
	July 4	38	12 .8		3 17 10 2			12,441,070
	Sept. 1	38	12 .9		3 17 10 2			13,202,460
	Nov. 3	38 2	13 .3		3 17 10 2			13,720,260
1798	Jan. 2	37 5	11 .1		3 17 10 2			13,759,940
	March 2	37 8	11 .8		3 17 10			
	May 1	37 10	12 .3		3 17 9		0 3 2 2	
	July 3	37 10	11 .3		3 17 9		0 3 2 2	
	Sept. 4	37 7	12 .3		3 17 9		0 3 2 2	
	Nov. 2	37 7	11 .6		3 17 9		0 3 2 2	
1799	Jan. 1	37 7	11 .6		3 17 9		0 3 2 2	
	March 1	35 6	5 .4		3 17 9		0 3 2 2	
	May 3	36	6 .9		3 17 9		0 3 2 2	

Year	Date	Hamburgh	In favor of London	Against London	Standard Gold per oz	Above its Mint Price	Bank of England notes in circulation
1800	Jan. 3	32 3		5 8.5	4 5 0	9 2 11 3	15,110,060
	March 4	31 4		7 3.5	4 5 0	9 2 11 3	15,213,520
	May 9	32 5		3 4.5	4 5 0	9 2 11 3	15,230,490
	July 1	32 6		3 5.9	4 5 0	10 8 8 1	15,450,970
	Sept. 2	32 2		4 11.9	4 6 0	5 18 9 1	16,365,206
	Nov. 4	31 10		5 6.2	4 2 6	9 2 11 3	
1801	Jan. 2	29 8		11 6.5	4 5 0		No account of the Bank notes in circulation appears to have been presented for this year, subsequent to March 25th.
	March 3	31 7		6 6.5			
	May 1	31 6		6 6.2			
	July 3	31 6		6 3.5			
	Sept. 1	31 7		6 4.5			
	Nov. 3	32 6		3 4.3			
1802	Jan. 1	32 2		4 3		7 4 5 2	15,956,016
	March 2	32 3		4 1.3	4 3 6		16,747,300
	May 4	32 8		3 1.3			16,141,636
	July 2	33 3		1 0.8			15,838,410
	Sept. 3	33 3					16,101,140
	Nov. 2	33 5					16,734,510
1803	Jan. 4	34 5	0 .9				16,622,510
	March 1	34 4	2 .2	2 .5			17,931,930
	May 3	34 4	1 .9				17,274,493
	July 1	32 10	1 .9				
	Sept. 2	34 4					
	Nov. 3	34 10	1 .9				
1804	Jan. 1	35 9	3 .4				18,033,383
	March 2	35 8	3 .9				17,194,133
	May 1	35 10	6 .1				16,881,306
	July 3	35 6	5 .9		4 0 0	2 14 6 3	
	Sept. 4		6 .4		4 0 0	2 14 6 3	
	Nov. 2		5 .4		4 0 0	2 14 6 3	

Year	Date	Hamburgh	Per centage in favor of London	Per centage against London	Price of Standard Gold per oz.	Per centage below its Mint Price.	Amount of Bank of England notes in circulation.
1805	Jan. 1	35 6	5 .4		4 0 0	2 14 6 3	18,407,880
	March 1	35 8	5 .9		4 0 0	2 14 6 3	17,367,740
	May 3	35 5	5 .1		4 0 0	2 14 6 3	16,449,020
	July 2	35 8	5 .9		4 0 0	2 14 6 3	16,753,490
	Sept. 3	35 5	5 .1		4 0 0	2 14 6 3	17,293,070
	Nov. 5	32 9		2 .8			17,085,150
1806	Jan. 3	33 3		1 .3			17,281,330
	March 4	34 2	1 .4				17,040,790
	May 2	33 8					16,618,390
	July 1	34 5	2 .8				17,536,400
	Sept. 2	34 4	1 .9				17,748,400
	Nov. 4	33 10	0 .4				16,930,200
1807	Jan. 2	34 8	2 .9				17,573,100
	March 3	34 10	3 .4				17,491,900
	May 1	34 10	3 .4				17,644,670
	July 3	34 3	1 .7				17,466,170
	Sept. 4	34 3	1 .7				17,560,060
	Nov. 6	34 4	1 .9				No account of Bank notes in circulation was pre-
1808	Jan. 1	34 4	1 .9				
	March 1	34 6	1 .4				
	May 3	34 9	2 .4				
	July 1	35 8	3 .2				
	Sept. 2	34 8	5 .9				
	Nov. 1	32 9	2 .9				
1809	Jan. 3	31 3		2 .8			
	March 3	31 6		7 .2			
	May 2	30 6		8 .5	4 10 0	15 11 4 3	
	July 4	28 6		9 .5	4 11 0	17 1 7 3	
	Sep...	00		15 .4			

J. TYLER, Printer, Rathbone Place.

BURT FRANKLIN: BIBLIOGRAPHY AND REFERENCE SERIES 382
Selected Essays in History, Economics & Social Science 90

Volume II.

THE EFFECTS

PRODUCED BY THE

EXPENDITURE OF GOVERNMENT*

DURING THE

RESTRICTION OF CASH PAYMENTS.

OBSERVATIONS

ON

THE EFFECTS

PRODUCED BY THE

EXPENDITURE OF GOVERNMENT

DURING THE

RESTRICTION OF CASH PAYMENTS.

BY WILLIAM BLAKE

BURT FRANKLIN
NEW YORK

Published by BURT FRANKLIN
235 East 44th St., New York, N.Y. 10017
Originally published: London, 1810
Reprinted: 1969
Printed in the U.S.A.

Library of Congress Card Catalog No.: 77-80229
Burt Franklin: Bibliography and Reference Series 382
Selected Essays in History, Economics & Social Science 90

THE following observations were written in the beginning of last year, but I forbore to publish them, because inquiries relating to the currency had ceased to excite much interest. The discussions at the late county meetings have induced me to think, that the publication of these observations now will not be wholly useless. It is necessary, however, to mention, that where allusion is made to the present state of things, it must be understood to refer to the month of February, 1822.

PORTLAND-PLACE.
March 3, 1823.

OBSERVATIONS,

&c.

THERE never, perhaps, was a period which presented to the political economist so many interesting objects of inquiry as that which has occurred during the continuance, and since the termination of the late war. Peace, instead of its accustomed attendant blessings, seems to have brought calamity and distress upon almost every class of society; and the circumstances in which we are placed appear to be so peculiar and anomalous, as scarcely to admit of a satisfactory solution. We have seen landed proprietors without rents; farmers and manufacturers without a market; the monied capitalist ready to lend, and the merchant not wanting to borrow; a redundant capital, yet a redundant population; and the industrious poor compelled to apply, like mendicants, at the parish workhouse.

To account for these appearances every one has his favourite theory, and believes or assumes the facts that will best support it. One sect of political economists asserts that there is a want of capital, another that there is an excess. One party recommends us to save from our revenue, in order to increase our capital; another, to increase our expenditure by converting capital into revenue. The agriculturist, although he has had for some years the monopoly of the home market, still petitions for protecting duties against foreign corn; whilst the manufacturer urges the necessity of keeping down its price, that he may not be undersold in the foreign markets. Upon one point alone all parties seem to be agreed, namely, that the value of our currency has been depreciated to the extent of 25 or 30 per cent.; and that in whatever degree other causes may have operated to produce the present distress, the evil has been aggravated by the too sudden return from a depreciated to an undepreciated currency.

Whether any depreciation of the currency, in the sense in which that term is generally understood by the public, has actually taken place, or to what extent it has taken place, I have long had considerable doubts. It appears to me, that very great delusion has prevailed, and continues to prevail, on this important question. As I have myself been heretofore under the influence of this delusion, I think it may be of service to state what are the facts, and the inferences from those facts, that have led me to modify the opinions I have given upon this subject.

The most sanguine theorists who have written on the alleged depreciation of the currency must, I think, have felt their faith shaken by the passing events that have occurred since the report of the Bullion Committee in 1810, and by the facts disclosed in the evidence before the committee on the resumption of cash payments in 1819.

There can be no doubt that subsequently to the restriction on cash payments in 1797, every symptom that indicates an over issue of paper circulation, and an alteration in the value of the currency, has manifested itself. We have witnessed a depression of the exchanges, to a degree, and for a countinuance, that has been unexampled. We have had the market price of gold exceeding the mint price, far beyond the limits that could have occurred if the Bank had been paying in specie. We have seen the legislature compelled to pass an act to make bank notes a legal tender, in order to prevent an avowed difference between payments in gold and payments in paper. And all this accompanied by a general rise of price in most of the articles of consumable produce.

Now I have no hesitation in admitting, that

all the symptoms just enumerated are *indications* of an excess of currency, and of depreciation: and further, that an over issue of currency could not exist for any length of time, without producing these symptoms.

I have, however, perfectly convinced my own mind, that all the results above specified may have arisen from causes not necessarily connected with an alteration in the value of currency; and, moreover, that such other causes are not hypothetical merely, but have been in actual operation.

Now if these premises can be substantiated, and there should appear to be two hypotheses, either of which is adequate to explain the very extraordinary symptoms just specified, it becomes an object of considerable interest to inquire which of the two has in reality been the efficient cause. The discussion will, in this way, resolve itself into a question of fact rather than a question of principle ; and it will remain to be decided, which explanation most satisfactorily accounts for the appearances.

A series of phenomena so remarkable, and so connected, cannot have arisen either from accidental or from trivial causes : they are of a magnitude too extensive to be referred to any ordinary interruption or fluctuation of commercial intercourse. I have very little doubt that the whole of these appearances may be traced, and will be found to have originated in the enormous expenditure occasioned by the late war, the extent of which has perhaps had no parallel either in degree or duration, and never before has been combined with a restriction on payments in specie by the Bank. My object is to show, that these effects not only may have arisen, but must have arisen, from such an enormous and continued expenditure, although the currency had remained in its most perfect state, and had been invariably kept to the due proportion which it ought to bear in relation to the commodities to be circulated by it*.

In order not to perplex the argument, it will be advisable to divide the subject into two distinct parts: in the first of which I shall endeavour to prove that the adverse exchanges, and the excess of the market price above the mint price of bullion, were mainly caused by the large *foreign* expenditure of government; and in the second, that the general rise in the price of all consumable produce was the necessary effect of circumstances connected with

---

* I do not pretend to ascertain that due proportion. There is some ratio which ought to subsist between the total amount of the currency, and the total value of the commodities to be circulated by it. If that ratio be constant, the value of the currency will remain unaltered.

the war, and the increased *internal* expenditure of government.

. That a large foreign expenditure of government will increase the demand for foreign bills, and produce an immediate effect upon the exchange, is admitted by all practical merchants, and by all speculative writers, who have adopted the distinction which has been made between the nominal and the real exchange.

It would be a waste of time, in the present advanced state of knowledge on this subject, to stop to prove, that the real exchange depends upon the proportion which the debts of a nation bear to its credits, or, in other words, between the payments it has to make and those it has to receive. An increase of demand then on the part of government for foreign bills must increase the premium upon them in proportion to its extent. Some judgment may be formed of the effect of this demand, from the fact, that the news of Buonaparte's landing in France from Elba, produced in one post day an advance of ten per cent. on the price of foreign bills, arising solely from the anticipation of this demand *.

Now as soon as the advance in the price of bills exceeds the expenses of transmitting

* See evidence of Mr. Haldimand, p. 67. Report on Resumption of Cash Payments.

bullion, the latter, if it can be procured at the usual price, will be sent abroad for the purpose of drawing against it, and deriving a profit from the premium on the bill. Before the restriction act, bullion could always be procured at the Bank by exchanging notes for coin: the coin was immediately exported, either in the state of coin, or melted into bullion, and no laws have ever been found effectual to prevent its exportation. An immediate reduction of the currency is the necessary consequence. As the law now stands upon this point, the coin is permitted to be exported, and therefore no alteration whatever would take place in the price of gold so long as the merchant exporter could apply at the Bank and convert the paper currency into exportable coin. If, in consequence of the increased demand for foreign bills, gold were to acquire an increased value, the currency by its contraction would augment in value at the same time, and, keeping pace with it, would prevent any excess of the market price above the mint price of gold. But suppose the currency to consist of paper only, and of paper not convertible into gold, what would then be the effect of this increased demand for foreign bills? In the first place, no gold could be procured at the Bank: the exchange-merchant must apply to the bullion-broker, who would be perfectly aware of the object of the application, and would, as a matter of course, increase his price in proportion to the profit that could be derived from its exportation. Let us take an instance: suppose the demand of government has continued long enough to raise the premium on foreign bills ten per cent.*, and that no bullion can be procured but at the bullion-brokers, and at the market price: suppose, too, that to transmit the bullion to the country with which the exchange is unfavourable would cost in freight, insurance, &c. 2 per cent. Is it not evident that the holder of bullion, by transmitting it to the Continent at an expense of 2 per cent., and drawing against it a bill which he could dispose of at a premium of 10 per cent., would gain 8 per cent. profit, and without risk. To conceive it possible, after such an advance had taken place in the price of a foreign bill, that an exchange merchant would think of offering the same price as he would have done before the advance had taken place, or that the bullion-broker would consent to accept it, is to

* It may be noticed here, that long before the premium on bills had risen to 10 per cent., the bullion of the country would disappear. A half per cent. above the charge of transit is sufficient to occasion its export. What remains is retained for the purpose of manufacture, and it remains because the price rises so as not to allow a profit on the export.

suppose that both the one and the other were utterly incompetent to their business. To draw this inference requires no knowledge of the practical dealings in exchange. It is manifest to common sense, that with such an alteration in the exchange, there must be a corresponding and proportional alteration in the price of bullion.

Now, if the paper currency of the kingdom is not convertible into coin, what is there in this demand for bullion that can have any influence on the amount of the currency? If the currency is in its due proportion to other commodities previously to the operation, there is nothing in the transaction between the bullion-broker and the exchange-merchant, that can in any way influence the general amount of the currency, or alter their proportion. Nothing more is required to insure the profit of the exchange-merchant, but that bullion should remain steady in its value at the place to which he intends to export it.

It is curious to observe, in the examinations of the merchants on this point before the committees of 1810 and 1819, the extreme perplexity they evinced, when pressed to explain how the value of gold could rise partially here, without a corresponding rise on the Continent; and with what complacency the examiners seem to have regarded the steadiness of its price on the Continent, as a proof that its high price here must have arisen from depreciation dependent upon over issue.

Now there is nothing whatever in the effect just described, that in the slightest degree indicates the currency to have changed its value in relation to commodities in general. It marks neither more nor less than that gold acquired an artificial increase of value in this country, in consequence solely of the premium on foreign bills.

The restriction on the specie payments of the Bank virtually precluding the accustomed contraction of the currency, it no longer rose to a level with the gold; and the excess of the market price above the mint price, marked the height to which the gold had risen.

Admitting then, that if the Bank had been paying in specie, the difference in the value of gold would not have shown itself, would it not be a strange confusion to say that the restriction was the cause of the increased value? It is the premium on foreign bills that gives the increased *value* to the gold, and the bank restriction having removed the accustomed counteracting remedy, occasioned that increase of value to be shown by the increase of *price*.

It will be contended, no doubt, that in acknowledging the increase of the price of gold, I admit the currency no longer to conform to the value of bullion, its only legitimate standard; and that, inasmuch as it will no longer exchange for the same quantity of its standard measure, it must be considered in a certain sense as depreciated. This is perfectly just; and if the term depreciation was confined to this sense alone, it might with such limitation be freely allowed that the currency had been depreciated.

But this is not the sense in which the term depreciation is understood by the public; it is meant to convey, and does convey, the idea of falling below the former level—a change in its value as compared with *all* other commodities. The moment the term depreciation is applied to the currency, it is assumed as the cause of the increase of prices generally. If an adverse exchange raises the price of bullion 20 per cent. above the Mint price, it is supposed to account for an increase in the price of commodities to the extent of 20 per cent. also ; than which nothing can be more fallacious.

Advantage is taken of the equivocal meaning of the word, and inferences are drawn from it which are not warranted. If this were merely a dispute upon terms, the inquiry would be of little importance; but it is a most essential distinction in fact, and a want of attention to this distinction has been the principal cause of the delusion which has misled so many. If any term had been invented or adopted, that should have expressed the·rise in the value of gold, we should never have heard such extravagant opinions respecting the depreciation of the currency. It is extraordinary that Mr. Baring, Mr. Tooke, Mr. Ricardo, Mr. Haldimand, should all agree in stating, that they know of no other criterion of depreciation than the value of the note as compared with that of gold. This unqualified assertion conveys a false impression, and proves them not to have been sufficiently on their guard against the inferences that result from the ambiguity. They must know that cloth, corn, manufactures of all descriptions, are criteria by which the altered value of currency may be determined. If no change take place in the price of these commodities, it is a tolerably certain proof that the currency remains at its level.

It is evident, therefore, they must in their own minds have limited the signification of the word, and have used it in a sense different from, and more qualified than, that in which it is understood by the public. Mr. Ricardo, indeed, expressly states, that when two commodities are compared together, gold and paper for example, it is impossible to say when they are varying; whether the one is failing, or the other is rising. Nay, he goes so far as to affirm, " that if the price of gold was at 5*l*. 7*s*. per ounce, he should say the currency was depreciated in proportion to the difference between that price and the Mint price of gold, that is above thirty per cent., *although the price of all other articles remained the same.*" And in another part of his evidence he says, " I think it quite possible that a bank note may be depreciated, although it should rise in value, if it did not rise in value in a degree equal to the standard *."

Now, as the purchases and sales of goods will be regulated by their value estimated in the currency, and the currency will thus be the measure of all contracts between debtor and creditor, is it not an inquiry of vast importance to ascertain, whether the paper has been steady in value, and the gold *risen* above the paper; or whether the gold has been steady, and the paper *fallen* below the gold?

This question—whether the currency or the gold had altered?—was continually put to the witnesses by the committee in 1810 and 1819, and never received a precise and definite reply. To read the evidence, one would imagine both

* See evidence of Mr. Ricardo, pp. 138 and 140. Report on the Resumption of Cash Payments.

the examiners and the examined were alike
perplexed. If the witness affirms, that gold
has risen in value because it is wanted for exportation (which is quite correct), he is immediately asked, whether it has risen in the general market of the commercial world, whether
there was any greater demand for gold on the
Continent, or whether there was any scarcity
in the supply there? And as he knows that not
to be the case, he feels himself baffled and confused, and begins to guess and imagine any
thing that will relieve him from the embarrassment of an apparent contradiction; that it is
wanted for the payment of the armies there, or
for metallic circulation, or for any other purpose that the examiner suggests. Whereas,
the true and proper answer would have been,
It has not risen in the general market of the
world; it is not in greater demand abroad;
there is no scarcity in the supply there. If
goods could be exported without loss, they
would answer the purpose as well as gold.
The demand is for foreign payment, not for
gold; and it rises in value in this country, and
this country alone, because the exchange has
become so adverse as to create a large premium
on a foreign bill, and a profit is to be obtained
by the export of gold. The steadiness of its
value abroad is the circumstance that renders

the profit certain. On this account the holder
of gold will not part with it, and transfer the
power of making the profit to another person,
unless at an advance in its price; which advance will be exactly measured by the difference between the premium on the bill, and the
cost of transmitting the bullion, with a small
additional deduction of perhaps a half per cent.,
constituting the profit of the exchange-merchant
who conducts the operation.

Now, although this effect of an increased
price of bullion could only take place within
very narrow limits, supposing the currency
were convertible into coin or bullion, it might
take place to any extent when the currency
was inconvertible, depending upon the amount
of foreign payment to be made, and yet without deranging the just and natural proportion
between the currency and the usual commodities that are to be circulated by it.

The price of corn, of cloth, of every other
commodity, might remain precisely the same,
and nothing alter but the price of gold. Not
only might it vary to any extent without altering the price of these articles, but for any
length of time too, provided the foreign expenditure continued upon the same scale
that first induced the adverse exchange, and
was constantly creating a fresh adverse ba-

lance, as the export of bullion or of other commodities was tending to liquidate it. This would depend on the extent of foreign payment required to meet an extraordinary exertion, and on the difficulties which might be thrown in the way of providing for that payment by the export of goods. For the bullion that could be procured to meet a large foreign expenditure would be very limited, and would disappear almost immediately unless kept in the country by increase of price.

It will be objected, no doubt, that the case which I have supposed does not apply to the actual circumstances we have witnessed during the late war; inasmuch, as the price of produce rose, and indicated the same depreciation of the currency in regard to *all* other commodities as in relation to gold. Of this I am perfectly aware, but I have no doubt of being able to prove, that this general rise in price was the result of another cause acting simultaneously with that which produced the high price of gold, but equally independent of any previous alteration in the value of currency. That it was in fact the result of circumstances connected with the war, and the increased expenditure of government within the country, creating a demand, which could not be supplied except at an increase of price. Now, if

I prove this, and moreover that the increase of price would of *necessity* arise, although the currency remained at its level; then the argument remains untouched by the objection, and is applicable in all its force as far as relates to the high market price of gold. The discussion of this point would lead me prematurely into the second division of my subject, and I must postpone for the present any investigation of this topic; only begging my reader will not suffer his attention to be diverted from the immediate subject of inquiry, *viz.* whether the excess of the market price above the mint price of gold is a fact, when taken alone, that *necessarily* implies an alteration in the value of the currency.

It will be asked, however, does not this excess imply a derangement in the currency? Does it not imply a greater amount of circulating medium than could have existed under similar circumstances, if the Bank had been paying in specie? Undoubtedly it does. If the Bank had not been restricted from cash payments, such a state of affairs must have led to a contraction of their issues; and the consequence would have been, that the value of the currency would have been elevated to the artificial value which the adverse exchange had given to the gold, and thus the difference between the market and the mint price of gold would have disappeared.

This was the accustomed mode in which the currency kept on a level with gold previously to the restriction act, in 1797; but it is evident, that, where the increased value of gold was occasioned by an adverse exchange, such a change in the amount of circulation did not restore a depreciated currency to its level; it raised the currency from its natural level to an artificial elevation; and thus, by an imperceptible influence, kept the currency *apparently* of an uniform value, and the exchanges steady.

It is clear, however, that this apparent uniformity of value was in truth a real fluctuation; and unless it had been confined within moderate limits, might have become a positive evil; and an evil, too, that scarcely admits of a remedy, unless the currency can be so regulated as always to bear its just proportion to the wants of the community, and can be continued at that exact proportion during the fluctuations of the exchange. But how is the currency to be so regulated? And to whom is the regulation to be committed? To the bank-directors? By no means. Much of unmerited odium, as I believe these gentlemen to have incurred, and giving them all possible credit for the moderation and forbearance with which they have exercised the power so improvidently committed to them; I am confident, that no human being, or corporation of human beings, is capable of executing so important a trust, as that of proportioning the amount of the circulating medium to the wants of the community. It is utterly impracticable to calculate what amount of currency would be required, for the purposes of distributing the annual produce amongst its consumers. No human foresight could anticipate the contingencies that might occur. If such calculations were possible, we should at once attain that great desideratum in political economy, an uniform measure of value : but not possessing such powers of calculation, we have no alternative but to adopt that circulating medium which is least liable to variation, and to leave it to find its level among the different nations of the commercial world, by export or import, by melting or coining, as circumstances may denote the necessity of these changes. Such was the state of our currency before the restriction act, in 1797. No other checks against fluctuation then existed, and they were found sufficient for all practical purposes, and in the main salutary in their operation.

After this examination it may be assumed,

that provided the paper be not convertible at option into coin or bullion, the price of gold will be advanced by an adverse exchange; and yet, that the currency may remain at its natural level, that is, unaltered in value, and be maintained in its exact and perfect relative proportion to the commodities to be circulated by it.

Let us then, before we quit this branch of the investigation, examine the facts disclosed by the evidence before the committees of 1810 and 1819; and see how far they tend to invalidate or confirm this opinion.

Assuming that the price of gold, when the currency is not convertible into bullion, may be augmented by either of two causes, that is, by an adverse exchange, or by an over-issue of paper; it might afford strong ground of inference which of the two had been the operating cause, according as a connexion could be traced between the one or the other with the changes in the price of gold.

Upon this point, the tables published in the Appendix to the Report of 1819 offer ample instruction. Not only is there a general accordance between the exchanges and price of bullion whether rising or falling, but if taken for any long periods of time the connexion

may be stated to be absolutely invariable*.
Whilst, on the contrary, no such connexion has
subsisted between the amount of Bank issues
and the high price of gold : nay, so far from it,
that for months together they are found to run
in opposite directions.

It was this want of connexion, between the
amount of Bank notes and the price of bullion,
that first led me to suspect the accuracy of the
theory, that attributed the high price of gold
to the over-issues of the Bank; and the suspicion gave way to absolute conviction upon
the events that took place on the peace in
1814, and the return of Bonaparte from Elba,
in 1815.

When the war ceased in 1814, the price of
gold bullion was five guineas per ounce, that

---

* Some few discordant instances occur of trivial import,
and trivial amount, where a specific quantity of gold and
silver might be wanted for consignment on the sailing of an
Indian Fleet, or for the immediate supply of Government;
and one or two slight discrepancies are also pointed out by
Mr. Baring. So far, however, are they from shaking his
conviction as to the necessary correspondence between the
exchange and the price of bullion, that he attributes them entirely to some inaccuracy in the statements of price by the
bullion-brokers of the Bank; for he observes, that such discrepancies would be impossible if the price of gold were correctly reported.—See Report of Committee on Cash Payments, p. 186. See also Evidence of Mr. Holland, p. 116.

is nearly thirty per cent. above the mint price, and it had been at that price upon an average, ever since the latter end of the year 1812. From May, 1814, it fell gradually, and was at 4*l.* 9*s.* per ounce before the following March, the exchange experiencing, *pari passu,* a corresponding improvement : on the arrival of the news of Bonaparte's landing in France from Elba, the exchange varied at once ten per cent. and continued falling, whilst the price of gold mounted as rapidly to 5*l.* 5*s.* per ounce. All the symptoms that had been considered as indicating a depreciation of the currency previously to the peace of 1814, immediately manifested themselves, and continued during the one hundred days of Bonaparte's power. The battle of Waterloo again put an end to the war, and from that moment the exchange gradually recovered. The price of gold fell back proportionably, and in the course of the following year was at 3*l.* 18*s.* 6*d.* per ounce, that is within 7½*d.* of the mint price.

During the whole of this period there was but little variation in the Bank issues, the numerical amount of the notes in the beginning of 1814 and the end of 1815 being about twenty-five millions. They had been at one time in the course of the two years as high as twenty-eight millions; but, by a perversity most unfortunate for the theory of depreciation, the issues of notes were continually augmenting whilst the exchanges were improving, and the price of gold falling : these events speak volumes. In the midst of peace, when all the symptoms of depreciation were gradually subsiding, when commodities were selling at prices corresponding with the amount then in circulation, a great political event occurs, entailing the probability of a new war and of a great foreign expenditure. In an instant, without any change in the amount of circulation, or of consumable produce, the exchanges fall between twenty and thirty per cent. ; and the price of gold mounts in the same proportion above the mint price. This state continues for one hundred days, and at the expiration of that period, when the battle of Waterloo and the march of the allies to Paris put an end to all further expectation of a continuance of the war, the currency still maintaining its relative proportion to commodities, all the movements begin to retrograde, and every thing returns to its former state of quiescence.

If the symptoms that occurred during this short interval are to be considered as *proofs* of an alteration in the value of the currency, it is in vain to continue the argument. To my mind they demonstrate incontestably, that the anticipation of a large foreign expenditure acted suddenly and powerfully on the exchange, and, as suddenly, through the intervention of the exchange, on the price of gold.

If alterations in the amount of the currency had been the moving force, the price of gold instead of rising ought to have fallen. Can there be a doubt then, that in this case the gold was raised for a time above the level of the currency and afterwards fell back to it? And if in this case, why not in others that occurred previously to the peace of 1814, when the same disturbing forces were in action?

This fact alone throws all the *onus probandi* on the advocates for depreciation; and yet, in the evidence they gave before the committee on the resumption of cash payments, they were utterly unable to give even a plausible explanation of these contradictions. Instances without end are adduced before the committee of 1819, not only of a want of connexion between the Bank issues and the high price of bullion, but of a direct opposition between them, and that not for short periods, but for months and years; and it is quite impossible to lend oneself to the various futile attempts that are made to reconcile the inconsistencies*. If an accidental coincidence can be traced between an enlarged issue of Bank notes, and an augmentation in the price of bullion, it is immediately insisted upon as cause and effect. When the want of coincidence is pointed out, then the witness replies, that the numerical amount of Bank issues is not to be considered as any criterion of excess of circulation, or the contradiction is attributed to some alleged interference of the issues of the country banks. When again the witness is asked, whether the amount of country paper is not regulated by that of the Bank of England? then the difficulty is referred to excessive importations occasioning stagnation of commerce.

* I subjoin the reference to some of the instances alluded to.

	Bank notes.	Price of gold.		
		£.	s.	d.
April to June, 1815	27 millions	5	4	0
July to Decem. 1817	29 millions	4	0	6
July to Decem. 1818	26 millions	4	2	6

Evidence of Mr. Ward, p. 74.

		£.	s.	d.
1813	24 millions	5	10	0
1817	28 millions	4	6	0

Evidence of Mr. Tooke, p. 129.

		£.	s.	d.
Latter part of 1817	29 millions	4	0	6
1819	25 millions	4	3	0
From July 1815 to Decem. 1816, three half years steadily at	26 millions	4 16 0 to 3 18 6		

Evidence of Mr. Ricardo, p. 134, 135.

In short, the high price of bullion is never to be accounted for by the adverse exchange; but both the one and the other are attributed, as a matter of course, to the over issue of circulating medium. Indeed Mr. Ricardo, whose opinions upon subjects connected with political economy will always be received with the deference due to one whose writings have so much contributed to the advancement of the science, entertains such very peculiar notions on the subject of exchanges, that I do not see how he can attain a correct view of the bearings of this question; for he seems to maintain in all his publications, that the variations of the exchange arise solely from the variations in the comparative value of the currencies of different countries, and does not admit that the exchange is dependant upon the balance of debts and credits. Mr. Wheatley, as far as I know, first stated this opinion in his work on the theory of money and commerce; and it seems to have been adopted in its full extent by Mr. Ricardo. As the opinions of these gentlemen are peculiar to themselves, and, in my mind, absolutely untenable and at variance with facts, I must, with all due respect for the weight of such authority, think it unnecessary to dwell upon them; I shall merely state a circumstance that I consider conclusive upon the subject.

I put this question to one of our principal exchange-merchants :—" If, in time of profound peace, with the currencies of France and England upon a perfect level in regard to commodities, and the exchange at par, you were to be informed that the English government had, for some purpose, no matter what, determined to transmit a subsidy, or loan, or present of ten millions to the government of France, would you, after the receipt of that information, draw upon Paris upon the same terms as before ?" The answer was, " Undoubtedly not. I should be aware that such an intention must increase the demand for foreign bills, and I would not grant a bill except at an increased premium." Now as the terms upon which this gentleman would draw upon Paris would, in fact, be quoted, as the exchange of the day, there needs little further argument to prove, that the amount of payments to be made compared with those to be received, must have a decisive influence on the exchange. Whilst considering this part of the subject, it may be advisable to point out a material distinction, which, from not being sufficiently attended to, has led to considerable confusion on the subject of exchange.

It is perfectly true, that if a difference take place in the relative value of the currencies of two countries, in consequence of one of them having increased the amount of its circulation so as generally to affect prices, such an alteration will immediately show itself in the exchange. The depreciated currency of one country will no longer buy the same amount of the currency of the other. This would be an adverse exchange arising solely from depreciation. Such a derangement can only be remedied by a removal of the cause, that is, by contracting the currency, and reducing the excess which occasions the depreciation. In this case, the alteration of the currency is the cause, and the adverse exchange is the effect. This accords with the theory of Mr. Wheatley and Mr. Ricardo, who suppose that no fluctuation can occur in the exchange without a *previous* fluctuation in the currency. But it is equally true, that the same *apparent* difference in the relative value of the two currencies will show itself, when from a disturbance of the relative amount of exports and imports an alteration first takes place in the exchange ; and this apparent difference may be produced without any real difference in the value of the two currencies.

For it would take place between two countries making use of the same metallic currency. In the case above supposed of the currencies of England and France being in the most perfect state possible, and a large payment of ten millions for subsidy being to be made from London to Paris, the premium on foreign bills would rise. Suppose it were to rise 1 per cent., it would then require £101 to purchase a bill upon Paris for £100; or £101 of English currency would appear to be of no more value than £100 of French currency, although not the slightest change took place in the proportion between the currencies of either country, relatively to the commodities to be circulated in each*. This fluctuation would be rectified

---

* I am quite at a loss how to reconcile such an exchange with the theory of Mr. Wheatley and Mr. Ricardo; for it is easy to conceive an intercourse between trading nations of the following description. England might send hardware to Spain, Spain might send wool to France, and France send wine to England; in which case the respective debts and credits would be liquidated through a circuitous remittance, known technically by the term arbitration of exchange. The direct exchanges, however, between England and Spain would be in favour of England; between Spain and France, in favour of Spain; and between France and England, in favour of France. If these exchanges are to be considered as indicating a corresponding difference in the value of the respective currencies, it would follow that the currency of England was more valuable than that of Spain; that of Spain more valuable than the currency of France; and the currency of France more valuable than that of England: that is, A greater than B, B greater than C, and C greater than A, which is evidently impossible. The contradiction arises from transferring that language to the currency which is only applicable to the bills.

quickly, if no obstruction to the commercial intercourse between the two nations interposed; because the £1 of premium on the bill upon France would be an extra profit upon all exports, and a diminution of profit upon all imports, and thus the derangement would be removed by an alteration in the proportion between the credits and the debts.

In addition to this remedy from the exports and imports, there is another powerful auxiliary to rectify the fluctuations of the exchange. For as soon as the premium on a foreign bill has exceeded the limits which will repay the exporter the expenses of transmitting bullion, the coin itself will be exported in payment of the adverse balance. This will lead to a contraction of the currency, and an artificial elevation of its value; and this elevation of the value of the currency, lowering the prices of produce, will still further increase the profits upon export, and diminish the profits upon import. Not so, however, when, after the disappearance of the coin, the currency consists of paper, and of paper *not convertible* into specie. As soon as this step is taken, some of the essential correctives which tend to restore the exchanges are removed: for, first, the price of bullion will then rise exactly to the point where it ceases to be profitable to export it; and consequently the remedy from the export of bullion can no longer be applied. And, secondly, the prices of all other commodities will *not fall.* Now it is this fall of price, arising from the forced contraction, that enables the exporting merchant to gain augmented profits upon all his exports; he would buy cheaper here, and sell at the same price abroad. For the same reason he could not *import* so advantageously as before; for he would buy at the same price abroad, and must sell cheaper here. The exchanges, therefore, could not, after the restriction, right themselves so rapidly. There would then be left but one correcting remedy; viz. the extra profit arising from the premium of the exchange on all exports, and the corresponding diminution of profit upon all imports.

It is clear, too, that the exchange would become more and more adverse in the compound ratio of the extent of payment to be made, and the difficulties thrown in the way of exportation. At the time of the Milan decrees being enforced, and when the ports of the Continent were shut against English goods, the depression of the exchange would no longer be measured by the accustomed test of the expenses of transmitting bullion. The exporter would have to contend against the charges on the conveyance of bulky goods; he must incur the expense and risk of gaining admission for his goods, and when admitted, would have to sell them at low prices, in consequence of the supply being so much beyond the usual demand for consumption*.

It might therefore be expected, that during the continuance of the large foreign expenditure the exchanges would continue to be adverse in a much greater degree than could have arisen under ordinary circumstances.— As soon, however, as the foreign expenditure ceased, this sole remaining remedy was found effectual in improving the exchanges, and lowering the price of gold. For long before the resumption of cash payments, the exchanges were gradually approaching to par, and the price of gold to the mint price. Up to the time of the passing Mr. Peel's bill in 1819, this improvement was in progress, notwithstanding a considerable increase of Bank issues above the amount circulating in 1813.

The country paper is said to have been much diminished between the years 1813 and 1819. I have not been able to ascertain to what

---

* Some estimate of the extent of these difficulties, and of the expenses of sending goods to the Continent, may be formed from the fact, that during the Milan decrees the insurance against the risk of seizure in the ports of the Baltic could not be effected for a less premium than from 20 to 30 per cent.

degree the contraction took place; and certainly, whatever it might be, as it was previous to the passing of Mr. Peel's bill, it could not be owing to that measure.

There is positively no ground for supposing that Mr. Peel's bill produced any effect whatever upon the value of the currency. I am convinced that the exchanges and the price of gold would have subsided tranquilly to their level, if that bill had never been passed, and without any effort on the part of the Bank to contract their issues. Indeed, looking at the last returns of the issues of Bank paper, it does not appear to me that the directors have taken any steps whatever to contract their notes*, or that the amount of the circulating medium, taking the notes and new coin together, is in any degree less than it was at the time of passing the bill, and certainly nothing like so low as it was in 1813.

I have thought it right to make this short digression on the subject of the exchanges, because I observe a constant disposition on the part of some of the witnesses before the com-

---

* This is now stated from authority. The Bank has never made any preparation for cash payments by contraction of their issues. The Bank directors have, on the contrary, been quite ready to make advances upon bills, but the merchants have not applied for them.

mittee on the resumption of cash payments, to represent the exchanges as dependent upon the estimation in which foreigners might hold the value of our pound sterling. Now, if the value of our pound sterling, as compared with foreign money, would be equally affected either by a depreciation of the currency, or by an adverse exchange with an undepreciated currency, it is a complete *petitio principii* to attribute the foreigner's estimation of our pound sterling to his guesses at the depreciation of our circulating medium. The foreigner would be as well aware as ourselves that the adverse exchange enabled him to purchase a bill payable in our currency with a smaller amount of the currency of his own country, in exact proportion to the depression of the exchange.

Having past experience alone for a guide, it was not an unlikely mistake for theorists to fall into, that such an adverse exchange could only arise from depreciation. For no such exchange had ever before arisen without an acknowledged depreciation; as, for instance, that which occurred previously to the reformation of the gold coin in 1774. And it is demonstrable, that no such adverse exchange could have taken place now, but for the restriction on the Bank. It seemed, then, a natural inference, that the Bank being relieved from the necessity of cash payments, had taken advantage of the privilege; and having created a depreciation by over issue, had produced those evils, which had never before been known to arise from any other cause.

It was stated in the evidence on the resumption of cash payments*, that on the return of Buonaparte from Elba, the pound sterling fell, in one post, on the Royal Exchange, to the extent of 10 per cent.; and this statement gave rise to the following questions and answers. " Have you ever known such a fluctuation un- " connected with political causes? Such fluc- " tuations I have never known unconnected with " bank-paper; they are caused by speculation on " the price of the paper.—Have you ever known " that fluctuation with paper unconnected with " some political event? I have never known that " fluctuation in so short a time, which I should " call an anticipation of the future value of paper " currency, except from political causes."

Here it is evident that the witness is answering under the bias of a preconceived theory. He is fully persuaded of the depreciation of the note (which he afterwards distinctly avows), and he states his opinion that the depreciation

* See page 67, Report on the Resumption of Cash Payments.

of the note is the cause of the adverse exchange, and of the high price of bullion. Whereas, if he had felt at the time a conviction that there would be precisely the same difference in the apparent value of the note from an adverse real exchange, and that the exchange was the cause of the apparent depreciation, his answer would have been—I have never known such a fluctuation but from political causes, and I should refer it to an anticipation of an adverse exchange, which would necessarily follow the large demand of government for foreign expenditure.

After this investigation, I may at least assume that there are two modes of viewing this important question : that there are two modes of accounting for the remarkable fluctuations that occurred, both in the price of bullion and the exchanges.

It is quite clear, at all events, that the high price of gold bullion is not a necessary criterion of the currency having fallen below its proper level ; and the reader must decide to which of the causes he will attribute the extraordinary effects that have taken place. In making up his mind, he would do well to reflect, that for the theory of depreciation there is no proof whatever, save that which arises from the symptoms alone. That this proof amounts to little more than an argument in a circle. The depreciation is assumed as a test of over issue of currency, and the over issue is inferred, because there is a depreciation; whereas, if he takes an increased foreign payment as the cause of an adverse exchange, he takes for his basis an acknowledged fact, and from that fact he traces a demonstrable result. He does not argue from symptoms back to a conjectural cause, but he has an *à priori* demonstration, that a large foreign expenditure must create an adverse exchange. That an adverse exchange must, at all times, and with the most perfect metallic currency, give the appearance of a fall in the value of our circulating medium as compared with that of other countries, and with an *inconvertible* currency, must raise the price of gold, without necessarily interfering with the price of other commodities. Having established this foundation, abstractedly from all practical application, he has the opportunity of comparing how the two theories correspond with the series of events.

If any one will be at the pains of reading the evidence before the Bullion Committee in 1810 and 1819, taking along with him this key, he will find the theory of depreciation opposed at every turn by facts in direct opposition to it. Exchanges favourable when they ought to be adverse; gold high when it ought to be low; and contradictions and inconsistencies without end; while the other theory has no difficulties to overcome, save such as may arise from our ignorance of the operations of government, and the precise amount of the foreign expenditure at any particular period of time. He will find the exchange most adverse, when we were making the greatest exertions abroad, either by our own military operations, or the subsidies to assist the military operations of our allies. He will find the evils aggravated, when obstructions were thrown in the way of our exports by the Milan decrees, or by large importations of corn. He will find the unfavourable aspects assume a different appearance at the close of the war, and be renewed during the hundred days of Buonaparte's return from Elba; and, in short, that general accordance between the events, and the actual or probable expenditure of government*, which could hardly be expected, unless they were connected as cause and effect. When the expenditure of government ceased, the adverse symptoms disappeared, and we passed gradually

---

* Mr. Rothschild states the expenditure of the British government in the years 1814 and 1815 to have been immense, and that it lowered the exchange nearly 30 per cent. See *Report on Resumption of Cash Payments*, p. 160.

and easily into our natural state, so far, at least, as regarded our relation with foreign countries.

Having disposed of this part of the inquiry, we shall now be better prepared for examining the remaining division of the subject, and for investigating the cause of that general increase of price of almost all consumable commodities which forms such a striking feature in this question, and which has been considered as another decisive proof of the depreciation of our currency.

If I have been successful in convincing my reader, that with a currency in the most uniform state in regard to other commodities, the high price of gold was the unavoidable result of our large foreign expenditure, and no proof whatever of a general depreciation of the currency, his mind will naturally be more disposed to admit any reasoning that may account for the rise of prices, without having recourse to the same theory. I have already stated, that this general increase of prices depended upon causes connected with the war, and the increased internal expenditure of government, and would have occurred although the currency had remained at its natural level. I shall now endeavour to establish this position, without any reference to the previous reasoning respecting the high price of gold. The two parts of the

argument being thus conducted upon independent grounds, will re-act upon each other,
and tend to the confirmation of both.

The first obvious cause of high prices is the
increase of taxation. Upon this point there has
been some difference of opinion, but none that
has any immediate practical bearing on the
question. It has, indeed, been contended, that
if taxes could be fairly distributed, so that each
person should pay his proportionate share according to the income he possessed, taxation
would have but little effect in raising price;
it would only tend to diminish the income of
those who paid the tax*.

In our present state of society, such a distribution is quite impossible. In the first place,
the income of the labourer is not much more
than sufficient to keep up the class of labourers;
and although I have little doubt that a very
large amount of the taxes is paid by this class,
yet they could not contribute any thing like
their individual proportion, without impairing
the funds absolutely necessary for subsistence.
Notwithstanding, therefore, that in consequence
of their numbers, they probably pay a large
share, they do not pay their proportionate share,

---

* See evidence of Mr. Tooke, Committee on Agriculture,
p. 292.

and, considering how limited their enjoyments are, it is to be hoped they never will.

The fact is, that the taxes are chiefly laid upon articles of consumption, and are generally imposed successively and partially. Such taxes, when levied on the producers, are immediately repaid to them in the increased price of the article, and fall upon the consumer; and the result is inevitable, because the producer has the remedy in his own hands. Unless the public will at once consent to pay the increased price, he will lessen the supply till his object is attained, and without which he could not continue his business. Part of the increased prices, therefore, paid for all articles of consumption during the war, has been owing to the increase of taxation, and would be confounded with the increased prices supposed to arise from a depreciation of the currency. Again, there are very few articles consumed by the most indigent classes of society, that are not in some way, more or less remote, dependent on the importation of foreign produce. The raw material of many, even the coarsest manufactures, is imported directly; various articles used in dying, and other processes of manufacture, are not the productions of our climate. Tea, sugar, and other varieties of food, come to us from abroad. Upon all these commodities there is, during war, an increased charge from high freights, insurance, and extraordinary duties of Customs; all these are so many sources of additional cost, and are causes of high prices, totally independent of depreciation. But the increase of prices does not stop here. If the articles consumed by the labouring poor become dear from taxation, and from the other causes just enumerated, the wages of labour will rise; and it becomes a subject of inquiry whether this increase of wages can be charged to the consumer in the same manner as the taxes.

Every manufacturer is aware, that during the pressure of unusual demand, he can well afford to pay higher wages to his workmen; because he not only reimburses himself for the extra advances, but is enabled to increase the price of his articles so as to augment his profits also. In a particular case then, his power of adding wages to the price will depend upon the demand compared with the means of supplying that demand. But the same reasoning will apply to the whole mass of manufacturers, provided a general demand arises for their commodities beyond the customary powers of supply.

The community consists of two classes of persons, one of which consumes and reproduces, the other consumes without reproduction. If all the society consisted of producers, it would be of little consequence at what price they exchanged their commodities amongst each other; but those who are only consumers form too numerous a class to be overlooked. Their powers of demanding arise from rents, mortgages, annuities, professions, and services of various descriptions rendered to the community. The higher the price at which the class of consumers can be made to buy, the greater will be the profit of the producers upon the mass of commodities which they sell to them; hence it becomes an object of great importance to inquire in what degree the demands of the consumers may vary in relation to the means of production.

Now, amongst the class who are only consumers, government holds the most prominent station; and before the subject can be satisfactorily investigated, we must examine more closely the effects produced by its expenditure. Dr. Hamilton states, that from the year 1793 to 1815, both years inclusive, the sum of nearly 509 millions of *sterling* money was borrowed by the English government*.

If the expenditure of this enormous amount

---

* Hamilton on the National Debt, Table 3, Appendix.

could be considered as an extra demand, in addition to the ordinary demand of the society, there would be but little difficulty in accounting for the increase of prices during the war; and were I content to build an argument on the opinions generally prevalent, I might assume this extra demand as a truth admitted by all practical men, and by very many able writers. It is a position, however, of too much moment to be thus lightly passed over. Political economists have considered the expenditure of government to be derived from a fund that would have been equally a source of demand if it had been left in the hands of the public; it becomes, therefore, absolutely necessary to inquire a little more scrupulously, whether this immense sum is to be considered as an additional demand, or merely as a transfer of demand.

Five hundred and nine millions, divided amongst the twenty-three years of war, give an average expenditure of about twenty-two millions per annum. Let us assume, for the sake of facility of calculation, that the government required twenty millions per annum. If this sum could be raised at once by taxes out of the income of individuals, it would be a mere transfer of income from the people to the government; it would make no difference in the expenditure or the consumption. The people would lose the enjoyment which twenty millions of expenditure might have afforded them, and the government, with its subordinate agents, would consume an equal value in their stead.

Considering that at the present moment we actually raise in taxes above fifty millions per annum, it cannot but excite regret that we should ever have had recourse to so improvident a system, as funding; entailing upon us a perpetual charge from which we might have been wholly exempt, if we had submitted to a greater sacrifice, when the country required a greater exertion.

It must be remembered, however, that it is by degrees only we have arrived at that state of opulence which enables us to raise so large a sum within the year, and that at the respective periods when the loans were contracted, the burthens might have been absolutely intolerable. To alleviate the pressure of this burthen, government has been in the habit of borrowing loans from the people, in return for which, annuities have been granted to the contributors, to be raised by taxes out of the future income of the country. This has been usually effected by applying to some banker or merchant of great credit, who contracts to furnish the amount by monthly instalments, or as the immediate wants of government may require.

The loan contractor has not, nor is he supposed to have, any such sum ; but he expects by his own exertions, and those of his friends who embark with him in the contract, to be able to dispose of the annuity in smaller annuities among the public, so as to provide for each successive instalment as it becomes due. Supposing then the annuities to be thus parcelled out, it is clear that in whatever manner the contributors had hitherto been employing their capital, they must have made up their mind upon this occasion to lay by a certain portion in the purchase of an annuity, and to withdraw it from active employment. Instead then of distributing that capital amongst their workmen, they transmit it to the loan contractor, who is thus enabled to fulfil his engagement with government. Whilst this process has been going on, the orders have been given for a supply of muskets, swords, cannon, gunpowder, &c. ; and upon the receipt of the twenty millions of money by the government, it is immediately reissued, in payment for the warlike stores which the manufacturers have furnished. When returned into their hands, it serves as a repayment for the raw materials, food, clothing, &c., and all the ingredients of circulating capital, which had been left without a demand, when the capitalist who furnished his funds to govern-

ment retired from business. By this circulation, every thing is apparently restored to its
former state ; except that there has been an
extra production of military stores, and a deficient production of the goods that would have
been fabricated by the capitalist, if he had not
lent his funds to government ; and the public
have been burthened with the payment of an
annuity of one million, to be levied out of their
income for ever, and no longer to be enjoyed
by the producers, but to be transferred to
the annuitants who have now become national
creditors.

In examining the links of this chain, it appears, at first view, as if the funds for the maintenance of productive labour had only passed into
other hands, and that the aggregate income of
the country had not been diminished ; inasmuch
as the taxes levied to pay the annuity have
added to the income of the national creditor
precisely the same amount that was taken away
from the income of the public. It seems too,
as if no destruction of property had taken place,
save that which arises from the consumption of
the wrought goods, of clothing, and of food
fabricated, or raised to meet the demand of
government. It must not be overlooked, however, that when government, or its troops, or

agents, obtain possession of the commodities thus raised by the exertions of the people, the commodities are consumed without any reproduction.

When the food, clothing, and raw material, which constitute the circulating capital of the country, are distributed amongst the working classes, their consumption is followed by a reproduction of similar materials, together with a surplus value, constituting the fund denominated revenue or income. The latter may be devoted to unproductive consumption, without in any way injuring the productive powers of the community. The efforts of the capitalists will be directed towards the supply of both these funds with such articles as are adapted to the different wants and tastes of the community. The demand of government will disturb the usual course of production; and that portion of goods destined to unproductive consumption must be augmented beyond what is commonly allotted for the ordinary consumption of the society, by all the extra quantity now required by government. If previously to this demand the productive powers of the country were exerted to the utmost, and there was no means of adding to the gross annual produce, then the government could only be supplied with the commodities it required, at the expense of that fund which had before supplied the capitalist.

If the circulating capital of the country is conceived to be represented by the number 100, the workmen in consuming that amount ought, at a return of 10 per cent., to reproduce a value equivalent to 110. In which case, 10 would represent the amount that might be devoted to unproductive consumption, without injuring the society; and there would remain a value equal to 100, for the purpose of carrying on the same process the following year. If government borrows 10 of that 100 in the form of a loan, and with that loan stimulates the producers to fabricate a quantity of commodities for its own particular use; the value of 110 would be reproduced as before, but under a different form. The surplus fund devoted to unproductive consumption would be represented by 20, and 90 only would remain to supply the labourers with subsistence and raw material for the following year. From the consumption of this quantity of capital, the workmen ought, at the same rate of 10 per cent., to reproduce in the second year a value of 99; of which, if the community consumed 9, and the government as before required 10, there would remain but the value of 80 to be distributed among the working classes, in the third year, and so on.

In this way the capital of the country might be gradually devoted tô consumption. As the process continued, the funds which supplied the working class would disappear, and nothing but impoverishment could ensue. If the capital of the country is always in the fullest activity, and no extra production can take place in any one employment of it, without a corresponding diminution of production in some other; it immediately follows, that the demand of government is no addition to, but merely a transfer of the ordinary demand, with this alarming consequence attached, that in every step of the progress, a certain portion of the powers of production is annihilated for ever. Let us then bring this theory to the test of experiment, and trace the effect that would follow from the expenditure of the actual sums which government has annually been in the habit of borrowing.

Assuming then twenty millions to be wanted for the service of the year, let us suppose that this amount of capital is taken from an employment where it is reproduced with a profit, and that it is transferred to be expended unproductively, so that at the end of the twelvemonth, no traces of it shall appear. This is precisely what is meant by converting capital into revenue.

Now twenty millions of circulating capital thus borrowed will, of course, throw out of work all the hands employed by the capitalists who lend it. The persons thus deprived of employment would be chiefly artisans, and might, one with another, earn £40 per annum each. At this rate, the twenty millions of capital would give employment to five hundred thousand workmen, and as many of these might be heads of families, there could hardly be (taking workmen and their families together) less than one million of souls depending for subsistence upon their employment. To prevent the convulsion incident to such a diversion of capital, let us suppose that government employs a certain number as soldiers, and that the remainder could find work in manufacturing the warlike stores and accoutrements, all of which are to be consumed, according to the conditions, unproductively. In this way, no inconvenience would be felt; the whole million of souls would be provided for, and it would be a fair representation of the change of productive capital into unproductive revenue.

Thus far the process goes on very smoothly; and were we to stop here, no other difficulty would ensue, except that which attends all violent transitions. But what is to be done the second year? Government requires a further supply of twenty millions, which is to be borrowed in the same manner, and with the same consequences. Five hundred thousand more artisans are thrown out of work, who with their families constitute a second million of persons wanting the means of subsistence, in addition to the million of the former year. Continuing, then, the same supposition, that government could apply, as before, the twenty millions of money in providing work for the discharged artisans, we should still have two millions of persons to support with a fund equal only to the supply of one million: the third year would give three millions of people to be employed by a fund of the same limited power, and thus in succession as long as the war lasted. So that at the end of the late struggle, after twenty-two years of war, there would be a destruction of four hundred and forty millions of capital, and twenty-one millions of souls would have been left without subsistence, or any possibility of finding employment.

A more striking example of a moral *reductio ad absurdum* could hardly be imagined; and

yet, extravagant and preposterous as this conclusion may appear, I am not aware of any
exaggeration. It is, as far as I know, a fair
representation of what would be called destruction of capital, or a diversion of capital from a
productive to an unproductive employment.
This view of the process may be rendered less
distinct, by distributing the capital over a great
extent of country, and a great variety of trades
and manufactures; but assuming that the capital of the country is always fully employed,
and that the expenditure of government is only a
transfer of demand, the conclusion at which we
have arrived seems to be inevitable. Forty
pounds per annum is assumed as a fair rate of
wages, near enough to the truth for the purpose
of illustration, and, as a round number, facili-
tating calculation; if a less sum be taken, the
evil would be aggravated, and the consequence
still more absurd.

Such a state of affairs is not only utterly in-
conceivable, but is at absolute variance with all
our past experience. The funds which gave
subsistence to twenty-two millions of people
cannot have disappeared without our being
aware of the loss; and during a period when,
instead of distress from want of employment,
we have witnessed the greatest activity in every

department of industry; every symptom of increasing capital, increasing' wages, and increasing population, affording the strongest evidence of prosperity and wealth. There must either be some gross and radical error in the theory that leads to such absurd results, or in making the application of the theory to the actual circumstances of the country some material fact must have been overlooked, that has either corrected or mitigated the desolation that would otherwise have ensued.

It appears to me that the error lies in supposing, first, that the whole capital of the country is fully occupied; and, secondly, that there is immediate employment for successive accumulations of capital as it accrues from saving. I believe there are at all times some portions of capital devoted to undertakings that yield very slow returns and slender profits, and some portions lying wholly dormant in the form of goods, for which there is not sufficient demand. I believe, too, that when capital accumulates rapidly from savings, it is not always practicable to find new modes of employing it. Now, if these dormant portions and savings could be transferred into the hands of government in exchange for its annuities, they would become sources of new demand, without encroaching upon the existing capital. Unless savings were actually accumulating simultaneously with the expenditure of government, it appears to me that all the mischief described in the foregoing pages would have followed, and that long before the expiration of the contest our efforts must have been completely paralysed.

Adam Smith has long since observed, " that the principle which prompts to save, is the desire of bettering our condition; a desire which, though generally calm and dispassionate, comes with us from the womb, and never leaves us till we go into the grave. It is this effort, protected by law, and allowed by liberty to exert itself in the manner that is most advantageous, which has maintained the progress of England towards opulence in all former times. The profusion of government must undoubtedly have retarded its natural progress towards wealth and improvement; but in the midst of all the exactions of government, the capital has been silently and gradually accumulated by the private frugality and good conduct of individuals, by their universal, continual, and uninterrupted efforts to better their own condition."

It will be contended, no doubt, that if the savings had remained in the hands of the capitalist, they would have equally been a source of demand as when transferred to the government; but this is the very point at issue. It is quite clear that the object and the consequence of the demand would be totally different in the two cases. Whatever amount of produce is withdrawn from the market by the demand of the saving capitalist, is poured back again, with addition, in the goods that he reproduces. The government, on the contrary, takes it away for the purpose of consumption without any reproduction whatever. The question then will simply be, What effect will be produced upon the general industry of the country and upon prices, according as the one or the other mode of employing this extra capital prevails?

Now, whenever savings are made from revenue, it is clear that the person entitled to enjoy the portion saved is satisfied without consuming it. It proves that the industry of the country is capable of raising more produce than the wants of the community require. If the quantity saved is employed as capital in reproducing a value equivalent to itself, together with a profit, this new creation, when added to the general fund, can be drawn out by that person alone who made the savings; that is, by the very person who has already shown his disinclination to consume.

When once the division of labour has taken place, the efforts of each individual are directed to the fabrication of some specific commodity. He fabricates it in the hopes that there will be a demand for all that he can produce. If every one consumes what he has a right to consume, there must of necessity be a market. Whoever saves from his revenue, foregoes this right, and his share remains undisposed of. Should this spirit of economy be general, the market is necessarily overstocked, and it must depend upon the degree in which this surplus accumulates, whether it can find new employment as capital. For it is quite evident, that to continue to fabricate the same sort of goods that have been already rejected would only tend to increase the evil.

Accordingly, Adam Smith remarks, that " As capitals increase in any country, the profits which can be made by employing them necessarily diminish. It becomes gradually more and more difficult to find within the country a profitable method of employing any new capital. There arises, in consequence, a competition between different capitals, the owner of one endeavouring to get possession of that employment which is occupied by another. But upon most occasions he can hope to jostle that other out of this employment by no other means but by dealing upon more reasonable terms. Their competition raises the wages of labour and sinks the profits of stock."

This opinion of Adam Smith has been controverted by the political economists of the present day, who have endeavoured to show that profits never permanently fall in consequence of the competition of capitalists lowering price by over production. They admit that there may be a partial glut of particular commodities from miscalculation of the wants of the market; but that over production can never induce a general glut, and that profits will not fall from this cause, but will be regulated by the rate of wages, and the rate of wages by the quality of the last land taken into cultivation.

This doctrine, I think, has been pushed a little too far. It proceeds upon the assumption that every addition to capital necessarily creates its own demand; but in applying the theory to the actual circumstances of mankind, some inseparable conditions appear to me to have been overlooked. It takes for granted, that new tastes, new wants, and a new population, increase simultaneously with the new capital; a supposition which is not consonant with the fact. The advocates of this theory contend that demand and supply are correlative terms, and must always exactly balance each other *. That any commodity being in excess proves the efforts of the capitalists to have been misdirected, and that there must be a corresponding deficiency in other things.

Nothing can be more clear than that in order to make a demand, you must have an equivalent to offer in exchange. Something must be produced to demand with. In other words, the terms demand and supply merely express, that one sort of supply is exchanged against another sort of supply. This is perfectly true as far as both sorts of supply are wanted for consumption. If one set of capitalists produce a given quantity of cloth beyond their own immediate wants, and another set of capitalists produce an equivalent quantity of corn, also beyond their wants, the surplus quantity of corn may be exchanged against the surplus quantity of cloth, and thus afford a profitable market to each other. But this proposition implies that there is not more corn and cloth in the whole than the two classes of capitalists want to consume. If more than that is produced, the surplus is absolute waste on both sides; and all

* This argument nas been most ably and adroitly conducted by Mr. Mill, in his Elements of Political Economy, and, granting that new tastes and new wants spring up with the new capital, appears to me unanswerable.

the labour thrown away. I shall be asked, no doubt, does not this arise from miscalculation on the part of the producers? Undoubtedly it does, but it is not an excess of one commodity, and a deficiency in another. It is an excess of both. Why then were the corn and the cloth produced? For this plain reason : neither the corn grower, nor the cloth maker, could know that there would be an excess till the excess occurred. Each depended upon a market, and was mistaken. If every thing could be foreseen, mankind would not miscalculate, and there would be no overstocking of the market. But they do miscalculate, and the market is overstocked. When savings are devoted to reproduction, each manufacturer employs the additional capital in fabricating that class of commodities which he has been in the habit of making. But if there was already more than sufficient, the addition must still farther increase the excess. How is it possible for this process to continue without a fall in prices, and a lower rate of profit to the capitalist?

The difficulty of finding employment for new capital is acknowledged by all practical men. They continually feel and complain that every channel is full. The evidence is brought home to them, by the general accumulation of commodities undisposed of, and stored in the warehouse. These are the records of so much capital in a state of actual stagnation, neither affording profit to the owner, nor employment to the workman, and discouraging all future exertion. The capital expended in the production can be replaced to the manufacturer in no other way than by the sale of the goods; and until that is effected, both capital and workmen are reduced to a state of inactivity. The difficulty is easily got over theoretically, by supposing the manufacturers to invent immediately new articles to gratify the tastes of consumers. The practical manufacturer, however, knows the risk attendant upon speculations of this description, and is afraid to encounter them. But let a new market be opened, and the impulse is given at once. If when the two sets of capitalists were producing more corn and cloth than could be consumed, a country were to be discovered which afforded other objects of gratification to man; and corn and cloth should be articles of request in the new market, the surplus is at once disposed of in exchange for the new productions: and that which was absolute waste, as corn and cloth, becomes in another form a source of enjoyment, and a stimulus to future exertion. So will it be with savings. Open but a new market, or invent new objects of desire, and either the savings are consumed in

another form by the persons who had previously
ceased to consume, or they are advanced as
capital to workmen, and the revenue arising
from that capital is expended in the purchase
of the new luxuries.

Now this is precisely what is effected by the
increased expenditure of government: a new
and immense market is at once opened for
consumption.   9

The immediate means of purchasing which
government possesses is derived from the sale
of annuities. The power of levying taxes in
perpetuity, and of transferring the income
arising therefrom to individuals, enables the
government to collect all those savings that find
no immediate employment as capital, and to
devote them to expenditure. The purchasers
of these annuities consist chiefly of the class
living upon fixed monied incomes, who are dis-
inclined personally to employ their petty savings
in business, and who prefer the security of government to that of private borrowers; or they
are of the class of capitalists, who finding the
returns upon their capital inadequate to the
trouble and risk, are glad to receive a stipulated
and certain return as interest, rather than an
uncertain one in the form of scanty profits.
The purchase of an annuity is a complete proof

that the owner of the capital has not the means of employing it advantageously.

The loan contractors thus become the channel through which all the accumulations of capital that are feebly employed, or that are without employment, find their way into the hands of government; whence they immediately pass into a state of complete activity amongst the producers who furnish the warlike stores, or such other commodities as the subordinate agents of government require. Whether this additional consumption be eventually beneficial to the country, is not the present object of inquiry; but there cannot be a doubt, that during its continuance, the effect must be precisely the reverse of what we have been endeavouring to trace during the progress of rapid accumulation of capital. Its tendency would be, to relieve all capitalists from excess of stock; to create a demand for their goods, whilst it diminished the competition of new capitalists, and thus to increase both prices and profits.

That this increase of profits has been the consequence of a war demand, we have all the evidence that historical evidence can afford.

No proposition is more generally admitted, than that the market rate of interest paid for the loan of capital is proportionate to the profits that can be made from the employment of it.

If profits, then, were regulated solely by those made upon the last quality of land taken into cultivation, we should observe in all countries a regular fall in the market rate of interest as the population increased, and was compelled to have recourse to inferior land. Now it is not denied that such has been the usual course of the rate of interest; but it is equally certain that there are very remarkable deviations from this law, and for long periods of time together.

In the twenty-six years of peace that followed the treaty of Utrecht, the market rate of interest ran steadily at 3 per cent., and 3 per cent. stock of government, previously to the war of 1739, sold as high as 107*. During the war, the 3 per cents. fell from 107 to 80, and after the peace of Aix la Chapelle, again rose to 106. In the year 1762, during the seven years war, they fell to 63, and rose during the peace to between 80 and 90. In 1782, during the American war, they fell as low as 54, and in the following peace again rose to 96†. During the French revolutionary war, the market rate of interest rose to 7, 8, 9, and even 10 per cent.,

* Hamilton, p. 317.

† Hamilton, on the National Debt, p. 317, 318.—I am well aware that the price of government securities is not a perfectly correct criterion of the market rate of interest, but it affords a fair approximation, and a scale of comparison for different periods.

although during the whole time lands of the very lowest quality were inclosed and cultivated. Since the termination of the war, the interest of money has again fallen, and the Bank are discounting at 4 per cent.

These facts are in direct opposition to the theory of profits being regulated *always* by the quality of the last land taken into cultivation*; they are a strong confirmation of the opinion of Adam Smith, that the profits of capital are subject to variation, from the proportion which the capitals bear to the existing population, and to the desires or powers of the community to consume. The fact, too, of the low rate of interest paid in the year 1792 is strong evidence, that previously to the breaking out of the French war, capital was accumulating faster than the means of employing it; and warrants me in the assumption, that savings from revenue were then going on, which might afford a fund for the war expenditure of government.

If, then, during the periods of peace, when, probably, there is a rapid accumulation of capital, I find that profits diminish; and that during periods of war there is a great increase

---

* This point has been very ably urged by Mr. Malthus in his Principles of Political Economy, and has not as yet received any satisfactory answer.

of profit, and that both these results ensue without reference to the quality of the land taken last into cultivation, how can I resist the conclusion, that savings from revenue, when devoted to further production, have a tendency to increase the quantity of commodities beyond the means of consumption, and thereby to lower prices.

When savings from revenue, instead of being devoted to reproduction, are transferred into the hands of government, no productive labourers are thrown out of employment, for the savings have never yet served as capital; the working classes are still fully occupied by the capital previously existing, in providing the gross annual produce for consumption. When government comes into the market with the funds supplied by the loan contractors, it makes a demand upon the producers for an extra quantity of work, to be furnished by the same number of workmen ; wages rise, but the master manufacturers, with the certainty of a market for their goods, gladly advance the extra stimulus. The whole industry of the nation is called into action, and new life infused into every employment.

That capital exists in a dormant state, and is capable of being called into increased activity by the application of the proper stimulus, there can-

not be the smallest doubt. Every day's experience
affords practical evidence of it. No sooner is a
market, or supposed market, opened at Buenos
Ayres, or elsewhere, than cargoes to an immense amount are shipped to take advantage
of it. The trade with India is thrown open,
and instantly the different presidencies are
glutted with English goods, without any diminution in the supply of the home market. Ask
the manufacturers at Leeds, Manchester, Birmingham, what would be the effect of a certain
sale for fifty millions of their respective manufactures? Can there be a moment's hesitation
that every workman would be called upon for
his utmost exertion. In the evidence before
the committee on the Agricultural Distresses,
Mr. Attwood states the productive power of
Birmingham to be double what its action
then was. Examine the evidence of Alderman
Rothwell, Mr. Rous, and various other witnesses, who all agree, that during the war there
was both greater production, and greater consumption. How could there be greater production from the same number of workmen,
without more exertion, and higher wages? The
hay season, and the harvest season, offer good
illustrations of the quantity of extra work that
can be done, under the stimulus of high wages.
Every one knows what exertions are sometimes

F 2

made when artisans are paid by the piece. Machinery may be made to work the whole twenty-four hours instead of twelve. Nothing is wanting to create this activity but high prices, and the confidence of a market *.

If savings are to be employed as capital, they must be distributed amongst a population not more numerous than before, and higher wages must be given; but, I contend, that there will be a disinclination to give the higher wages, or to employ workmen at any wages, when the goods produced have to seek for a doubtful consumption by competition in a market already fully supplied. When the savings are expended by government, the manufacturers feel the market

* The following information was obtained from an intelligent woollen manufacturer in the neighbourhood of Leeds. He occupies a large mill, and has the necessary proportion of manual labour for the power of his engine. He was very much pressed for the kind of goods he manufactures, and in order to meet the increased demand, called on his labourers for their utmost exertions. The ordinary day's work is from six o'clock in the morning to six in the evening, allowing time for meals. He overworked his hands from two to three hours per day, thereby making from seven to seven and a half days work per week for each hand; and although for a few months in summer under such circumstances, he is of opinion that an increase of ¼th *in production* might be obtained in his mill; yet to continue to extract as much as possible from manual labour for any considerable length of time, would not produce an increase of more than one-seventh.

to be declared and manifest, the demand urgent, and the customer prodigal and improvident in his bargains. It is to be remembered also, that the demand of government is not only for goods, but for men. The army and the navy must be recruited. Whilst more commodities are required, government withdraws a part of the power that is to produce them, and wages are still more enhanced by this new competition. The natural consequence that results from this increased activity is, a very great extra demand for agricultural produce, and for sustenance of every description. That part of the loan which is distributed in pay to the troops is mostly expended in provisions for their maintenance. Probably a greater quantity may be consumed by them as soldiers, than if they continued in their usual occupation; and this is much dwelt upon by some writers, as the great cause of extra consumption during war; but, I think, more importance has been attached to this species of waste than can be justly ascribed to it. The demand, however, of a large manufacturing population, receiving high instead of low wages, and *in full employment,* is an efficient and powerful cause, that must produce an immediate effect upon consumption, more especially of food and the raw materials of coarse clothing.

The numbers in the higher classes of society

bear no sort of proportion to that of the working class. We are apt to dwell upon the expenditure of the former, as if their revenues
were the great source of national demand; for-
getting that the bulk of the gross annual produce is consumed by workmen whilst preparing commodities to gratify the tastes of capitalists. A return of 10 per cent. has been
thought a fair profit to the possessor of capital.
For every £100, then, of circulating capital that
is distributed amongst workmen as wages, which
is the measure of their consumption, the possessor himself can consume but to the extent
of £10.

If, in consequence of brisk markets, the
artisans are employed fourteen hours a day instead of twelve, and they receive wages in proportion, the demand for goods suited to their
consumption will be increased in the same ratio
as the wages. An increased exertion amounting to one-sixth would be tantamount to an increase of population to the same extent; and a
population, too, possessing the means of effective demand.

It has been said, that the " desire of food in
every man is limited by the narrow capacity of
the human stomach." I am satisfied, however,
that the consumption of a labouring man and
his family, when in the receipt of high wages,

admits of considerable latitude; and that one can hardly form a definite idea of the increase of demand for agricultural produce, for coarse goods, and the homely luxuries of the poor, that might be created by a manufacturing population suddenly enjoying a great augmentation of revenue from full employment.

When more work is performed, more wages must be given to the labourer. If the increased wages are exactly proportioned to the increased quantity of work, his rate of payment remains the same, although the actual amount he receives is greater. An artisan, working six days, at twelve hours per day, and receiving 18s. for his weekly wages, would, by working fourteen hours, be entitled to 21s. per week. In this case, without altering the rate of wages, his demand on the market would be increased one-sixth.

The same may be observed in regard to profits. When the capitalist furnishes an extra quantity of goods, he acquires a greater amount of profits, but not a greater rate of profits. If, however, in consequence of a great demand from unproductive consumers, and the difficulty of obtaining the extra produce to meet it, he can obtain higher prices for the work done than the extra cost of production from higher wages would entitle him to; he would receive not only more profits, but a higher rate of profits.

There cannot be a doubt that during the war more produce was raised, and more work done. This would be a source of greater profits and greater wages, even without any alteration in the rate of either, and would create an increased demand in the markets. But it does appear to me, that not only was there an increased amount of wages and profits from the extra work done, but also an increased rate of both, and that this was effected through the medium of prices.

With a greater demand for work, and a part of the workmen withdrawn for the army and navy, I cannot conceive it possible that the rate of wages should not be enhanced by the competition. If one hundred pieces of cloth were required instead of fifty, not only more looms would be employed, but more would be paid by the piece to the weaver. I am, therefore, disposed to concur with Mr. Malthus, that the rise of wages which took place during the war did actually afford a greater remuneration to the labourers.

Whatever doubt there may be on this point, there can be none respecting the rate of profits. For the market rate of interest rose to 6, 8, 10, and even 12 per cent. at some periods of the war; and I would ask, how it is possible to account for this rise in the sum paid for the use of capital, unless a greater profit was to be derived from its employment.

The depreciation of money, supposing it to exist, could in no way affect the interest paid for its use. If £200 of currency became of no more value than £100, ten pounds paid as interest for the £200 would be of no more value than five pounds. Whatever affected the value of the principal, would equally affect the value of the interest. Whatever affected the value of the capital, would equally affect the value of the profits. It could not alter the ratio between the two. Some other cause then, besides depreciation, must have raised the rate of interest, which is the index of the rate of profits.

It has been contended, that the rise of wages, if general, would diminish profits, but not raise prices, and that if it did raise them, no producer would be benefited; because he would lose as much upon all that he bought, as he gained upon that which he sold. But this reasoning is not applicable to a state of society in which a large class are not producers. If A, having a certain capital, and employing a certain number of labourers in raising corn, has to exchange his produce with B, who, with a similar capital and number of workmen, is fabricating cloth, it is evident that no advantage could accrue to either of them by increasing the price at which they interchanged the corn and the cloth. But if both A and B have to contribute a fixed sum for the expenses of government, for the payment of public creditors, for the interest on capital borrowed, for the support of the clergy, it is their interest to interchange commodities at the highest prices that can be obtained. Wherever there exists a large class living upon fixed incomes derived out of the produce raised by the industrious classes, the sum that is levied upon the producers becomes virtually diminished in proportion as the prices of commodities are increased. Thus a new distribution of the annual produce takes place. More than the just share is obtained by the producers at the expense of that portion, which of right belongs to the class who are only consumers.

In times of peace when more is produced than finds a ready consumption, there is a difficulty in raising prices as wages rise. But in time of war, when there is an unusual demand, when the markets are more scantily supplied in proportion to the extent of consumption, when the supply can only be obtained by increased exertion on the part of the capitalists and the labourers, then it is that the working classes reap their harvest, and acquire not only the increased wages and profits to which they are entitled from the addition to the annual produce, which their extra exertion has created, but an increased rate both of wages and profits.

It is an acknowledged fact, that the money value of wages rose during the war, and the market rate of interest proves that the rate of profits also rose. Now, how could the capitalist, having more to pay to his workmen, realize even the same rate of profits, except from an advance in the money price of commodities?

A given number of workmen, and a given number of capitalists employing them, are called upon to furnish an extra quantity of work. Is it possible to conceive that they will not take advantage of the urgent necessities of the buyer, even if they could produce the articles wanted without additional sacrifices? But, if the men are to work thirteen hours a day instead of twelve, and the machinery is to be watched night and day, and the employers to devote more time to superintendence, are they not entitled to a greater remuneration? The sacrifice of personal comfort is greater, and must be paid for, or the commodity will not be produced.

In the comparison of these two modes of employing the savings from revenue, we have taken for granted that the savings devoted to capital would still remain within the country. Now this is granting more than the facts will justify. When the capital accumulates rapidly, and profits fall, it will have a tendency to remove to Spain, to Naples, to Columbia. It will be engaged in the carrying trade, or in employments that do not set much labour in motion; in all which cases but little stimulus will be given to the home producer. When the savings are employed as loans to the government, the demand finds its way immediately into the market, and either relieves it by taking off the produce that remains on hand, or stimulates to the production of more.

During the progress of the war, five hundred and nine millions sterling were in this way devoted to the purchase of commodities intended for consumption, instead of being devoted to reproduction. And I ask whether it be necessary to resort to depreciation, in order to account for the high prices which such a market for consumption must have occasioned? It is to be observed, too, that though in the first instance the demand might be for the materials of war, it would gradually extend to almost every commodity ordinarily consumed by man.

When once the loan is in the hands of government, it is distributed in a thousand different channels. When paid to the troops, it passes into the market for provision, for necessaries, and for clothing; when to the Admiralty, part of it is applied to the purchase of hemp, tar, tallow, timber, and part for provisions of every kind for victualling the navy: when to the Ordnance, it is expended in accoutrements of all descriptions: when to the Civil Departments of the State, it would form a source of demand in the same manner as the income of private families. Whatever direction the expenditure took, it would be a call upon the capitalists to exert themselves, and to produce the commodities wanted for consumption. The war had scarcely commenced before its effects were made manifest. Nothing more was wanting to stimulate the industry of the country than a new market, where the producer was certain of a sale for his goods. It not only afforded a source of extra profit to all the capital then in existence, but offered the strongest temptation for the accumulation of more. There cannot be a more decisive proof of this than the immediate change in the rate of interest. If such a demand had arisen at once, no ingenuity in the application of the powers of machinery, and no increased exertion of the physical powers of the industrious classes, could have provided the means of meeting it. But it was diffused through twenty-two years of war, in the very mode most likely to produce the effects we have witnessed. In the commencement the extent of our operations was not upon the scale they assumed towards the conclusion of the contest; during the last four years of which, the expenditure of government, independently of the supplies raised by the property, and other war taxes, was not less than a hundred and forty-seven millions sterling.

This increase of expenditure, therefore, came upon the country when it was more prepared to meet it. For, although five hundred and nine millions sterling was the amount distributed amongst the working capitalists of the country, the value received by government in return would be charged with the extra profits of those capitalists, and the extra wages of their workmen. These profits and wages would, therefore, form a part of the increase made to the general income of the country, and be an additional fund to contribute to the enjoyments of the people, if destined to consumption ; or, if not so consumed, would offer a further source for the accumulation of capital.

When commodities become high priced, and continue so for a length of time, it is sometimes argued that this circumstance of itself is proof of a depreciation of the currency. I have no other objection to this phraseology, if it be consistently adhered to, than that its tendency is to mislead. Commodities are higher priced, and *therefore* money is no longer able to purchase the same quantity as before. Be it so: but let us understand each other. Let us not wander so far from common sense as to affirm, that the altered value of money is the cause of the high prices, instead of the effect. Let us not invalidate the fixed contracts between man and man; and when commodities fall back from high prices to their level, be allowed to resist the stipulated payment under the pretence that the money has altered in value, and not the goods. Well might Locke say, " Words being intended for signs of ideas to make them known to others, not by any natural signification, but by a voluntary imposition; it is plain cheat and abuse when I make them stand sometimes for one thing and sometimes for another, the wilful doing whereof can be imputed to nothing but great folly, or great dishonesty."

If every increase of price is to be designated as a depreciation of money, let us revise our language; and when a bad season, or difficulty of production, or taxation, has raised the price

of corn, of cloth, of leather, and of any other
article that we consume; let us say that corn,
cloth, and leather have not risen, but that
money has fallen in value from depreciation.
If the object be to confound all our conceptions,
and all our reasonings on this subject, there
cannot be any more certain mode of effectuating
the purpose than by adopting this equivocating
language.

There is great difficulty, I admit, in defining
what is meant by currency remaining at its
level; but supposing the quantity of circulating
medium to be at any period whatever in its due
proportion to commodities, I should say it remained at its level, if its increase or diminution
corresponded exactly with the increase or diminution of the value of commodities to be circulated by it; that is to say, if the circulation of
commodities of four hundred millions required
a currency of forty millions, and that this proportion of one-tenth was the due level, estimating both currency and commodities in gold;
then, if the value of commodities to be circulated increased to four hundred and fifty millions, from natural causes independent of depreciation, I should say the currency, in order
to continue at its level, must be increased to
forty-five millions; or that the forty millions

must be made to circulate with such increased
rapidity, by banking or other improvements, as
to perform the functions of forty-five millions.

If, then, more business was done, more commodities produced, more interchanges made,
and those interchanges made at higher prices,
more circulating medium would be required, or
a greater rapidity of circulation. Such an augmentation, or such rapidity would be the consequence, and not the cause, of the increase of
prices. Accordingly, we find on examination
of the evidence before the committee on the
agricultural distresses, that as far as any increase
or diminution of the circulating medium can
be connected with prices, such was the order of
precedence.

There is scarcely a shade of difference in any
of the evidences respecting the time when the
advance in prices began. It does not correspond with the increased issues of the Bank,
nor with the high price of gold bullion, which
latter effect indeed did not even show itself till
the year 1800; whereas the prices paid by
Greenwich Hospital, as given in the Appendix
to the Report on the Resumption of Cash Payments, denote an increase before the year 1797;
notwithstanding the remarkable contraction of
the currency, both of the country banks, and the
Bank of England, during the years 1795 and

1796. Prices, too, began to fall immediately after the termination of the war. Although the Bank issues were, upon an average, constantly increasing from the year 1813 to the year 1819; and since that period, and since the resumption of cash payments, there really does not appear to have been any material diminution of the circulating medium, as far at least as the issues of the Bank of England form any criterion by which to judge of the amount; inasmuch as the quantity of coin and bank notes together form a larger amount than when Mr. Peel's bill passed into a law.

It seems to be generally admitted, indeed, that since the year 1813, there has been a considerable diminution of country bank paper; but here again we must take care not to confound the cause and the effect; for, as Mr. Malthus observes, " it is of the utmost importance to recollect, that at the end of the war prices failed, before the contraction of currency began. It was, in fact, the failure of prices which destroyed the country banks, and showed us the frail foundations on which the excess of our paper currency rested *."

I have no intention of pushing this argument farther than it will fairly bear, but it is quite

* I may be allowed to quote the fact, without admitting the implied inference of an excess.

clear, that with no other criterion for depreciation than a rise in prices, and with a demonstration that a rise of prices must have been induced from natural causes, such as increased taxation, increased wages of labour, and increased demand for consumption, in proportion to the means of supply, we shall be venturing to sea without helm or compass if we suffer ourselves to guess what part of the increase has been owing to depreciation, and what part to the natural causes just referred to.

It is of no avail to argue, that such a state of things could not have existed if the Bank had been paying in specie. Of that I admit there can scarcely be a doubt; but in what way would the increase of price have been prevented? By a contraction of the circulating medium, that would have reduced prices below their natural level; would really have altered the value of currency, and have given it an unusual elevation. The foreign expenditure and adverse exchange must necessarily have forced the Bank to reduce the amount of its paper, and the prices at which commodities would have settled would have been some intermediate point between the high prices occasioned by the influence of the war, and the low prices occasioned by the contraction. Prices acted upon by these opposite causes might have varied, as either the one or the other predominated, or have remained nearly stationary.

The Bank restriction has, in fact, unfolded what would have been the consequence if the act of 1797 had never passed. The currency must have been reduced, until it was raised to a par with gold; I have no hesitation in saying, such ought to have been the consequences. The community having established gold for their standard, should never have departed from it. But I think it by no means improbable, that with the immense and continued expenditure that has occurred, the fluctuation of the currency, without a restriction, might have been very considerable; and, that in consequence of that measure, its level may in reality have been less disturbed.

It would be idle to affirm, that during the period of the restriction act, the currency had been so nicely adjusted by the Bank directors, as never to exceed or fall short of the due proportion it ought to bear to the value of commodities; it is probable, that in the course of the period they have erred sometimes on one side, and sometimes on the other. But it is evident, that in assuming the price of gold as the measure by which to estimate the deviations of currency from its level, we should be adopting a criterion that would afford but little insight into the real fluctuations of an inconvertible currency, and would expose us to every degree of exaggeration.

It may be thought, perhaps, that with these views, I consider the Bank restriction to have been practically beneficial: I am glad to have this opportunity of entering my protest against any such inference. The measure appears to me to have been fraught with extreme danger to the public; to have occasioned a considerable loss to the government, entailed additional taxation on the subject, and to have been attended with great injustice to all creditors. Most dangerous; inasmuch as it was giving to the Bank directors a power of controlling the circulating medium of the country, which was liable to the greatest abuse. Most impolitic; because the loans required by government would have been less, in exact proportion to the increased value of the currency, if it had been allowed to contract, as of necessity it must have done without a restriction on specie payments. The whole debt incurred would consequently have been less, and the future taxation diminished in the same ratio. It has interfered, too, with all contracts between debtor and creditor; for as the creditor is subject to the fluctuations that occur in the value of gold, and must submit to receive, in liquidation of his claim, the same nominal amount, whatever be the diminution in the value of the metal itself, he is justly entitled to receive the same nominal amount of gold, when any accidental circumstances occur to raise its value.

I therefore hail the measure of resuming cash payments as one of the greatest boons that could be conferred; and, more particularly, as it took place at a time when from the progress already made in the fall of the price of gold, any contraction in the amount of the currency was rendered unnecessary.

In settling the rights of debtor and creditor, it is of great importance to determine, clearly, what were the actual changes that took place in the value of our money; such a question never could have arisen, but for the restriction of specie payments, and is another proof, if more were wanting, to show the mischief of tampering with the currency of the country. At the present moment, there is a strong feeling against the claim of the public creditor. It is contended, that the debt was contracted in a depreciated currency, and the dividends are henceforward to be paid in an undepreciated currency. Now granting, in the first place, this supposition to be true, if the contract were made between the creditor and the public,

under an express provision that he was to have
a specific dividend, and that that dividend was
to be paid in the legitimate currency; and
farther, that during the whole period of borrowing, there was a law in force, that the dividends should be paid in specie within six
months after the conclusion of the war, there is
no pretence whatever for flying from the terms,
even if they were to become more oppressive
than they really are. But if the currency has
not been depreciated, if the value of gold has
arisen from the accidental cause of a large
foreign expenditure, and on the cessation of
that expenditure has returned to its original
level; then the public debt was contracted in
money of the same value as it is at present,
and there is no pretence in law or equity that
we should relieve ourselves from paying what
is justly due. The very raising of this objection to the claims of the public creditor
demonstrates unequivocally that it is no longer
a dispute upon terms, or whether this meaning
or that shall be attached to the word depreciation; but whether the rights of a large class
of individuals are, or are not, to be violated.
We have already done them one wrong, in
passing an act that prevented the currency
from rising; and instead of giving them any
redress, there is a strong feeling to commit

a second wrong under the pretence that not rising has the same signification as falling.

I have now brought to a conclusion the observations I proposed to make on national expenditure, and its effects on currency and produce. No person can reflect upon the points that have been discussed in the forgoing pages, without anticipating the few remarks that remain to be made on the causes of our past and present difficulties. It appears to me, that in whatever degree minor circumstances may have co-operated, the great and mighty source of the distresses felt by all classes of producers has been the transition that took place at the termination of the war. Not the transition from war to peace, in the usual acceptation of those terms; not the transition that arises from the diversion of capital from one employment to another employment; not the transition from the waste occasioned by the extra consumption of troops, either at home or engaged in actual warfare; but the transition from an immense, unremitting, protracted, effectual demand, for almost every article of consumption, to a comparative cessation of that demand. And this change, too, accompanied with almost every circumstance that could aggravate the evil. For the producers had been so long habituated to the extraordinary call

made upon them by the increased expenditure
of so many millions, that their means of supply
has been formed with a reference to the system
and an expectation of its continuance.

Hence, no sooner had the large profits
which their exertions enabled them to obtain
exceeded their immediate wants, than they
began to multiply the sources of production.
The savings from these increased profits, as
soon as realized, were vested in new and more
powerful machinery, or improvements of the
old. There appeared to be no limits to the
extension of these powers, yet, were they kept
in full and active employment. Machinery,
which under ordinary circumstances always
throws out of employment the greater part of
those who had been supported by the circulating capital before it became fixed, seemed
to be deprived of its temporary noxious effect
upon the condition of the labourer; for the
rate of wages never fell from the high level it
reached soon after the commencement of the
war, and proved that the increased demand
would admit of no relaxation, and still out-
stripped the ordinary rate of production.

The excitement was not confined to manufactures. It extended to the producers of the
raw material in every branch of employment:

the mines of copper, tin, lead, iron, coals, were all in activity.

The farmers felt the immediate influence of the demand, in a still greater degree than the manufacturers: food and raw material were in great request, but they had not the power of resorting to machinery. Whatever could be effected by drainage and permanent improvements, by manure and dressing, and what has been called high farming, was done; but the produce from the old lands could not keep pace with the demands of government, and of manufacturers of all descriptions in full employment. The price of corn, therefore, rose more in proportion than that of any other article.

Notwithstanding that one thousand seven hundred and ninety-eight inclosure bills passed the House of Commons, during the twenty years, between 1795 and 1815, giving an average of eighty-eight for each year, the supply was still found to be inadequate; and foreign countries were put in requisition to make good the deficiency. The resources of our machinery were brought into action not only to furnish commodities for our own immediate consumption, but to supply a surplus quantity to be exported in return for corn.

They enabled us to search every quarter of the globe to procure the means of subsistence, and to obtain the effective ingredients of circulating capital, by the importation of food and raw material from every country within the circuit of commercial intercourse.

In the midst of this excitement, and with all the powers physical and moral in full action, the war ceases, and with it the demand of government and its subordinate agents. What other result could follow than distress throughout every employment in which productive capital was engaged? The reservoir intended to supply the national consumption was filled as before, but the great mains that were to carry off this supply were stopped. Every market overflowed with commodities, and gave no encouragement for further production*.

There cannot perhaps be a more striking con-

* It has been said that the increase of revenue is of itself sufficient proof that there is no falling off in demand and consumption. I would merely observe in reply, that when once the demand has so far diminished as to cause produce to sell at what may be called a glut price, the same consumption, or even an increased consumption, may take place, and add very considerably to the revenue, without affording any benefit to the producers; the consumption then goes on at their expense, and without repaying to them the costs of production. The cheapness of food, too, would enable the lower classes, who are the chief consumers, to expend a larger amount in beer and spirits, snuff, tobacco, and other excisable articles.

firmation of the opinion here enforced than the change that has taken place with regard to the importation of corn. At the time of passing the Corn Bill, it was universally believed that we did *not* grow enough for our own consumption. The promoters and opposers of the bill were alike impressed with the idea, and they acted upon this impression. The promoters expected that the price must necessarily be sustained at 80s.. and the opposers thought it never could be less. Both parties were borne out in their conclusions by the necessity of a constant importation; and I have no doubt that such necessity then actually existed. No sooner, however, did the war cease, and with it the great expenditure of government, than the discovery was *suddenly* made that we *did* grow enough for our own consumption. Can any body conceive this change to have arisen from the mere cessation of the wasteful consumption of war? Can any body believe that from that moment we should have had a succession of abundant harvests? Is it not clear that the great superfluity of all produce was the effect of the diminished demand? First, the diminution of the actual demand of government itself in the corn market, and, secondly, the diminution of demand from all the subordinate agents, and from the manufacturers and their workmen, to whom the expenditure of government had given full employment. It seems probable that the effect of this demand was felt through all countries from which we imported corn; for we find similar complaints of glut and low prices at the same period in almost every part of Europe, Canada, and the United States. This might arise partly from the cessation of our own demand, and partly from the cessation of demand which the war expenditure of other governments had created

The universality of this distress is not to be accounted for on any other supposition, and can hardly be attributed to abundant harvests for so many years together, in all the different quarters of the globe. More especially as there does not appear to be any conclusive evidence of such abundance, except what is inferred from the lowness of price. Moreover, the low prices are not confined to corn alone. It is well known that manufactures are less in quantity, and less in price also. A simultaneous fall of price takes place in almost every commodity, and in almost all countries. It cannot be abundant harvests; for it affects articles with which harvests have no connexion. It cannot be alteration in the currency; for it is felt in those countries where no change in the currency has taken place*. To what then can we attribute this universal effect, but to the general diminution of demand? There still remains the capital, and the labourers, and the commodities, but no longer the same market for consumption.

To those who imagine consumption not to be a necessary ingredient of demand, and that in order to make a market for commodities, it is only necessary to produce more, these phenomena offer problems not very easy of solution; nor is the difficulty less for those who conceive the previously existing capital to have been diminished by being converted into revenue. Accordingly, every drowning theorist has caught at the various straws that crossed him. It was the preparation for cash payments, or the raising the value of the currency 25 or 30 per cent., or adopting gold as a standard, instead of silver, or the importation of corn, or the blessings of

* A gentleman from Piedmont informs me, that the same measure of corn raised upon his own estate, which during the war sold at 9 francs, now sells at 3; and has done so ever since the peace, although, during the whole period, the circulating medium of Piedmont has consisted of coined money in its most perfect state. A letter was shown to me, written by a merchant in Holland to his correspondent here, stating that the rent of land about Utrecht had sunk to one-third of its former amount, owing to the great fall in prices.

a good harvest, or taxation, or the want of reform in parliament, or any thing but the obvious cause, that the supply was too great for
the demand.

I would put this single question. Was there
ever an instance of a *permanently* low price,
that is, a price which would not remunerate the
producer, except from the supply continuing
too great for the demand? Why then are we
to busy ourselves in finding out remedies for
an evil which, if left to itself, must always work
its own cure? The producer has the remedy
in his own hands. No man will continue to
carry on a business that is attended with loss,
or even with less than the ordinary profit of capital. If the capital is generally redundant, from
the falling off of consumption, the capitalist
must submit to receive a lower rate of profit,
until new markets, or the growth of new tastes,
and new sources of enjoyment, offer further
motives for increasing employment and consumption.

The distress that has pervaded all classes of
producers, since the termination of the war,
has been greater perhaps than ever was known
before. The manufacturers are said to be re-
covering; and it may be so: but I suspect the
masters can only find a market by selling their
goods at a very low rate of profit, and the artisans

can only find employment by working at a low rate of wages.

The state of the agriculturist is calamitous beyond all former example; and the extent of capital embarked in this pursuit, together with the extent of country over which it is distributed, brings it home to every man's feelings. One cannot contemplate a situation more distressing than that of an industrious and honest class of the community embarking their capital in a pursuit which for years has been attended with the greatest possible encouragement, and, without any fault or negligence on their part, suddenly finding their commodities without a market, and themselves reduced to comparative poverty.

It is a hard doctrine to preach to men in this situation, that their only remedy is to produce less. They naturally ask, Will this restore our capital? How are we to recover what we have invested in the permanent improvement of the land, if we are to give up its cultivation? Who is to begin? Will not every one endeavour to obtain the greatest possible produce? I have no wish to bruise the broken reed, but I fear there is but one answer to these melancholy questions. Those who are the least able to bear the pressure, must be the first to submit to the hard terms of necessity. It is the lot of all who embark their capitals in any enterprise, to take the risk of its success or failure. Such distressing fluctuations are continually occurring in trade, from circumstances over which the parties have had no control. At one time the West India planters were reduced to the verge of ruin, and many have suffered most severely. They are suffering now perhaps more than any other class, yet without exciting much commiseration. Sometimes the Baltic trade is distressed; then the Canada trade; or that in silk or foreign wool. Instances of this kind might be adduced without end. But it never has been, or can be expected, that the parliament or the public can guarantee individuals from the uncertainty incident to all human speculations. Nor can they, with any justice, be called upon to make good the loss which different interests have suffered, or may suffer.

The farmers, as a body, merit every consideration; and nothing should be left untried that is likely to afford assistance, or palliate their misfortunes. But let us beware of the empirical nostrums that are offered in such profusion, by the country gentlemen assembled at our county meetings. Let us beware of holding out the prospect of relief, by loans or purchases of corn by government; or increasing the currency, with a view to raise prices. Such remedies, if they were practicable, which they are not, would never reach the seat of the disorder. The farmers are suffering from over-production. They are not producing more, perhaps, than at the time of the high-prices; but the great demand has ceased, and the same quantity becomes relatively an excess. Nothing, therefore, can be attended with more fatal consequences, than to adopt any measure which by leading them to continue the production, will only perpetuate the disease.

For above twenty years they have had a golden harvest, and many have gathered largely into their garners. But they have not been prepared for, nor did they foresee the sad reverse; and they find themselves suddenly, by the fall of prices, and the lessened value of their stock, bereft of half their capitals.

I do not apprehend, however, that the change will have the effect of throwing any great extent of land out of cultivation. The lessened production will principally arise from an abandonment of what has been called high farming. This will have a two-fold operation: the expenses of cultivation will be diminished, and there will be less produce from the same extent of land. Such lessened produce will be sold at higher prices; and this appears to me to be the natural and the only remedy.

The inevitable consequence of this remedy must be a general fall in the nominal amount of the whole landed rental of the kingdom. This appears to be a momentous result, but will not eventually be attended with so much pressure as is commonly imagined. I have examined this subject with some care, and have come to the conclusion, that taking past and present times together, the class of landholders have not much reason to complain. In expressing therefore my opinion on the state of the agriculturists, I must confine my commiseration to the farmer alone, whose interests I consider to be essentially different from that of the landlord, although for a particular purpose it has of late been found politic to represent them as the same.

There is so much difference of opinion in the evidence of the land-agents examined before the committee on the agricultural distresses, that it would be unwise to place implicit reliance on any one. It may be safely assumed, however, that in the course of the last thirty years, the rental of the landed proprietors has, *at least*, doubled; and taking this fact along with daily experience as to their mode of living, there can hardly be a doubt, that during the whole period of the arduous struggle in which we have been engaged, they have scarcely suffered a single privation; whilst the receiver of a nominal income was actually sinking under the pressure of increasing taxation, and increasing prices; the landed proprietor was enabled with every rise of price to augment his rental proportionally, and to indulge in all the enjoyment that a constantly improving income could afford.

During the whole period of the war, speculations were entered into with borrowed money, under a full persuasion that land could scarcely be bought too dear*. No price, however extravagant, but what was found to repay the speculator by the increasing rent; and now when the accident that gave rise to this artificial value has ceased to operate, and prices are returning to their level, the landholder, grafting his application on distresses which more immediately relate to the farmer, appeals to the legislature for protection, as if the accidental high value was to be guaranteed to him by the state.

---

* I believe that the great clamour respecting agricultural distresses has arisen chiefly from the ruin that has attended these speculations.

I do not mean to deny that there are many landholders who are at this moment suffering from the fall of rents, and from farms being thrown upon their hands; but I do contend that their sufferings are attributable in a great measure to their own want of foresight. Without any merit or exertion on their part, they were supplied with the means of providing against any reverse that might occur : if, instead of that, they preferred present enjoyment, they must take the sweet and the bitter together : but can hardly be allowed to allege their former good fortune as the ground of relief, to be obtained at the expense of the other classes of the community.

It is universally admitted, that even now, farms are let at higher rents than in the year 1792; but the increase of taxation, and the pressure of the national debt, are dwelt upon as more than counterbalancing the advantage. Does not the observation imply, that up to the time of the fall of rents, the landholder had escaped from the increasing pressure of taxation? Why is the possessor of landed property to be exempt from paying his share of the public burthen? Have not all annuitants and receivers of a nominal income been paying these increasing taxes during the whole period of the war, without any means of relieving themselves?

In the midst of all the present complaints of injustice and distress, there is not, I firmly believe, a single landholder in the kingdom that would fairly change places with a fundholder of 1792; that is to say, if his estate were to be sold at thirty years purchase upon the rental of 1792, and vested in the funds at the then price of the day. I believe that no landholder would consent to give the present value of his estate, and the rents that he has received since 1792, for the amount of the stock it would then have purchased, together with all the dividends since that time.

It requires more than ordinary patience to examine, with temper, the various sophistries that have been resorted to, in order to uphold the system of high prices and high rents. I shall not enter into the arguments that occupied the public attention during the passing of the Corn Bill; but no man in his senses has ever doubted, that the object of the bill was to keep up the price of corn, and to afford what was called a remuneration to the grower.

That measure has entirely failed, because we have ceased for the present to be an importing nation. The great object which the advocates of that measure professed to have in view is attained. We *do* now grow enough for our own consumption. Still it is affirmed, that the grower has not a remunerating price. What is to be done? Higher protecting duties would be of no avail. The farmers have already the monopoly of the home market. The phraseology has therefore taken a new turn; as prices cannot be kept up, they must be rendered remunerating, by diminishing the expenses of cultivation; and as taxation is alleged to be one great source of this expense, the farmers are to be relieved by diminishing taxation. Was it not the general cry of all the landholders, that we could not meet the competition of foreign corn, because taxation had so raised prices, that it was impossible to cultivate upon the same terms as the foreigner? Be it so. What is this but admitting that taxation does raise prices? And without such admission, can any one doubt the fact? Must it not then raise the price of corn as well as of every other manufacture? With all this taxation upon its cultivation, corn has settled to its present price. If there had been no taxation, would it not have settled to a still lower price, and have left as little for remuneration as before? There is no escaping from the horns of this dilemma.

I have looked through the evidence of the witnesses' examined before the committee on the agricultural distresses, with the view of ascertaining what part of the expenses of cultivation arise from taxation; and the result is not only curious and amusing, but shows how little reliance is to be placed upon the estimates of men, whose minds are strongly biassed in favour of some special measure. It was the object of most of these witnesses to represent the expenses of cultivation as high as possible. In their statements, which were professedly derived from practical experience, they were at liberty to rate the expenses of manuring, wear and tear, and various other items, at a vague estimate : but the taxes were capable of exact calculation, being a certain amount on their windows and farm horses. The result is, that in magnifying the gross amount without the power of magnifying the actual taxes, they have left the proportion which the direct taxation bears to the whole expense of cultivation so exceedingly small, as scarcely to produce any perceptible effect either upon prices or expenses. Taking the average of Mr. Ellman, jun., Mr. Ilott, and Mr. Edmonds, the present direct taxation, now that the horse tax is abolished, does not amount to more than $\frac{1}{220}$th of the expense of cultivation, or about nine shillings of tax in every 100l. of gross expense*.

The landholders complain too of tithes and poor rates, as taxes that fall partially on the land, and from which the other classes of the community are exempt. It is perfectly well known, that no partial tax can ultimately fall upon a producer. Are there not partial taxes laid upon almost every branch of industry? If the brewer were to complain, that he could not continue his business on account of the tax upon beer, would not the landholder be one of the first to tell him, that the tax was repaid to him in the higher price charged to the consumer? Take the tax upon salt, the highest in proportion to the value of the article, and in that sense the most partial that can be conceived:—Is any one simple enough to imagine, that this tax falls upon the preparer of salt? How then does it happen, that the farmer alone is an exception to the general rule, and has not

---

* See Mr. Ellman's Evidence, pp. 112 and 113.

    Direct taxes -   -   £2 16 0

    Gross expense -   - 379 0 0 is $\frac{1}{135}$th.

  Mr. Ilott's Evidence, p. 140. Direct taxes 6d. on a gross expense of 6l. 17s. is $\frac{1}{274}$th.

  Mr. Edmond's Evidence, p. 184.

    Gross expense - £3988 0 0

    Direct taxes   -   9 4 0 is $\frac{1}{440}$th.

the means of repaying himself for any partial
tax that may be laid upon his produce.

Sometimes the tithes are represented as a
charge upon the landlord, and as a deduction
from rent. Now I would ask, did ever any
man pay the same price for an estate chargeable
with tithes, that he would give for an equally
productive estate tithe free? Does it not form
a part of his calculation when he estimates the
rent, and the number of years purchase that
he means to give? And if he buy an estate
subject to tithes, does he not make a proportionate deduction? In truth, he buys the right
to nine-tenths of the produce, the remaining
tenth never has belonged to him. It is quite a
different question, whether tithes be an eligible
mode of providing for the clergy; but such being
the law, the clergy have as good a title to *their*
portion as the proprietor has to the remainder.
In point of fact, the clergy scarcely ever receive
their full right. Tithes, therefore, as now collected, are practically a benefit to the landlord,
inasmuch as he obtains a part of that portion
which belongs to the church; and for which, at
the time of purchasing the land, he never paid.
There is a very effectual remedy, however,
against the burthen of tithes, both as it affects
the landlord and the farmer; although, I admit

its practical application would be attended with
some difficulty. Let the land be divided between the landlord and the clergyman according to their respective rights, and each
might let his portion tithe-free. But, how
many landlords, even in those cases where the
remedy was practicable, would accede to this
equitable division?

The poor-rates are not exactly upon the same
footing with the tithe, because, when estates
were purchased, there was no foreseeing the
height to which they would rise. It could
not, therefore, form a definite item in the calculation; but even in this case, all estates purchased since the establishment of poor-rates
have been subject to the contingency, and a
less price paid in consequence. The poor-rates
have, in fact, increased to their present enormous amount, in a great measure through the
contrivance of the landholders and the tenants,
who have upon all occasions endeavoured to
keep down the wages of labour, by paying a
portion of them out of the poor-rates. In this
way, they have been used as the means of
making the proprietors of houses contribute
towards the payment of the farmer's labourer.
If the poor-rates had been less, the wages of agricultural labour must have been higher. It has
been urged, too, on the part of the land-owners,

that they have not only their own agricultural poor to support, but the manufacturing poor also. That the greater part of the poor-rate is paid by the land, there can be no doubt; but it is equally true, that a very large amount is paid by the towns; and falls upon houses and manufacturing capital*. The charge against the manufacturers of not supporting the whole of their own poor has some foundation; but it must be remembered, that the landowners have derived the greatest possible advantage from the augmented numbers of the manufacturers, who have afforded the principal market for their produce, and must be considered as the original source of their wealth. The steam-engine has done more for agriculture than any bounty that ever was offered; and I have little doubt, if the subject was closely followed up, that the great change which took place when we were converted from a nation exporting corn to one requiring its importation might be traced to the perfecting of that stupendous instrument of manufacturing power.

* The rental of lands is estimated by Mr. Lowe at forty-five millions, and that of houses at sixteen millions.—State of England, by Joseph Lowe, Esq. p. 66. This publication exhibits a variety of facts and tables, collected apparently with great care and industry; and is a valuable contribution to our stock of statistical knowledge.

When any particular produce comes into competition with that of foreign countries, then, undoubtedly it becomes a question, what sacrifices the government will make to encourage or protect the home growth, or the home manufacture. And if the partial tax that has been levied has so raised the price that the commodity will no longer bear the competition, it may be and often has been found advisable, to impose a countervailing duty on the imported corresponding articles.

Taking then this principle for a basis, what ought to be the countervailing duty on imported corn, so as to balance the partial tax of tithe and poor-rates.

The evidence before the committee on the corn laws, and the agricultural distresses, furnishes the data for this calculation. On referring to the table, published by the Lords' committee on the Corn Laws in 1813, I find, that on an average taken from forty-two counties, the tithe and poor-rates, and all other rates, are together less than half the rent. Upon land of twenty shillings rent, the tithe and rates would be about nine shillings. Mr. Ellman states, that the produce of wheat on land of this value is three quarters per acre; consequently, this would give three shillings

per quarter as the countervailing duty to balance the tithe and poor rates.

As land, however, does not produce wheat
above once in four years, some allowance must
be made for the lower value of the other crops,
which, when estimated correctly, gives an average produce of wheat per acre of about one
quarter and a half, and therefore 6s. per quarter
for the countervailing duty*. Such would be
the claim to which the farmer would be entitled,
in order to protect his corn from foreign competition, as far as regards the direct taxes of
tithe and poor-rate.

In respect to the indirect taxes, inasmuch as

---

* Mr. Ellman's calculation of three quarters per acre on
land of 20s. seems rather too high; taking the produce at
twenty bushels per acre, the countervailing duty will still be
less than 7s. per quarter. Mr. Ilott gives the following crops
as the produce of land paying 25s. per acre rent, and about
12s. tithe and rates.

	£.	s.	d.
Turnips, per acre	2	0	0
Barley, four quarters per acre, at 24s. .	4	16	0
Clover, one ton and a quarter, per acre .	3	0	0
Wheat, twenty bushels at 7s. per acre .	7	0	0
Gross produce of four years . .	4	16	0
Average produce per annum . .	1	4	0

which estimated in wheat at 7s. per bushel, gives an average
wheat produce per annum of twelve bushels per acre; the
tithe and rates are therefore 1s. per bushel, or 8s. per quarter.

they are incapable of being calculated, and
further, that all other articles are alike subject
to them. no manufactures could be sent out to
pay for the corn that had not been liable to
these indirect taxes in the course of their fabrication. Now, as the corn imported must
pay for the manufactures sent out in exchange,
the imported corn is thus, in fact, subjected to
all the indirect taxes that are levied upon the
home corn*, besides the additional charges of
freight and insurance upon so bulky an article,
which from Dantzic to London does not amount
to less than 10s. 6d. per quarter.

It has been necessary to dwell somewhat
longer upon this point, because we have
heard such extravagant opinions respecting the
amount of duty necessary to protect the home
grower. If we are to keep up a scale of artificial
prices that shall remunerate the cultivation of

---

* As the indirect taxation bears more heavily on produce
raised by circulating capital or human labour than on that
fabricated by fixed capital or by machinery, it is a question
open to discussion, how far agricultural produce is or is not
more affected than manufactures? I am inclined to think,
that the quantity of human labour employed in raising corn
bears a larger proportion to the amount of fixed capital than
it does in manufactures; and that on this principle the agriculturist might fairly claim some additional protection. But
the point is doubtful, and could not be ascertained without
very minute and precise investigation.

our most barren soils, there is no limit to the amount of duty that must be imposed; but there is a limit to the sacrifice which those who are to pay the duty will submit to. The great difficulty of the present moment is, to prevent our capital from flying to other countries where corn is cheap, and the wages of labour low. Infinitely more danger, as it strikes me, is to be apprehended from the flight of capital, than from the risk of having our supply of food interrupted, supposing we were to depend more than at present on corn of foreign growth.

The whole question of the degree of protection to be given to the landed interest rests upon this point. The most sanguine agriculturist would think it absolute madness to encourage the cultivation of Bagshot Heath. Where to draw the line, and to what degree the country shall submit to the disadvantage of wasting its capital and productive powers on barren land must be left to the discretion of the legislature. In deciding, however, it would be well to remember, that there is at present a strong tendency to remove capital to foreign countries, and that personal property is already subjected to a very severe pressure in the form of legacy duty, from which the landowner is entirely exempt. On every succession to personal property, even to that of a parent, 1 per cent. legacy duty is paid, and for more remote relations from 3 to 10 per cent. By inquiry at the Stamp Office, I find that these duties are, upon the average, very nearly 3 per cent.*; and the average duty upon probates and letters of administration is about 2 per cent. more, making together nearly 5 per cent. This tax is levied upon the amount of *capital*, and is repeated at every succession. Now it has been ascertained, that where property passes in a direct line from father to son, there will be a succession about once in thirty years; and where collateral descent is included, the succession takes place about once in twenty years. As the succession to property by will, in this country, not only includes collateral relations, but absolute strangers, the succession might be still more rapid; let us assume it, however, to take place once in twenty years †; then 5 per cent. upon capital once in twenty years, is the same as 5 per cent. upon the income of that capital every year, and the legacy duty and probate are, in fact, equivalent to a perpetual income tax of 5 per cent. upon all personal

---

* The average duty is 2*l.* 18*s.* 3*d.* per cent.

† Many copyholds are held upon payment of a fine at the death of the tenant. The value of these fines is calculated, at the insurance offices, upon the basis that there will be a succession once in twenty years; and the fact is found to correspond with the calculation.

property. If any one possessing land should be disposed to underrate the pressure of this tax, I beg him to consider what his feelings would be, if upon every succession by death one twentieth of his estate should pass into the hands of government.

The expenditure of government has been so intimately connected with the changes in the value of property, that I could not conclude my observations, without taking a short review of the relative situations of persons enjoying landed property, and those possessing personal property. A spirit has of late manifested itself, which I can hardly designate by any less qualified term than that of fraudulent, but which has been awed and checked by the strong feeling of integrity that still pervades the great bulk of society. Opinions have been delivered on the necessity of breaking faith with the public creditor, which, twenty years ago, no man of character would ever have ventured to hazard, and to which no audience of English gentlemen would have listened without indignation. Paley defines the law of honour to be a system of rules, calculated to facilitate the intercourse of gentlemen with one another; and he adds, " That injuries done to tradesmen by insolvency, or delay of payment, with numberless examples of the same kind, are accounted no breaches of honour; because a man is not a less agreeable companion for these vices, nor the worse to deal with in those concerns which are usually transacted between one gentleman and another." I trust it is not reserved for some future moralist to adduce the instance of a breach of national faith, as one of those departures from common honesty which is sanctioned by the law of honour. Great allowance may be made for the soreness that men feel when the brilliant prospects of increasing wealth fade before them; but it never can justify an attempt to relieve themselves by the sacrifice of the general interests of society.

If the positions I have endeavoured to establish be correct, the possessor of personal property has derived no more advantage by the return of prices to their former level than he was justly entitled to; and the landholder, after twenty years of increased enjoyment, still finds his situation better than it was in the year 1792. Of those who, near the conclusion of the war, changed their property from the funds to land, or from land to the funds, probably neither the one nor the other foresaw the consequences, and they have experienced very opposite turns of fortune. With their speculations and the result of them, the public have no concern.

During the war the profits of farming capital

have been far above the general average, and
the great demand for agricultural produce kept
the prices at so high a level, that many were
tempted to invest their property in the purchase
of land, and many to embark in its cultivation.
At the present moment there is a great pressure
upon the agricultural interest. But I have no
doubt when production shall have gradually
accommodated itself to consumption, the difficulties will disappear, and the land, as heretofore,
afford a due remuneration to those who will estimate their stock fairly at the present prices. In
the course of the last six or seven years, farming
capital has sunk to nearly half its value, and
this loss must be submitted to. If the owner
expects that the present produce is to yield the
usual rate of profit upon the former estimate,
it can only end in disappointment.

But it is unnecessary to pursue this subject
further, and I shall take my leave, by recapitu-
lating, as briefly as possible, the conclusions
which the preceding investigation tends to
establish.

It appears to me, that the expenditure of
government, through its various channels and
subordinate agents, has occasioned a demand
for almost every species of produce. That the
supply required to meet this demand could only
be obtained by the increased activity of the ca-

pitalists and working classes. That the savings of the community, when borrowed by government in the form of loans, became the fund which, being distributed amongst the capitalists and their workmen, stimulated them to this extra exertion. That the markets were relieved from all superfluity in consequence of the demand for consumption exceeding the ordinary supply. That in consequence thereof prices began to rise at the commencement of the war, previously to the restriction on cash-payments, even during a period of considerable contraction of currency. That when the expenditure ceased, prices fell, before any contraction of currency took place, and that consequently the contraction was the effect and not the cause of the low prices. That agricultural produce increased in price more than manufactured goods, because machinery could not be brought in aid, and because we were compelled to have recourse to inferior lands, and to importation, with high freights and high war charges. That the full employment of the working class augments greatly the demand for coarse goods, and for corn; and that the least excess of demand for corn beyond what the home growth could supply would of necessity raise its price above the limit of 80s. That when the demand ceased, and the la-

bouring classes had no longer full employment, the same quantity of produce became a
glut, whilst the artificial state induced by our
corn laws precluded all relief from exportation.
That the foreign corn growers felt the influence
of our demand, at the same time that the war
expenditure of other governments contributed
to the same results, and that consequently the
distresses of the agriculturists have been nearly
universal. Such a change could scarcely have
occurred from abundant harvests in distant
countries, and under different climates, and
still less from alteration in the value of their
currencies; for the fall in prices was felt in
countries where there had constantly been a
metallic circulation; and in commodities, the
supply of which did not depend upon harvests
or seasons.

That the foreign expenditure contributed
equally with the internal expenditure in giving
full employment to the artisans, inasmuch as
there is no mode of providing for a foreign expenditure of such extent and continuance but
by the export of some valuable commodity.
That although under ordinary circumstances
goods can only be exported when higher prices
abroad afford a profit to the merchant, the export may be considerably enlarged under the
operation of an adverse exchange, since the

merchant obtains an advantage from the premium on foreign bills, in the same degree that
the exchange is depressed. That when the
currency consists of paper not convertible into
bullion, and the export of goods is insufficient
to keep pace with the foreign expenditure, the
high premium on foreign bills advances the
price of bullion, without interfering with the
prices of other commodities. That if there
had been no restriction on specie payments, the
contraction of currency induced by the adverse
exchange would have raised its value above the
natural level, and created a fluctuation in favour of all creditors, to which they were justly
entitled, and of which they were deprived by
the Bank Restriction Act. That all contracts
for purchases and sales were regulated by prices
estimated in currency, and not in gold; and
that to invalidate those contracts, under the
pretence that currency had fallen rather than
that gold had risen, would be to commit a second wrong instead of redressing the first. That
if an *inconvertible* currency could have been so
regulated as neither to be in excess nor deficiency, but to be a perfect measure of the rise
and fall in the value of commodities, the internal and foreign expenditure of government
would, with such a currency, have induced
higher prices both of commodities and gold.

That, consequently, these symptoms are not necessarily proofs of an alteration in the value of currency. That as far as we can judge from facts, the symptoms cannot be traced to excess of circulating medium, but are immediately connected both in time and circumstance with the increased expenditure of government; and we are warranted in concluding, that the expenditure and consumption occasioned by the war have been the chief causes of the increased production during its continuance, and of the distress that has prevailed since its termination.

It has not fallen within the limits of my inquiry to examine how far it is ultimately beneficial to the country, that the capital should gradually increase by saving, rather than be prevented from accumulating by the expenditure of government. This is more a question for the legislator than the political economist. My object has been confined to tracing its effect on prices. If the view which I have taken should lead to the inference, that war is not immediately attended with the calamitous effects usually ascribed to it, I beg to warn my reader, that whatever encouragement the expenditure of government gives to production, no permanent benefit arises to the country if the increased production is all destroyed by a corresponding consumption. Notwithstanding the excitement occasioned by a sudden and immense demand, there will still remain the perpetual burthen of increased taxation as a clog upon all future exertion, and for which I fear no remedy will be found available.

I am well aware of the errors into which a theorist may be led by attempting to generalise too far, and by referring moral effects, as he would physical, to unmixed causes ; neither do I wish to exclude the influence of collateral causes, if they should be thought necessary. The one pointed out seems adequately to account for many of the difficulties that have presented themselves. It cannot be denied that the expenditure has taken place : that the symptoms may have arisen from this source is matter of demonstration. The reader must decide whether that which is proved to be the possible, is not also the probable, nay, the actual cause of the phænomena to be explained.

THE END.

THE WAR AGAINST THE JEW

By the Same Author:

Concise Dictionary of Judaism
Dictionary of Philosophy
Hebrew Impact on Western Civilization
Letters to My God
Lost Legends of Israel
Of God, the Devil and the Jews
On the Nature of Man
Pictorial History of Philosophy
The Soviet Impact on Society
Treasury of Thought
The Wisdom of the Kabbalah

The War Against the Jew

by

Dagobert D. Runes

PHILOSOPHICAL LIBRARY

New York

To the memory of my mother,
victim of the fury of Anti-Semitic Prejudice

Raise not your children in disdain of Israel;
I say unto you, take out the venom from your
Scripture so that my people may live!

PREFACE

This is not a book of writings. This is a book of war.

There are many chronicles of war; of war lasting four days and of war lasting thirty years, even one hundred years, but then the war was over and peace followed.

My book is of a different war, a war forever, a war seemingly indissolubly attached to the creed of a billion people, a war that has become a dogma with the aggressor, a holy war with the most unholy consequences, a war deeply imbedded in the hearts of the bellicose, a war that never had an ending—even the rare armistices were not kept—a war so full of hate and cruelty for so long that history lacks any parallel, a war in which neither children nor invalids, the unarmed or ill, women or the aged, not even the newborn—who, our sages say, sleep in the wings of angels—were spared:

The War of the Christian Churches against the Jews!

This war is sometimes not declared but nonetheless pursued; when not pursued, the declaration still stands. Sometimes the war is cold,—cold hate preached in the Christian churches, seminaries and Sunday schools. The clergymen do not tell you whom to kill; they just tell you whom to hate.

Killing follows hate as combustion follows intense heat. The Christian clergymen start teaching their young at the tenderest age that *The* Jews killed the beloved gentle Son of God. That God Himself, the Father, punished *The* Jews by dispersion and the burning of their holy city. That God holds *The* Jews accursed forever and that the Romans (who had sacked every city in the Mediterranean cradle of civilization from Syracuse to Alexandria, from Carthage to Athens) tried to save the suffering Son of God, but the

ix

Jews apprehended the child-loving Savior, insulted Him cruelly, beat Him, thorned Him and finally nailed Him to a cross. Indeed, the Jews even wished to break the dying God's bones.

This is no place to reason with faith.

Reason says that if a man or group of men have decided to judge and execute one of their own—even if their judgment be wrong, totally wrong—no one can be held to account but they themselves. Three out of four Hebrews did not live in Palestine at the advent of Jesus; nine out of ten of the Israelites in Palestine inhabited towns and villages outside the city of Jerusalem; and of the inhabitants of the holy city, only a few hundred could possibly even have heard the trial of Jesus on the hill of the Temple.

Why pursue with fire and sword the descendants of the few hundred, even were they guilty?

Why pursue the descendants of the Israelites who heard of the trial a hundred years later? Why pursue the descendants of the Israelites who lived a thousand miles away at the time of the trial?

Why pour vengeance on the innocent for thousands of years?

Vengeance for what? For being a member of *the* people chosen by God to give flesh to His Son; a people who gave Jesus a father who was named as His ancestor in body; a people who gave Jesus all His Apostles and Evangelists during His earth-living years?

Vengeance on the only people who listened to His words, the only people who believed in Him? Were they one hundred, or five thousand, Jews were the only followers of Jesus in His wanderings. He had none others He could speak to; He knew neither Greek nor Persian, Egyptian nor Roman. Hebrew and the vernacular Aramaic were all He spoke; it was God's tongue. As Jesus said, "I speak to my people in their synagogue."

His message was meant only for the Jews. No other nation expected or wished a Messiah (*Christos,* in Greek).

Any and all descendants of the kin and family of Jesus

shared the horrible fate of the dispersed Jews. They fought against the Romans led by Titus, and a hundred years later fought again under Bar Kochba against the enemy. It was then that half a million perished at the point of Rome's sword. Again, many of the defeated Jews fled north and west.

What became of the suffering wanderers from Israel? The kin of Joseph and Mary, no less than other Jews, suffered at the vengeful hands of the Christian oppressors. Later, one-third of the Jews of Spain were brutalized by the Catholic Inquisitors; one-third of the Jews of France were put to death by savage Catholics who libeled the people of God as blood drinkers, plague carriers, Host defamers and God killers. And much later, in our time, one-third of the Jews of the world were choked to death with noxious gases, by Protestant and Catholic Christians alike, in whom the fruit of the thousand-year-old teaching of Jew hate came to full bloom.

For all the two thousand years, there was no act of war against the Jews in which the Church did not play an intrinsic part. And wherever there was a trace of mercy, charity, or tolerance to be found amid this savagery, it came not from the Church but from humanitarians in the civil world, as in Napoleonic France or during the American Revolution.

America is the one and only Christian country that offered Jews freedom and security when the pyres were still flaming under the charred feet of Jewish women and children. Some fancy that these brutal outrages of the Catholic Church occurred only in the Dark Ages, as if this were an excuse. Nay, when George Washington was President, Jewish people were burning on the spit in Mexico.

However, need I remind anyone that the supreme holocaust took place only a few decades ago under the very eyes of Christian Europe; that the bishops of Austria and Germany blessed the arms of the killers, and the Vicar of Christ looked out of his window in Rome while Jewish children and women were dragged to extermination camps?

But the churches are not only guilty of ignoring the doom of a million Jewish children, choked to death along with their parents and grandparents.

The churches are guilty of directly inciting this massacre by their persistent religious teaching based on this thesis: *The* Jews killed God, therefore *all Jews* are damned.

Somehow, through the efforts of the one and only Pope free of Jew hate, John XXIII, the Jewish "problem" was put on the agenda of the Ecumenical Council. But the good Pope died and we were left with a former undersecretary of state of Pope Pius XII, the on-looker of Rome.

This new Pope, Paul VI, in 1965 in his Passion Sunday sermon, opened the Ecumenical Era with an alarming news report: The Prince of Peace was set upon by *the* (*sic!*) Jews; first *they* insulted Him, then *they* tortured and finally murdered Him.

This same Pope came in the fall of 1965 to New York, the greatest Jewish center of the world, and after a noble liturgy about peace on earth, touching on all nations of the world, he reserved for the Jews a brief reading: Jesus appeared after His agony to His disciples, who were assembled behind closed doors in fear of *the* (!) Jews.

Pope Paul VI further advanced Ecumenism by placing at the head of his Curia, charged with the task of "solving the Jewish problem," Bishop Luigi Carli of Segni, a professional anti-Semite during the Hitler era, a man whose outrageous behavior during the first sessions of the Council compelled even his conservative colleagues to stop his followers, the Carlifatti, from distributing racially poisonous literature to the delegates.

This monstrous man was put in charge of finding a "solution" to anti-Semitism.

He found one *for* anti-Semitism.

Carli's version of the noble schema proposed by John XXIII to absolve the Jews once and forever from the ridiculous generalization of Deicide, and to condemn anti-Semitism as a heresy, came out with a re-emphasis on the Jews as Christ killers and a sly "deploration" of anti-Semitism.

Carli won over John XXIII. Satan won over Christ.

To make certain that he was not being misunderstood, Carli followed his pronouncement with a lengthy article explaining that Judaism is condemned by God. Whoever follows Judaism cannot but be damnable.

Pope Paul's choice as head of the Ecumenical Curia also decreed that "all people of Israel were faithless" and that "the term deicide applied to all Jews is theologically faultless and the only apt definition."

It is doubly tragic to have to report that Pope Paul VI not only approved Carli's version of the Ecumenical declaration but actually sponsored it.

The fact that Vatican "liberals" managed to add to the vicious denunciation of *the* (*sic!*) Jew as Christ killer the sop, "Of course not all Jews of today are to be considered guilty of deicide," would be ludicrous were it not so tragic. No Catholic in his or her right mind ever considered the Jewish plumber across the street as being literally and specifically a killer of Jesus.

The farce is over and, the "Uncle Tom" Jews notwithstanding, the Vatican only *made believe* it had taken a great step toward the Jews' freedom from Catholic insolence and calumny!

The Vatican has merely taken a short step to the right and has cleverly sidestepped the cardinal issue: to cease once and forever teaching its youth that *the* Jew is a killer of God. And, furthermore it has sidestepped the issue of teaching its youth that anti-Semitism is a heresy and therefore damnable.

The Catholic Church has condemned Freemasonry but refuses to condemn Nazism.

It resolved that you cannot be a Catholic and a Mason, but you can still be a Catholic and a Nazi.

Perhaps Hitler was right when he exclaimed in 1933 at the Concordat Conference: "I am only continuing the work of the Catholic Church: to isolate the Jews and fight their influence."

*

xiii

The war of the Christian churches against the Jews began with the relentless attack of the early Church Fathers against the "stubbornness" of the Israelites who refused to accept Jesus as the Messiah. During the lifetime of Jesus a considerable number of Israelites followed Him—indeed, they were the only people who did. After His execution by the Romans who dominated the Palestine tip of Roman "Syria" with typical severity, Saul, a Talmudic student, and others began to develop a sect with grandiose mythological implications. Finding little acceptance for their unhebraic Christology and eschatology, they ignored the fact that the Messiah was to come to redeem Israel and Israel alone, and began to spread the gospel of the Messiah among the pagans.

Their propaganda was most effective, especially among the multitude of the lowly, and by the beginning of the fourth century Constantine, a pagan king, who had personally rejected the Christian faith, found it politically suitable to make Christianity the dominant and only religion for the whole Roman Empire, with the Bishop of Rome as its all-powerful head.

Among the citizens of Rome, patricians and equestrians alike took a highly sophisticated attitude toward the official Greek and Roman gods. They regaled themselves in word, song, and painting with the amours of Jupiter in the shape of a bull, swan, fish, even a cluster of coins. The plebeians, masses of proletarians, and slaves adhered to sundry traditional ritualistic customs which had as little firm theology as they had abundance of variation.

In this ocean of disbelief and superstition, the Jews were the only ones to maintain a *religio licita* in its true sense.

The Jews would not give up their spiritual heritage and faith in the guidance of the Torah. They did not accept Jesus as the Messiah, although they permitted evangelists, as they had permitted Jesus Himself, to preach in the synagogue.

They believed in one God, the Father of all, and the

Jewish people as His chosen servants. By this they were ready to live and by this they were ready to die.

In those crucial centuries of the growth of Christian religion from an obscure sect to the all-powerful Church of Rome, the early theologians of the Church turned about and opened the war against Israel.

Craving and finally getting Roman approval as *The* Church, they published papers and pamphlets, said prayers and delivered sermons making the Jews out to be the killers of Jesus, although in all Palestine's history there never was a single person crucified except by Romans, and by Romans alone. This being known, the early Church Fathers made the Jews the *instigators* of the Crucifixion. This suited them very well, since the Jews coldly rejected the Roman brand of Christianity, while the Romans, on the other hand, were expected to, and did grant the rapidly spreading Christian Church absolute religious power.

The early Church Fathers—Eusebius, Cyril, Chrysostom, Augustinus, Origen, Justin, Jerome—carried on a venomous campaign against the Jewish "killers of Jesus," and when the New Testament was finally put together, it was laced with anti-Semitic statements. Pilate, of course, was made out to be a gentle Roman judge. The police chief became the personification of eternal justice, *lex Romana.*

The Jews, on the other hand, as the Christian Gospels were made to read, were bloodthirsty persons, torturers of the Savior, pitiless killers, traitors who sold their souls for thirty pieces of silver, moneychangers who desecrated the Temple, more cruel than beasts in demanding that the bones of the dying Christ be broken—the Jews were the sons of the Devil.

Such was the propaganda campaign of the early Fathers of the Catholic and Orthodox Church. These inflamed charges, which they demanded be taken as gospel truth, were followed by admonitions to the secular powers to expel the Jews, to isolate them, to burn their synagogues, to destroy their Talmud and Torah.

These same Fathers also charged the Jews with drinking the blood of Christian children, with poisoning the food and water of true believers, with conspiring with the Asian enemies of the Christians, with desecrating churches and crucifixes, and so on.

The War against the Jews had begun. From pulpit to pulpit, every Sunday and holy day, in every Church of Christ, cold hate was released against the hapless Jewish families. And this teaching of hate has not ceased to this very day.

Soon the cold hate turned into fiery action, and from one end of Europe to the other the almighty Catholic Church put the Jews to the pyre and sword. No child, no woman, no invalid was spared.

The wretches who fled one bishop were soon overtaken by the mobs incited in another diocese. To make the victims easily recognizable they were made by the Catholic Church to wear the leper sign. They were corralled into foul ghettos, easy prey to the wanton cruelty of the sermon-crazed Christians.

Wild agitators of hate against the Jews, armed with supreme powers by the Church, were sent through all Christian lands. Wherever they passed, the pyres were built up, with whimpering flesh dying an agonized death at the hands of executioners with the big silver cross dangling from their necks.

Three and a half million Jews died in this Church War against the Jews. When Hitler embarked on the road to kill another six million of the people of the Lord, he found to his admitted amazement that his Eichmann and Kaltenbrunner were as little opposed by the Germans as Cardinals Jiménez and Torquemada of iniquitous memory had been by the Iberians.

The German Christians had centuries of preparation for Jew slaughter, first by the Catholic Church and then by the renegade monk Martin Luther, who wanted the "killers of Jesus" made slaves of the serfs, because they were

the sons of the Devil and should never touch a free Christian's hand. Luther demanded that the synagogues be burned, the books of the Hebrews destroyed, and Jewish homes laid waste.

What Hitler did was only putting Luther's war plans into reality. Indeed, everything Hitler did to the Jews, all the horrible, unspeakable misdeeds, had already been done to the smitten people before by the Christian churches, especially the Catholic Church.

The isolation of Jews in ghetto camps, the wearing of the yellow spot, the burning of Jewish books, and finally the burning of the people—Hitler learned it all from the Catholic Church. However, the Church burned the Jewish women and children alive, while Hitler granted them a quicker death, choking them first with gas.

Yet all these horrible acts are only part of the evil done to the Jews. As in all wars, much of the bestiality remains forever hidden. Never has man been more cruel to man than the Christians have been to the Jews.

Will the infamy of this war ever end?

How can it, so long as the Christian churches continue to teach their youth that the Jews are the brood of the Devil and *the (sic!)* Jews are killers of their God?

How can this crime cease, so long as the churches tolerate anti-Semitism as a natural attitude of Christians and refuse to declare it sinful heresy?

The young Christians of today have been given the same lessons in hate as the young Christians a generation ago. The cold war teachings of anti-Semitism have not ceased. The Christians tomorrow will be as ready to fall upon the Jews as they were yesterday.

Neo-Nazism is again born out of Christianity. It is the same old teaching: the Jew is pariah. In Poland, in the Ukraine, in Argentina—wherever there are Christian churches there is anti-Semitism.

The Gospel of St. John, the teaching Gospel of the Christian churches, contains thirty-two references to the

Jews. Every one is meant to debase and degrade the Jew and make him hateful to the core. ("The Jew is the son of the Devil." John 8:44)

Rip out these sentences from your Gospels, for if your Gospels have to stand or fall by these few anti-Semitic lines, they certainly do not deserve to live on.

These sentences were put there by hate-maddened, primitive theologians of fifteen hundred years ago, and kept there by the power-seeking Bishops of Rome.

You have burned to ashes almost ten million of our people, a million of our children, because of your hate, and you are ready to burn more when the time is ripe, when the cold hate again turns into the flames of war.

Every Sunday of every week your youth is being readied for the supreme task of extermination. There is not a week when a Jewish cemetery or synagogue is not desecrated somewhere in the Christian world.

All reports and surveys make it clear that Christian youth overwhelmingly have a disdain or hate for Jews because of their religious training.

Make not your Church the headquarters of the war against the people of Jesus, Mary, and Joseph. You have burned to death one-third of their kin. Do you wish to burn the others?

The War against the Jews is almost two thousand years old, and still you continue your preparations for the next massacre!

I do not know where such an outbreak will take place. I did not know a few decades ago that it would happen in Germany.

I do not know where the next burning will occur. The air of Spain, of Portugal, of England, of Italy, of Germany, of Austria, of France, of Mexico, and of Brazil—the air of all holds the memory of burned Jewish flesh.

Do you really want to stop this massacre or do you want to be "neutral" like the Vicar of Christ, and then benignly say a prayer over the victims?

It is in your hands; we are only a few, among a billion Christians.

*

Some indifferent historians argue that, after all, the German Christians had to perform the Jew killings as a matter of enforced war duty; and all along that has been the alibi of the most sadistic concentration camp commanders. Of course the argument is as weak as the desire of those people to unmask the truth.

The truth is that Hitler, a graduate of the Linzer school of clerical anti-Semitism, was sure of his victory once the Catholic Church, through the untiring efforts of Pacelli, later Pius XII, joined him in the infamous Concordat of Collaboration, which turned the youth of Germany over to Nazism, and the churches became the stage background for the bloodthirsty cry: *"Pereat Judea!"*

The Protestants went them one better and, with hardly an exception, joined in a religious Fatherland Front. The most influential Bishop Müller even dedicated a sermon, which was widely publicized, to "Hitler and Christ." Of course, Christ came out second best.

To begin with, Hitler's desire to exterminate all Jews was on public record in his *Mein Kampf*. Pacelli knew that, as did all German Christians, in the pulpit or in the pew. Still, the German nation overwhelmingly voted for Hitler, and in Austria the Catholic Church through its Cardinal Innitzer openly asked its citizens to vote for union with Nazi Germany. Even before this "union" Innitzer signed his pastoral letters: "Heil Hitler." His painting in full regalia still decorates Catholic public buildings in Austria, the country that in the Middle Ages had burned alive hundreds of Jews.

Innitzer helped burn a thousand times that many.

The Christian Germans voted Hitler in—he was not a usurper—they followed him through his travels and festivals with delirious enthusiasm. There are a mass of street and stadium photographs available showing the Nazi killer

exhorting the populace to Jew slaughter, with the faces of the Teutons shining with adoration for the beloved leader, and down in front there are always the Christian clergy with benign smiles on their lips.

It was the same smile on the faces of the priests of the Spanish Inquisition, taking down the whispered confessions of tortured Jews, the same smile on the face of Peter the Hermit crying for the blood of Jews during the march of the Crusader hyenas, the same smile on the bishops of England watching Jews being burned in York, the same smile on the monks in France accusing Jews of well-poisoning and plague-carrying, the same smile on the Ukrainian Orthodox priests watching Jews being sorted out and shot in Babi Yar.

The churches of Europe rang the bells when Hitler won a victory, as they rang throughout Germany whenever the last Jew of the town was deported to perdition.

The Church, however, was not a silent witness. The priests and ministers preached sermon after sermon, published in their religious as well as the commercial press, on the greedy, the usurious, the nefarious, the power-mad Jew —and, of course, as an undertone, on the Jews as crucifiers of Christ.

The Church was then, as it is now, the prime bearer of anti-Semitic tales, ancient and new.

The barbarism of the German Christians toward the Jews is the direct result of the teaching of the anti-Semitic Church. The Germans did not deliberately kill a single Christian child or woman.

The killing of Jews, child and adult, the Christian Germans carried out with indifference, indeed, often with a sense of pride. They had learned from childhood to regard the Jew as vermin, as the son of Satan. Killing Jews was a duty, advised during the Middle Ages again and again by the Church.

Hitler only carried out the avowed policy of the Christian Church. Because of his talent for organization and

modern scientific acumen, he exceeded even the excesses of the Church.

Anti-Semitism begins with the Christian Church and can only end with it, certainly not without it.

Where is the first man of God among the Christians who will come forth in the name of Pope John XXIII and cry out, "We have sinned against the Jews by massacring the people of Jesus, and we have sinned as free men of the twentieth century by holding Jewish children responsible for a deed that may have been done two thousand years ago"?

Such men of courage and vision will come, and this book is meant to help them understand the gravity of their judicial crimes committed upon a little nation that has done no wrong except being the kin of Christ.

*

I say to the Catholic Church: Where are the Jews of Spain, of Portugal? You killed them. Where are the Jews of Italy, of France? You killed them. Where are the Jews of England? You killed them. Where are the Jews of Hungary and Austria? You killed them.

I say to the Protestants of Prussia and the Catholics of Bavaria: Where are the Jews of Germany? You killed them.

I say to the Orthodox of Russia and the Ukraine: Where are the Jews of the Czar? You killed them.

The Christian churches of Europe have killed and maimed the Jews from the days of the Visigoths to the pogrom in Kielce, Poland, in 1946.

If not for Cain with cross and sword, the Jewish nation would today comprise a hundred million people instead of fifteen million. As the centuries went by, Israel lost its majorities through conversion and the torch.

Will Cain ever face the Lord?

*

I am no respecter of the Cloth. Peter the Hermit wore the monk's hirsute shirt when he reviled the Jews as a

xxi

brood out of hell and so opened the Crusade with the blessing of an ax over our people's heads.

Cardinal Torquemada wore the Cloth when he watched agonized victims of torture "confessing" to monstrous crimes.

Martin Luther wore the Cloth when he damned the Jews to slavery and to having their homes and temples and holy books burned.

Cardinal Innitzer of Vienna wore the Cloth when he asked the Austrians to join Hitler.

I call a spade a spade, not the less when I see it in the hands of my gravediggers.

*

The War against the Jews led by the Christian churches has for the time being shifted to a cold war. We Jews are standing now between outbreaks of open violence, as we stood between the various Crusades, as we stood between vampire trials and Black Death accusations, as we stood between the Count Rindfleisch campaign and the Hussite wars, as we stood between the Chmielnicki bloodbath and the Russian pogroms, as we stood between the Rumanian barbarism and the Nazi holocaust.

There has not been a century in which the churches have ceased their malevolent sermons against the Hebrews, the moneychangers, the killers of beloved Jesus, instilling in the children entrusted to them an eerie fear of and contempt of devils, these Shylocks, these Judases, these Jews.

How shall I speak of these dark men of the cross?

They were no better than the Nazis, merely less powerful, less thorough.

There is no town in any Christian land of Europe where the ministers of Christ have not incited and led the mob as well as the nobles and kings to burn the Jew!

The extermination camps of the German Christians were only the culmination of the holy terror that Catholic clergy conducted for fifteen hundred years.

Some say we should forgive. I can forgive them the killing of my mother but cannot forget the million little

xxii

ones they choked to death as you would not a cat or a dog.

They want us to forgive the killing of six million Jews—and cannot forgive us the alleged killing of one.

They did not even bury our dead. They burned them and threw the ashes into the dirt, the Catholic bishops no less than the Brown Shirts.

If these sanguinary men believed in God, they could not burn children or choke them or stamp them to death. They must be certain that God is dead and that they now hold His reins.

No believer in God can be as cruel, as merciless, as bestial, as the Catholic Church has been to us. No man can watch a million children choke to death and not raise a finger unless he has lost all faith, all faith forever!

As I write these lines, reports are coming in that the Neo-Nazi Party in Bavaria, the *Nationaldemokratische Partei Deutschlands,* has won over 10 percent of the votes of this Catholic province, with the priests giving their gains a benevolent consent; reports come from Warsaw that the Jews in Poland, whose schools are totally in the hands of the Catholic Church, are subject to constant derision and abuse as Christ killers; reports come from Kiev that the Orthodox Christians of this town have for twenty years been using the burial place of its Jewish population massacred by the Nazis, Babi Yar, as a dumping ground, and that the Jews, as in earlier papal days, are not permitted to build synagogues or raise their children in their faith, celebrate their holy days, or even read their prayer books; reports come from Catholic Argentina, which has become the haven of Nazi criminals, that the youth are infected by the clergy with anti-Semitic prejudices which frequently lead to hostile acts against the Jews; reports come from Protestant England that academic dictionaries of the English language, such as those of the Oxford University Press, have still not ceased defining Jew in the old church manner of Reverend Prynne as "cheats, usurers, unscrupulous bargainers."

It is too late to raise one's voice when the ax has fallen,

and it *will* fall again on the heads of our kinsmen if we do not succeed in persuading the Christian clergy to cease the teaching of contempt and hate for the Jew.

Cleanse your catechisms and cleanse your scriptures, I say, of the malevolent Roman references to our people.

Those who honestly wish to make an end to the scourge of anti-Semitism, be they Jew or liberal Gentile, let them speak out now and move to correct the vicious texts of the churches and make an end to the Jew-baiting sermonology!

Let us not sit out this cold war until the inevitable pogrom; let us fight now!

They are a billion strong, and we are few, but tomorrow is in the hands of the Lord.

*

I have chosen only sample events and personalities implicated in the wanton War against the Jews. My book makes no claim to completeness. One need not know the gory totality of the anti-Semitic carnage to be appalled by its magnitude.

Even an enumeration of all the known sanguinary occurrences would fall short; infamy often does its work in darkness and silence, unbeknown to the wide public.

How many Jews were subject to persecution in the two thousand years of Christian domination no one will ever know. But of what we know, I have endeavored to give you a brief record.

If the facts are abhorrent, there is much more I have refrained from advancing, to spare my people who read this book.

I fervently hope that enough liberals will be found among Christian theologians and ministers to reach the true depth of contriteness and set upon the great task of freeing Christian teachings of the sin of anti-Semitism.

For the serious student I have added a bibliography offering documentation.

No one has to hate the Jews in order to love Jesus.

A

ABRAHAM A SANTA CLARA (1644-1709)

wrote, when the Turkish invasion threatened Vienna and brought about general misery: "After the Devil the Christians have no greater enemy than the Jew. They pray daily that God destroy us by pestilence and famine. Are there any greater scoundrels than Jews?"

This vicious Augustinian monk mounted the pulpit in school and church to accuse the Jews of bringing the plague.

ABULAFIA, SAMUEL HA-LEVI (1320-1360)

Treasurer of Don Pedro of Castile. The Catholic clergy conspired against him and had him tortured to death.

ADVERSUS JUDAEOS

General term for anti-Semitic literature, especially that authored by the early Church Fathers. The most vicious of all was John Chrysostom (Saint) of the fifth century, who ran wild at the mouth against the Jews: "They are rapists, pushy, deceitful, hucksters." Further, they are: ". . . Lustful, rapacious, greedy, impure, debauchers. . . ." A worthy predecessor of the Nazi Streicher.

AGOBARD, SAINT (779-840)

Archbishop of Lyon who directed his church activities to spread anti-Semitism. In his essayistic epistles he

1

"proved" that the Jews were born slaves, were stealing Christian children and selling them to the Arabs, are accursed by God and should be so regarded by all Christians.

Again, many statements of this high-placed clergyman have found willing ears among modern anti-Semites.

AHLWANDT, HERMANN (b. 1846)

Journalistic anti-Semite of Prussia. Strongly supported by the Protestant clergy. Helped prepare ground for Nazism.

AKSAKOV, IVAN SERGEYEVICH (1823-1886)

Journalistic Russian anti-Semite, strongly supported by the Orthodox clergy.

AKTION REINHARD

The code name for the detailed plan to plunder the property of the Jews in Nazi Germany; so titled after its director, Reinhard Heydrich.

A guideline for this plan could be found in nation-wide expropriations by the Catholic Church in conjunction with various rulers. The Catholic Church provided many models for expropriation combined with execution or expulsion of Jews on repeated occasions. The Nazis merely streamlined an old operation.

ALBA, DUKE OF (1508-1582)

Repugnant anti-Semite of the Spanish aristocracy. Prohibited the printing of Hebrew books in the Netherlands. Similar prohibition is attributed to Joseph Stalin, a former Christian seminary student, who gave up the faith of his youth but not his anti-Semitic prejudices. The Stalin prohibition still holds good in the Soviet Union, minor exceptions for propaganda purposes to the contrary.

2

ALBERTUS MAGNUS (1206-1280)

A bishop of the Catholic Church and one of its revered philosophers, he presided over the tribunal that condemned the books of the Talmud in 1248 as pernicious literature. In the Hitler era German theologians often borrowed quotations from this "trial," such as "Talmud Jews."

ALBI

In this French town in 1320 the total Jewish population was annihilated by the Catholic authorities.

ALBRECHT OF BRANDENBURG

This Roman Catholic Archbishop initiated in 1516 a movement to expel all Jews from Germany. He was only partly successful. Completion of the pious task had to wait almost five hundred years.

ALEXANDER I (1777-1825)

Czar of the Russians who expelled the Jews from villages to certain restricted towns and forbade them to keep Christian servants (August 10, 1824 and January 13, 1825). A reversion to the anti-Semitic attitudes of medieval Catholicism.

ALEXANDER III (1845-1894)

The anti-Semitic attitude of this Russian Czar was manifest. As soon as he ascended the throne pogroms broke out in 160 places. Jewish women were publicly outraged, and thousands of persons of the Hebrew faith were mutilated or killed and their property put to the torch. The clergy of Russian Orthodoxy spread the terror, finding it opportune to sermonize on the Christ killers.

In Warsaw persecution of the Jews began on Christmas,

1881, as an aftermath of Church services. The military as well as the civilian authorities were so deeply imbued since childhood with anti-Semitism that instead of protecting the Jews they turned against them.

As usual, unscrupulous opportunists turned to anti-Semitism as a means for blackmail, and solicitation of funds from wealthy Jew haters.

In 1890, American liberals appealed to Czar Alexander to give the Jews access to economic opportunity in the arts, crafts and professions, and freedom to move about, since their condition was the most wretched of all people in Europe. The pious ruler quoted a sentence from the Patriarch of Kiev: "Let us never forget that *the Jews* [*!*] crucified our Lord and spilled His precious blood."

What piety and nobility—almost matched by that other Alexander III, the Pope (1159-1181), who reproved King Louis VII of France for treating the "killers of the Savior" like Christians.

A thousand miles away, a thousand years apart—yet but one thought in two namesakes united by the bonds of faith.

ALFONSO X (1252-1284)

Under this Castilian King, the Seven Part Code (*Las siete partidas*) was devised by the Catholic hierarchy. One part reads: "We order that no Jews shall dare to bathe in company with Christians."

The exclusion of Jews from Castilian beaches and baths intrigued Hitler. He made the Castilian Code valid for Germany. In later years, however, in Catholic Spain as in Nazi Germany, Jews were to be found only in cemeteries.

ALFONSO DE SPINA

Noted Spanish theologian, who proved (in his book *Fortalitium fidei*) by the Talmud itself that the Jews were children of the Devil.

4

ALGIERS

When anti-Semitic mobs attacked the Jewish shops in Algiers (February, 1898), *La Croix,* a leading Catholic newspaper in France, claimed that Christ Himself had protected the Christian shops. Did the devout fathers who edited *La Croix* know that the Jewish shops of Algiers had been marked the night before with a white Star of David?

The marking of Jewish places of business was successfully used by the Brown Shirts fifty years later. Did Christ protect the Christian shops in Berlin?

AMBROSE, SAINT

A fourth-century bishop of Milan and one of the four Latin Doctors of the Catholic Church, he reprimanded Emperor Theodosius for ordering the rebuilding of a synagogue in Mesopotamia that had been destroyed by a monk-led mob. In his zeal the good saint himself offered to burn the synagogue in Milan. Unfortunately other Christians had done so already.

AMULO

This Bishop of Lyon (841-852), successor of the notorious Agobard was also a prolific epistle writer. He claimed like our present-day Bishop Luigi Carli (who, for God knows what reason, was placed by the Vatican at the head of the four-man Curia committee to offer a "Schema on the Jews"), that the Mosaic religion was an accursed faith. His vile references to the Jews were often used by the German Jew haters.

ANJOU

In this French city in the years 1236, 1239, and again in 1271, thousands of Jews were put to the sword by monk-

5

accompanied Crusaders. Contemporary chronicles describe the monstrous events.

ANSBACH

The Jewish population of this Bavarian town was put to death in 1349 by flagellants singing hymns of Christian love. Not one Jew escaped.

ANTICHRIST

is depicted by the clergy from the thirteenth century on as an offspring of Jews, and supported by Jews, who, with Satan's guidance, would destroy the true faith and re-establish Judaism as the dominant power. In medieval illustrations and plays, the Devil wears the Jew badge, has a hook nose and curly hair.

ANTI-SEMITISM

This term is first found in *Der Sieg des Judenthums über das Germanenthum* ("The Victory of Judaism over Germanism") by Wilhelm Marr (1879).

ANTI-SEMITISM IN ABSENTIA

is one of the many facts in evidence that Jew hate is hardly ever caused by the specific acts or behavior of Jews in the community, but rather by the deplorable educational process of the Christian church. Indeed, the three most anti-Semitic countries in recent decades are Austria, Poland and Bavaria. None of these Catholic lands now have any Jewish residents to speak of, yet the majority of the rural youth of Austria, Poland and Bavaria, who have most likely never seen a Jew, never competed against one, or been hurt or affected by one, carry hearts full of hate for "the Christ killers."

Similarly, for many centuries the populace of England,

Spain, Portugal, and other lands where the Jews had been expelled or put to death, retained a blind fury against the "children of the Devil," who "tortured their Savior."

All that these Christians, young or old, knew of the Jew was what they learned from their liturgy, but this was enough to set their minds in perpetual hate. It is not the presence of Jews that creates anti-Semitism, rather the persistence of Gospel teachings in their hate-instilling form.

We find the same situation in all of Western and Southern Europe in the early part of the eighteenth century. Those among the Jews who escaped the fury of the Church had fled to the Moslem countries, or to the "under-developed" Russian East, where Jewish skills and know-how were needed. Yet, in spite of the small number of Jews left in such countries as Germany, France, Italy, Spain, England and Switzerland, the Church managed to keep the issue of anti-Semitism alive by repeating again and again, from pulpit and printing press, the great lies of the Jews being God killers, the Jews profaning the host, the Jews being vampires, the Jews being poisoners of the very wells they were themselves using, the Jews bringing the plague to the very same streets they themselves were frequenting, the Jews bringing the Mongols and Moslems to destroy the Christian Church, and so on.

As stupid as these and the other anti-Semitic fabrications sound today, nevertheless, the populace of Europe— illiterate for the most part, and those few literate confused and browbeaten by the fanatics and power-mongers of the dominant Church—the populace absorbed Jew hate and acted upon it at the pleasure of Dominicans, Franciscans and the malevolent Vatican itself.

If there was any lull in the anti-Semitism of the first eighteen centuries of Christianity, it came from secular sources, never from the Church.

APULIA

In this district of Southern Italy the Dominican order in the fourteenth century destroyed all Jewish cemeteries and converted the synagogues into churches.

The Jewish population was given the choice of baptism or the stake by King Charles I. Eight thousand accepted conversion, the others fled.

AQUINAS, SAINT THOMAS

Catholic philosopher (1227-1274), defender of slavery for Jews, who wrote: "The Jews refuse to work, they never do anything, that's why they become more and more avaricious."

ARAGON

In this province of Spain in the fourteenth century thousands of Jews were either baptized or killed. Under King Martin, those who remained alive after the bloody excesses of Father Vincente Ferrer had to wear the badge and destroy their Hebrew books.

The schismatic Pope Benedict XIII, forced to seek refuge in his native Aragon, in 1415 issued a bull *Etsi Doctoribus Gentium* that barred Jews from holding any office or following the profession of physician, chemist or merchant. All Jews over the age of twelve were required to listen to proselytizing sermons three times a year.

ARBRIES, PEDRO (1441-1485)

A Spanish canon, one of the most fiendish inquisitors into faith. He was finally assassinated by a Marrano. Pope Pius IX canonized this monster (1867).

ARGENTINA

Today anti-Semitism as represented by Tacuara is running along "Christian" lines. Its spiritual head is the Catholic priest Dr. Alberto Contreras. Nazi-type mass meetings with Hitler salute, etc., are held in front of the Cathedral of St. Francis with full knowledge of the Archbishop.

ARLES

In this French city on April 8, 1484, mobs led by monks attacked the Jews, compelled about fifty to accept Christianity, and murdered the rest. Contemporary chronicles hail this "victory for Christ."

ARMLEDER

A murderous group in Alsace, under the leadership of John Zimberlin, who took it upon themselves in the fourteenth century to avenge the crucifixion by cutting down Jews. Their outrages were only a prelude to the Black Death massacres in Central Europe.

ARNOLD OF CITEAUX

A protégé of Pope Innocent III (1198-1216), this Cistercian monk, at the head of a crusading army against the Albigenses, killed 200 Jews of Béziers in France. A few in despair grabbed for the Crucifix to escape death.

ARYAN CHRISTIANITY

In a pastoral letter of 1939 Archbishop Konrad Gröber argued that Jesus was totally different from the Jews and therefore they crucified Him.

Bishop Hilfrich of Limburg "reasoned" that Christianity was not to be regarded as a product of Israel; it was

therefore not un-German. In fact, it finds itself in intimate union with the German spirit. (1939 Pastoral letter).

These and similar articles, as well as books of Christian anti-Semitism, bore the imprimatur. Bishop Alois Hudal, head of the German church in Rome, declared that the Nuremberg Laws were a necessary self-defense against the influx of Jewish elements into Christian Germany.

ATHANASIUS, SAINT

A fourth-century bishop of Alexandria, honored as the father of orthodoxy; insisted that Rome use the sword to deal with the Jews and that tolerance toward Jews was treason against Christ.

AUGUSTINE, SAINT (354-430)

Bishop of Hippo and the most influential Catholic theologian, he called Judaism a corruption. "The true image of the Hebrew is Judas Iscariot, who sells the Lord for silver. The Jew can never understand the Scriptures and forever will bear the guilt for the death of Jesus."

In the judgment of this fountain of Christian love, the Jew must forever spend his life as a slave.

AUSSEE

In this Austrian town in 1722 the synagogue was burned down by orders of the Catholic Church because a priest who had entered the house of worship uninvited on Jewish High Holy Days, was prevented from delivering a conversion sermon.

AUSTRIA

This little Catholic state can justly claim the dubious distinction of being for one hundred years the most anti-Semitic country of Europe. Austria is not only the home-

land of Adolf Hitler, but the stamping ground of such professional Jew baiters as Father August Rohling, Georg von Schoenerer and Karl Lueger, who, with the help of the clerical organizations and press, worked for the exclusion of the Jews from all economic and cultural life. The Jew was depicted as a monstrous creature from the pulpits of the many Catholic churches of Austria and of course received similar treatment in the clerical press, from the *Reichspost* of Vienna to a precursor of *Der Stürmer* called *Kikeriki*.

This type of propaganda found willing listeners among the Church-educated Austrians, who elected the candidate of the clergy, Karl Lueger, as Mayor of Vienna, and swamped the Austrian Parliament with Jew haters (1897).

As late as 1925 the deans of all Austrian universities and schools of higher education passed a resolution that no Jews be given academic posts.

Today these same universities and schools of higher education, which have for a hundred years been a hotbed of Jew hate, are still deeply infected with anti-Semitic clericalism. One of its most virulent representatives is the Catholic lay leader, Taras Borodajkewycz, Professor of Social History at the Viennese College of Commerce, who, despite—or because of?—his pre-Hitler Nazi background received and retained his important post. I was in his classroom in March of 1965 when, during one of his tirades against world Jewry, Austrian students took up the cry: "Out with the Jews!" and "Long live Auschwitz!—(*Lang lebe Auschwitz!*)" This same Borodajkewycz is one of the contributing editors of the academic monthly *Eckartsbote,* which is no less anti-Semitic than the *Deutsche Hochschullehrer Zeitung.*

In 1965 the University of Vienna appointed the Nazi Helfried Pfeiffer professor of history. Pfeiffer wrote in 1941: "Hitler was Austria's greatest son." Pfeiffer's lecture series in 1965 was entitled "The Essence of Democracy."

The treatment of Nazi criminals in Austria has nat-

11

urally been most lenient. In 1961, of sixteen mass killers tried, eleven were acquitted and the others released after having received token sentences. At almost every trial, however, an invited public was loudly expressing its resentment of Jewish "vengeance seekers."

Of the top judges who presided during the Hitler era over "Special Courts" of extermination, one is professor of law at the University of Innsbruck; another became co-author of the Penal Code of the "new Austria."

AUTO-DA-FE

Solemn ritualistic burning of Jews and other "heretics" at the behest of the inquisitional authorities of the Catholic Church. "Trials" were conducted in the presence of the clergy and invariably ended in confession under torture by fire, skinning alive, bone-crushing, etc. The verdict was almost always: burn them alive.

AVIGNON, COUNCIL OF

Proposed cessation of all intercourse between Christians and Jews (1567). It forbade Christians to employ Jewish physicians, to enter Jewish homes, to participate in Jewish festivals, to seek employment by Jews, or to serve as their masons or barbers. The Jews were rigidly confined to ghettos.

In 1616 the Pope expelled the Jews altogether from Avignon. Prior to their expulsion a number of Jewish children were secretly baptized by Dominican monks and so lost to their parents.

AVILA

In this Spanish town near Madrid in 1491 a child from "La Guardia," a village that never existed, was allegedly found dead. A Jewish shoemaker, his brothers and father

12

were accused by the Church of having killed the child (later canonized) and drinking its blood for Passover. The accused admitted, under torture, all points of the indictment. Following their burning, all Jews in this little town were murdered and their homes sacked. The Catholic clergy appropriated the synagogue for a church.

AVITUS, SAINT

This bishop of Clermont, France, in 576 gave the Jews in his diocese the choice of baptism or exile. The synagogue was burned.

B

BABI YAR

Ravine near Kiev. Here, in the Second World War, German *Einsatztruppen* shot and killed over forty thousand Jewish civilians, mostly women and children.

The Ukrainian population, its anti-Semitism long nurtured by the clergy, used the place of mass burial as a dumping ground. World pressure is being exerted on the Ukrainian authorities to erect a memorial to the victims.

Kiev remains today a center of anti-Semitic activity in the Ukraine, and its Academy of Sciences has repeatedly published tracts against the Jewish religion and ideology.

BAKUNIN, MICHAEL (1814-1874)

Offspring of wealthy Russian aristocracy, he was raised in the "Zid" (Jew) hating atmosphere of a Czarist Greek Orthodox parochial school and an officers' training center.

Intrigued by anarchistic ideas, he left the service and spent his time as a semi-journalistic do-nothing. A colorful demagogue and pamphleteer, he fell out with socialists of all denominations. However, one thing the Christian social-

13

ists and Communists had in common was hate for the Jew, which they had acquired with their earliest reading and listening.

Proudhon, like his deadly adversary Marx, accused the Jews of being capitalistic parasites, refusing to work and aiming to conquer the Christian world through Jewish capitalism. The Jews, he claimed, killed the first socialist, Jesus Christ, and will continue to do likewise. However, claimed Bakunin, Jewish socialists and Communists were actually crypto-capitalists who worked hand in hand for a Jewish victory. In fact, Bakunin wrote, Marx and Rothschild were two of a kind.

It is remarkable how close this type of "thinking" comes to that of Bakunin's contemporary, the French Catholic leader, Drumont, who like Hitler, later charged Jews with being both ultra-capitalist and ultra-Communist.

Credo quia absurdum.

BARCELONA

In this capital of Catalonia took place the public dialogue between Moses Ben Nachman and Pablo Christiani in 1263. Dominican friars, who later took a bloody hand in the Grand Inquisition, compelled the Jews to listen to their conversion sermons. The priesthood, as it gained power, pressed for laws restricting the Jews. A Jew or Jewess meeting a priest had to kneel down in the street.

In 1391, while the massacre of Jews at Palma on the island of Majorca was still going on, bands of Church-incited marauders stormed the Barcelona ghetto in a rampage of slaughter and plunder. Most Jews died defending their families; a few converted to the loving Church.

Barcelona was *"Judenrein."*

BARRIOS

Spanish equivalent of "concentration camps," established during the fourteenth and fifteenth centuries by order

of the Catholic authorities for Jews and Semitic Christians (Marranos). By decree of the Cortes of Toledo (1480), all Jews who had not fled the barrios in the city were to be burned later.

The barrios of Toledo were similar to the "model" ghetto of Theresienstadt established in Czechoslovakia under Hitler, in that Jews were given a certain amount of self-government. The outcome in both enclosures was identical.

BASEL

In this Swiss canton the populace was subjected to anti-Semitic sermons late into the nineteenth century. In 1839 Basel expelled all Jews. On November 17, 1857, a law was passed forbidding Jews to settle, trade or ply a craft.

For the Medieval roots of Basel's Jew hatred, see *Black Death*.

BASKET TAX

The right to collect this tax on Kosher meat, trade licenses and traditional Jewish wearing apparel was leased to the highest bidder by Czarist Russia. It is a carryover from a privilege granted to Catholic monasteries. Even on skullcaps and the wigs prescribed for women they levied a burdensome taxation. In Russia the tax was first decreed on December 31, 1844, and remained in force until the twentieth century.

BAUER, BRUNO (1809-1882)

Influential Protestant theologian in Germany who sermonized persuasively that the oppression of Jews by Christians was justified, they being the killers of God. Also, that the Jews had never contributed anything to civilization, unlike the Germans, who were the essence of mankind.

15

BAVARIA

In this German state, the birthplace of Nazism, few Jews remained after the expulsion ordered by the Elector Max Emanuel on March 12, 1715. It was a pitiful few, their ancestors having been put to death on flimsy Church-inspired accusations of host-nailing, blood-drinking, well-poisoning, plague-creating, crucifixion-defiling, etc.

Burned in Munich, in 1285, were 180 Jews for allegedly having bled to death a Christian child in the synagogue. In 1298 a priest was responsible for spreading the rumor that Jews were driving nails through holy wafers, thereby crucifying Christ again. Among those murdered that year because of a maddened cleric were 628 Jews in Nuremberg (Mordecai ben Hillel, the famous scholar, was one of the victims).

In Deggendorf, in 1337, the whole Jewish population was butchered because a Jew supposedly broke a holy wafer. A memorial chapel was erected on the spot of the butchery and pilgrimages were arranged by the Catholic Church which still go on.

Ten years after the Deggendorf "purification" the Bavarians, driven by their priests, fell upon more than eighty Jewish communities in their land with pitchfork and sickle and killed every man, woman and child. Ten thousand fell, victims of this latest, the "Black Death," accusation.

Numerous chapels and churches still stand in the heartland of Hitlerism, erected in commemoration of the "cleansing." These churches were consecrated to Mary, holy mother of Christ. It is quite likely that among the ten thousand Jews murdered then—as among the six million murdered later—there were direct relatives and descendants of the Jewish gentlewoman and her Hebrew spouse Joseph.

BELGIUM

As late as 1898 a solemn procession of Belgian clergymen paraded through the streets to commemorate a bloody

and torture-ridden trial of 1370 for "desecration of the Host."

The Church has a long and vindictive memory. In 1370 someone imagined he saw a Jew break a wafer, and a hundred of Christ's kinsmen, children among them, were roasted like chickens—only no one roasts a chicken live, and even cannibals kill their victims by knife, not by slow fire.

*

Gauthier de Castillon (c. 1160), provost of the Chapter of Tournai, distributed a three-volume set of calumnies against the "Christ killers" that deepened and spread anti-Semitism throughout all churches of the land.

*

In 1261, Alix of Brabant, widow of Henry III, inquired of Thomas Aquinas, the renowned doctor of philosophy if she could—without harming her Christian conscience!—deprive her subject Jews of their funds. The sage Dominican in a brilliant piece of casuistry reassured her that she could, provided she left the God killers enough to carry on.

What price scholasticism?

*

In 1370, "five hundred Jews were dragged through the streets of Brussels and without distinction of sex or age mutilated until dead." Eighteen tableaux showing Jews driving nails through holy wafers and blood flowing from the host were painted in the cathedral and can still be seen.

BELLOC, HILAIRE (1870-1953)

Most articulate spokesman of English Catholicism, propagated the idea that the Jews pursue only one object: money. The Jews have no true interest in science, philosophy or the arts; they look only for material gain.

Goebbels frequently took a leaf from his writings. Along with Chesterton, Belloc was repeatedly honored by the Catholic Church.

17

BENEDICT VIII (1012-1024)

On Good Friday of 1021 an earthquake followed by a hurricane occurred in Rome, creating havoc in the city. The Pope arrested a number of Jews, who allegedly had put a nail through a holy wafer the day before, as the probable cause of God's wrath. They all confessed and were burned.

Good Friday is a bad day in the Jewish calendar and Holy Week the terror of the year. Religious persecution of the Jews rises to its peak at these times.

BENEDICT XIII

This schismatic Pope in 1415 prohibited the "existence" of the Talmud and prescribed that every Jew attend official Church sermons under penalty of death.

BENEDICT XIV (1675-1758)

One of the monsters to wear the Tiara. In 1747 he issued a bull that all Jewish children over seven years of age could be baptized, even against the will of their parents.

He also reactivated the law of 1732 which prohibited Jews from spending even a single night outside the ghetto.

The year 1732 was the birth-year of George Washington.

BERNANOS, GEORGES (1888-1948)

Dominant French Catholic writer, "obligatory" author in French high schools and colleges. This gentle "friend of every priest" wrote "When the right moment comes, clean out the Jews, the way a surgeon removes an abscess."

I suppose Hitler and Eichmann should be named "Surgeons of the Century."

18

BERNARD OF CLAIRVAUX, SAINT (1090-1153)

Founder and abbot of a Cistercian monastery, adviser to popes, author of books on "Humility," "Love of God," "Grace," "Charity," etc.

Of the Jews the saintly philosopher said: They are no better than beasts, in fact "More than bestial . . . They are of the Devil."

Julius Streicher urged the killing of all Jews as the "offspring of the Devil."

BERNARDINUS OF FELTRE (1439-1494)

Fanatical Franciscan friar who traveled through Italy, as a self-appointed protector of Christian children "whom the Jews want to steal and crucify." He had a strong appeal to the devout masses of Italian serfs and servants, who were incited to bloody riots along the trail of the mad Franciscan, especially during Holy Week.

For a donation, the poor and ignorant got a drop of "Holy Water" from the priest to cleanse their shabby homes of Jews and devils. The friar depicted all Jews as moneybags who exploited the Christian masses—another of the saintly predecessors of Hitler.

BERTHOLD, BISHOP OF STRASBOURG

Presided at a meeting of the Council of Towns of Alsace, held in 1348 amid the wave of Black Death accusations against the Jews. The learned Bishop demanded that all Jews be exterminated *"Mit Kind und Kegel"* ("bag and baggage"—literally, "with child and brat"), an expression that Hitler later adopted.

BEZIERS

In this French town it was the custom for many hundreds of years during the Middle Ages to stone Jewish

homes on Good Friday, when the death of Jesus was commemorated. Good Friday and Palm Sunday sermons throughout the Christian world have given the cue to attack or insult Jews as killers of God.

BIROBIDZHAN

A Siberian ghetto colony established by Joseph Stalin in 1934, the year of the great anti-Semitic purge, so that the Jewish people of the Soviet Union could be shipped off into permanent isolation. Stalin was well acquainted with the papal as well as Lutheran utopian projects for permanent segregation of the Jews.

The Birobidzhan plan failed because the Stalin government was unable at that time to spare the Jewish scientists, administrators and professional personnel needed by a Russia engaged in crash industrialization. However, Stalin's youthful orthodoxy in religion prevailed and he vent his anti-Semitism, like the earlier Orthodox leaders of Russia, in systematic police pogroms against the Jews. Over fifty thousand "expendable" Jewish writers, artists, teachers and political figures were executed, while Russian Orthodox priests scraped favor with their Communist masters by preaching against the Jewish menace and all "internationalists."

The Hitler war interrupted the anti-Jewish measures, which were taken up by Stalin again, as soon as peace was assured. This time the Jews were assailed with the age-old Christian accusation of being engaged in an international conspiracy to conquer the world (the New York-Tel Aviv Axis). Ancient statements by early Christian Church Fathers (Chrysostom, Eusebius, Justin) were dug up to support the contention that the Jews were using the synagogues to smuggle currency (moneychangers of the Gospel) and, in general, to plot evil against their neighbors.

The Judas people were hiding enemy silver (American) in their Torahs and prayer shawls. Indeed, Stalin's propa-

20

gandists only repeated the priest-inspired charges of Constantine, that the synagogues were places of ill repute.

During the Stalin era, Jew hate rose to high pitch. Hundreds of Jews were shot for "economic" offenses in widely publicized "trials," in which great emphasis was placed on the "Jewish origin" of the accused. Torahs, Talmuds, prayer shawls, even Yarmulkas were offered in "evidence" to show where Jews were hiding American money.

In Russia's satellites, Jewish officials from ministers on down were executed as Judases. Slansky in Prague and Anna Pauker in Bucharest were only two of those singled out for inquisition treatment as enemy Jews.

In 1953, the inquisition terror culminated in the "Jewish Doctor Accusation." Following closely the Catholic and Orthodox admonition to Christians that Jewish physicians always plan to kill Christians, Stalin accused his own Jewish doctors of just such deviltry. Anti-Semitism flared higher and higher. Telegrams poured in from the Orthodox Patriarch and priests alike demanding immediate execution of the Jew doctors.

Only Stalin's death prevented a repetition of a German-style massacre of the Hebrew people in the Soviet Union. The Tiflis seminary student joined his fellow priests of anti-Semitic persuasion wherever such men go, and he left a heritage of revived Jew hate that will take generations to obliterate.

BLACK DEATH

On January 9, 1349, all the apprehended Jews of the Swiss city of Basel were burned by a mob, infuriated by Church sermons which accused the Jews of deliberately giving the current plague, known as the Black Death, to Christians. The Jewish cemetery was destroyed—the burned require no burial—and the old tombstones with their Hebrew inscriptions used for the building of fortifications.

Again the Catholic Church preceded the Nazi Germans

21

in blasphemy. The Church killed Jews without giving them even the dignity of burial and consigned consecrated tombstones to war use. The clergy transformed the synagogue into a church.

It was only in 1869 that Jews were readmitted to Basel. The poison of Jew hatred lingers on.

BLOOD DRINKING, RITUAL. See Vampires.

BLOOD PURITY

with the Germanic strain, of course, representing the pure and the Semitic the corrupting element, was most successfully promulgated by the untutored Austrian, Adolf Hitler; the Führer sent out a "welcome-wagon" of florid racial propaganda, and thousands of German philosophers and theologians jumped on it to create a new anthropology, with the Jew next to the gorilla and the Teuton next to Christ.

All this was hardly new. Rampaging Castilian priests of the fifteenth century denied even the dubious sanctuary of Christianity to the desperate Jews of Inquisition Spain because of their impure Semitic blood. (Question: Was Christ of Iberian or Teutonic blood?) Hitler's clamor for "purity of blood" was only an echo of inflamed Spanish Catholicism which used the identical phrase. See *Limpieza de sangre*.

BLOY, LEON (1846-1917)

Leading French Catholic author, who wrote of the Jews: "It is impossible to earn the esteem of a dog if one does not feel an instinctive disgust for the synagogue." Further: To love Jews is a suggestion at which "nature revolts." Bloy's works are standard texts in all French high schools and liberal arts colleges.

BOOK BURNING

was another one of the ways in which the Christian churches expressed their hate of Judaism. We find it throughout the history of Christianity. As late as 1731, the Dominican Giovanni Antonio Costanzi instigated a drive to collect and burn all "Jewish" literature.

In September of 1553 all Hebrew books in the city of Bologna, Italy, were burned at the behest of Pope Julius III. He was only one of many book burners in the Vatican.

Despite their theological differences, on the point of anti-Semitism and especially the burning of Jewish literature Protestants and Catholics were hand in hand then, and for hundreds of years later.

In 1753 Pope Benedict XIV renewed the search in the ghettos of the Papal States. The notorious book burnings by Goebbels were only one of the many "mild" forms of anti-Semitism for which the Christian churches supplied a historic precedent.

BORION

in North Africa; it was, in 535, the site of concentrated clerical anti-Semitism. All synagogues were closed and Jewish religious practices, such as Matzoh eating, circumcision, bar mitzvah, marriage and burial rites, were outlawed.

BOSSUET, JACQUES BENIGNE (1861-1925)

This benign church leader of seventeenth-century France, appealing to both Catholics and Protestants, sermonized: "The Jews are monsters, hated universally. They are beggars and the butt of the world's jokes. Thus has the Lord punished them for killing His Son."

Such sentiments are typical of church preaching in this era.

BRESLAU

was the scene, together with Erfurt and Mainz, of large-scale extermination of Jews in the fourteenth century. Plague-ridden Germans took their vengeance on the Christ killers.

BROGLIE, VICTOR-CLAUDE (1757-1794)

President of the French Revolutionary Assembly, this representative of a princely Catholic family led the opposition against emancipation of the Jews. He was defeated.

BROWN CARDINAL

On March 9, 1939, Cardinal Theodor Innitzer was summoned to Rome by Pope Pius XII, together with the three German Cardinals: Adolf Bertram, Michael von Faulhaber and Karl Josef Schulte. After his reign of only one week the former German Nuncio, Pacelli, decided to send a lengthy handwritten letter of well-wishing to German Chancellor Hitler, who by then had already put underground thousands of Jewish children and hapless civilians, had burned all synagogues, etc., etc.

The good Pope had already sent through his office the usual perfunctory well-wishing messages to all other heads of state; with Hitler he felt compelled to communicate by his personal pen.

Cardinal Innitzer at this historic meeting suggested that His Holiness address the Führer with the respectful "Thou" (*Sie*). He emphasized that in the spirit of the Pacelli-Hitler Concordat of 1933, all teaching priests no longer greeted their pupils with the ancient "Praised be Jesus Christ" but with the new "Heil Hitler, praised be Jesus Christ."

Cardinal Faulhaber of Munich had already in March of 1934 greeted the Nazi Minister of the Interior, Adolf

Wagner, with "Heil Hitler" and Cardinal Innitzer regularly signed his name with "Heil Hitler."

On March 18, 1938, the month of the annexation of Austria by Hitler, which the Cardinal strongly supported, he wrote to the Gauleiter of Vienna, Josef Bürckel: "I enclose a declaration of loyalty by our Bishop, from which you can take that we Bishops *voluntarily and without duress* have fulfilled our duty. Thus our declaration will follow fine mutual cooperation."

And indeed the Cardinal and the Gauleiter worked hand in glove until the very end of the Austrian regime.

On March 15, 1938, two days after Hitler's arrival in Vienna at the head of the Nazi troops, Cardinal Innitzer met Hitler in a special audience in the Hotel Imperial and assured the Führer of the loyalty of his church. This is the day when Hitler spoke dreamingly of a "Religious Spring" in Germany.

On March 27 the Cardinal composed a pastoral letter, the text of which was first sent to the Gauleiter for approval and signed by Innitzer "with special assurance of esteem and Heil Hitler."

This document, oozing with subservience and Hitler adulation, was read from the pulpits of all Austrian Catholic churches on the last Sunday of March, 1938.

As a postscript Innitzer added that the struggle of Hitler is "visibly a subject of the blessings of divine providence."

On March 31, 1938, Innitzer wrote to the Gauleiter Bürckel: "I wish to emphasize that the support of the Hitler plebiscite by our Bishops is principally to be considered as the voice of our common German confession."

Like his Pope, Cardinal Innitzer uttered not a single word of protest when a quarter of a million Viennese Jews were shipped to fearful forms of execution.

BRUNNER, SEBASTIAN (1814-1893)

A Catholic priest and journalist who published violent anti-Semitic attacks in Vienna. His personal journal, *Wiener Katholische Kirchenzeitung,* was finally silenced by court action. At the sensational trial in Vienna it came to light that his anti-Semitica were largely plagiarized from older sources. His whole campaign was revealed to have only one purpose: money, gained by the time-worn technique of publishing scandalous material to increase circulation. Father Brunner was a precursor of Julius Streicher.

BRUNO, GIORDANO (1548-1600)

Eristic member of the Dominican order, who referred in his *Spaccio* to the Jews as a mangy and leprous people who "deserve to be exterminated."

This Catholic nonconformist, himself in later life a victim of prejudice, wished of the Jews that their offspring might be exterminated before birth!

One of the many steps of Christian theologians toward *Die Endlösung* of the Jewish "question."

BRUNSWICK

and other German provinces suffered severe anti-Semitic riots in 1540 in response to the hate polemics of Martin Luther. The Jews' position remained barely tolerable until the Napoleonic era.

BUCHAREST

In 1801 the Orthodox populace of this Rumanian city fell upon the Jews, who were accused of ritual blood drinking by the Orthodox clergy. This charge had been made against the Jews almost fifteen hundred years before by the favorite saint of the Orthodox, Chrysostom. One hundred twenty-eight Jews had their throats cut.

BUERGER

Hitler's edict depriving the Jews of all citizen's rights is only an emulation of a similar order issued under heavy Catholic pressure by the Stadtrat of Frankfurt, a/M. in 1480. Jews who, by direct command of Pope Pius II (1458-1464), had been restricted to a ghetto in Frankfurt, were referred to as *Hundejuden* (dog Jews) in all city records since 1460.

BURNING OF SYNAGOGUES

A feature of the infamous *Kristallnacht* in Germany of a generation ago, it was widely practiced in the years of the early Church Fathers: In Cortona, Italy, the local bishop incited the mob to arson and built a church in the synagogue's place. At Portus Magonis on the island of Minorca; at Tipasa in Africa, synagogues were burned and destroyed. Burning and savage attacks went on throughout the empire. When Theodosius II (408-450) wished to restore the synagogues, he was severely criticized by Simon Stylites (Saint!).

C

CANTERBURY, ARCHBISHOP OF

Closed all synagogues in his diocese in 1282. Under pressure from the Archbishop in 1290, all Jews still in England were expelled by King Edward I, with the Crown expropriating the property of the exiled. Seventeen thousand, the last Jews of medieval England, left for France and Belgium; many of them, however, never reached the shores of Europe, being thrown into the sea by avaricious ship captains.

CANTONISTS

Jewish boys in Czarist Russia who at the age of twelve were forcibly taken from their parents and forced into army service for twenty-five years. During these years they were subjected to weekly conversion lectures by Orthodox priests and monks and invariably "converted" to the Christian faith. Statements by such converts were employed in the Beiliss ritual trial case (1911).

CAPISTRANO, SAINT JOHN (1386-1456)

Fifteenth-century Franciscan propagator of the faith, papal appointee to head the Inquisition in northern countries, nicknamed "Scourge of the Jews," he ordained: "To fight the Jew is a duty of the Catholic, not a choice."

Many of Capistrano's malevolent practices were repeated by the twentieth-century propagators of Christian faith, such as Himmler, Frank and Eichmann. Hitler paraphrased the papal messenger of death by saying: "I am acting in accordance with God's Will by defending myself against the Jews; indeed, I am doing the Lord's work."

CARIDAD

A fifteenth-century Spanish religious association organized by the Bishop of Cordova that excluded all Marranos and other racially Semitic Christians from membership. As in Hitler Germany many of the Catholics of Semitic origin were finally put to a cruel death by the roving mobs of the bishop.

CARNIVAL

A pre-Lent period of public amusement in Rome established by Pope Paul II, in which the local Jews were made to play contemptuous parts, ending in injury or death.

The church-incited riffraff of Rome prevented the Jews from ending their forced run, and otherwise assaulted and molested them.

Not until January 28, 1668, was there an end made to this "sport." Instead, the papal authorities accepted a yearly "tax" of 300 scudi which was extorted from the Jewish population up to the accession of Pius IX in 1846.

Even the delivery of the extortion money was accompanied by abuse, kicking and slander of the Jewish delegates.

CASA SANTA

The "Holy House," reserved for the examination of men and women suspected of heresy by the Dominican friars of the Inquisition. In Spain their favorite "guests" were Jews who had converted to Christianity and their descendants.

Many of the instruments of "investigation" to be found in the *Casa Santa* were copied to a nail by the Gestapo for their latter-day headquarters.

CATECHESE CHRETIENNE ET LE PEUPLE DE LA BIBLE, LA

A basic work by the French priest Paul Démann, examining a great number of French-language religious texts used in France, Belgium, Switzerland and Canada. Here is how some of the parochial school books tell the Gospel stories:

"The crowd followed Jesus, the majority were Jews, His enemies [!], who wished to see Him die."

"Now those evil [!] men, they were Jews [!], spoke."

"But the [!] Jews were heartless [!] and yelled, Crucify Jesus!"

"The heart of the [!] Jews was as stone."

"The wicked [!] Jews took delight in watching Christ's suffering."

29

The above are verbatim quotations appearing in the survey of catechisms by the distinguished French theologian, Father Démann.

It is not surprising that graduates of such religious schools welcomed Hitler's arrival in France with satisfaction rather than dismay, and that a great number of French priests cheerfully fell in with the anti-Semitic program of the Nazi-Vichy government.

CATECHISM

"Sidic" a new ecumenical journal edited in Rome by Catholic clergymen, published in its June, 1967, issue a series of critical reports on the distorted picture of the Jew drawn in Catholic catechisms. Current German and Spanish texts continue to send seeds of "gospel-anti-Semitism" through its liturgical literature.

CATECHISMS

and other liturgical manuals of the Church are characteristically interspersed with anti-Semitism.

The celebrated catechism of Abbé André Hercule de Fleury (1653-1743), which in two centuries went through 172 editions, reads: "Did Jesus have enemies?—Yes, the carnal Jews.—To what point did the hatred of Jesus' enemies go?—To the point of causing his death.—Who was it who promised to hand him over?—Judas Iscariot.—Why was this city [Jerusalem] treated in this way [destroyed]? —For having caused the death of Jesus.—What became of the Jews?—They were reduced to servitude and scattered throughout the world.—What has become of them since?— They are still in the same state.—For how long?—For seventeen hundred years."

Such lessons were read to millions of children all over the Catholic world *and still are being read with hardly any change.*

Here is a section from the catechism of Gambart, written especially for the uneducated:

"Some insulted him; others, with the backs of their hands, struck his noble and gentle mouth; others spat into his face (for it was the custom of the Jews to spit into the faces of those whom they cast out from among themselves) ; others tore out his beard or pulled at his hair, and thus trampled under their accursed feet the Lord of the angels. . . . And still spitting into his noble countenance, they struck his head with a stick, so that the thorns of his crown sank into his head and made the blood flow down his cheeks and over his forehead. . . . Pilate commanded that in this shameful and inhuman state he be led before all the Jewish people, who had remained outside in order not to sully themselves on the day of the Sabbath. But these accursed sons of the Devil all cried out with one voice: Take him away, take him away, crucify him."

Is it surprising that our people consider the Christian Sunday schools and seminaries no better than schools of defamation of the Jewish race, that we are convinced that the disdain for Jews taught in the churches to the young will remain with them emotionally no matter what manner of rationalization is offered them in later years? Theories acquired in formative years can be corrected, but prejudices and hates not so readily. The horror stories about the Jews remain in the hearts of Christians who have long given up the faith and teachings of the Church. That is why the better among them, who would not hurt a living creature, could watch with equanimity while tortures and death were perpetrated on Jews.

The hate mythology of the Gospel and the catechism makes it impossible for the Jews to be accepted by their Christian neighbors as mere people. In the soul of almost every Christian there lies a deep-set repugnance for the killer of God, a traumatic instillation of his youth. Indeed, he may no longer remember that it was in the church edifice that he acquired the *bacillus anti-Semiticus.*

The catechetical disease remains endemic, according to *Sidic,* a journal devoted to reform of Christian-Jewish relations which is published by the Catholic Sisters of Sion in

31

Rome. While "very good beginnings" are noted in the elimination of anti-Semitic references from catechisms in France, the United States, and some other countries, *Sidic* finds little comparable effort in Italy and complains that "seeds of Christian-type anti-Semitism" are to be found in current German texts. The journal's chief editor has been quoted as saying: "The Christian problem is to change a whole mentality, and this will take a lot of hard work."

CATHERINE I (1684-1727)

Devout Czarina of Russia who, upon the direct request of the Ukrainian clergy, expelled all Jews from their territory (1727).

CATHOLIC SCHOOLS

According to a report published in 1966 under the title *Catholic Schools in Action* (Notre Dame University), Catholic schools in America produce in 53 per cent of the students an unfavorable image of the Jew. The same report shows that only 33 per cent manifest a bias against the Negro.

CENTINELA CONTRA JUDIOS

Collection of Spanish tales published in 1728, which resurrected vicious fables about the Jews—among them one referring to "Jews that were born with worms in their mouth, descendants from a Jewess who ordered the crucifixion blacksmith to make the nails blunt."

CHAMBERLAIN, HOUSTON STEWART (1855-1927)

Son-in-law of the vitriolic anti-Semite Richard Wagner, authored *Foundations of the Nineteenth Century,* a racist volume that became the bible of German "anthropologists" in the thirties. By claiming superiority of the Teutons over

all other people, Chamberlain's book flattered the strident inferiority complexes of the Hitler era. Julius Streicher published sections of it (illustrated) in his *Der Stürmer*. He called it the greatest book since the Gospels.

CHAMBRES ARDENTES

The "burning rooms" of France in which converted Jews, accused of "back-sliding" by the Catholic clergy, were put to death. Inquisition trials continued in France up to 1772.

CHAUCER, GEOFFREY (1340-1400)

Author of *The Canterbury Tales,* in which he recites the ritual murder story of a sweet-singing little Christian lad, set upon by evil Jews, who slit the child's throat and then throw the body into the privy pit.

"The Prioress's Tale" is an early example of Jew hate, spread originally by the English Church Schools, which has become embedded in classic literature to influence one generation after another of secular readers. Its author was the first of English literature's anti-Semitic three—the second, William Shakespeare, propagandized the Jew as a malevolent usurer in his *Merchant of Venice,* while the third, Marlowe, defamed a Jew as a well poisoner in his *Jew of Malta.*

Here are some of Chaucer's loathsomely sweet verses which perpetuate the infamy heaped on the hapless Jews of England:

In Asia once there was a christian town
In which, long since, a Ghetto used to be
Where there were Jews, supported by the Crown
For the foul lucre of their usury,
Hateful to Christ and all his company. . . .
As I have said, this child would go along
The Jewish street and, of his own accord,

Daily and merrily he sang his song
O Alma Redemptoris. . . .
First of our foes, the Serpent Satan shook
Those Jewish hearts that are his waspish nest,
Swelled up and said, 'O Hebrew people, look!
Is this not something that should be redressed?
Is such a boy to roam as he thinks best
Singing, to spite you, canticles and saws
Against the reverence of your holy laws?'
From that time forward all these Jews conspired
To chase this innocent child from the earth's face.
Down a dark alley-way they found and hired
A murderer who owned that secret place;
And as the boy passed at his happy pace
This cursed Jew grabbed and held him, slit
His little throat and cast him in a pit.
Cast him, I say, into a privy-drain,
Where they were wont to void their excrement.
O cursed folk of Herod come again,
Of what avail your villainous intent?
Murder will out, and nothing can prevent
God's honour spreading, even from such seed;
The blood cries out upon your cursed deed. . . .
The Provost, praising Christ our heavenly king
And His dear mother, honour of mankind,
Bade all the Jews be fettered and confined. . . .
The Provost then did judgement on the men
Who did the murder, and he bid them serve
A shameful death in torment there and then
On all those guilty Jews; he did not swerve.
'Evils shall meet the evils they deserve.'
And he condemned them to be drawn apart
By horses. Then he hanged them from a cart.

CHESTERTON, G. K. (1874-1936)

Catholic writer, standard author in parochial schools of
today, expressed his regret that the Crusaders who slaugh-

tered Jewish men, women and children and then plundered their homes could not be canonized.

CHILE

The long arm of the Inquisition reached out from Rome and Madrid to the New World to arrest, torture and burn hundreds of Marranos, usually spotted and spied on by "familiars" of the Holy Office.

The records show only wealthy "offenders," which would seem to indicate that here, as in other places, the greed of the authorities was a larger motive than zeal against "heresy."

As late as 1852 the Jewish musician Michael Hauser escaped a "trial" only by flight. Anti-Semitism in Chile has never subsided. The churches keep it alive with fiery sermons.

CHMIELNICKI, BOGDAN ZINOVI (1595-1657)

Hetman of the Zaporogian Cossacks in the Ukraine; like Stalin, a devout student of the Greek Orthodox faith. It was not difficult for him to persuade his Cossack followers that the Jews, accursed by God, should be obliterated.

His butchery of the unarmed Jewish civilians in Poland and the Ukraine was so horrid as to forbid description. Europe was aghast at the atrocities perpetrated on hundreds of thousands of women and children.

In his early years Chmielnicki was a pupil of the Jesuits as well as Orthodox priests. He seems to have retained little from either denomination except fuming Jew hatred. His memory lives on in the Orthodox Church as a blessed defender of the faith.

In the Second World War the Germans were able to recruit from among the Ukrainians, perennially subject to anti-Semitic propaganda by the Greek Orthodox clergy, millions of Nazi collaborators and a whole army corps of volun-

35

teers for Hitler. The Ukraine is still the most anti-Semitic segment of the Soviet Union.

CHOSEN PEOPLE

The Ecumenical Council reiterated that the Chosen People were no longer the Jews but rather the faithful of the Catholic Church.

Unhappily, Julius Streicher, Hitler's man with the whip, had already lectured on this subject: "If somebody tells you the Jews were the Chosen People, don't believe him. Believe us instead. A chosen people does not practice ritual murder. You German youth must shout: 'We Germans hate the race which Jesus said came from the Devil.'"

The Gospel of St. John was correctly quoted: It says that the Jews were sons of the Devil.

Is it not time to clean up the book so the Streichers cannot use it?

CHRISTIAN ANTI-SEMITISM

There is none other. Political animosities in the present Arabic world are time-bound and ism-bound, like those among many other national or state groups. Pre-Christian quarrels of the Jews with Romans, Greeks, Egyptians, Persians or Syrians were local in time and place.

It is only the Christian religion as formulated in early Catholicism that has its very faith based on Jesus, the Son of God, and the Jew, Son of the Devil, the Killer of God. Christianity has anti-Semitism built in as part of its dogma.

Every one of the hundred references in the New Testament to the Jews is anti-Semitic. There is not one redeeming remark in the Christian Gospels concerning the Jew. The Jew is evil itself, killer of Christ, negator of Christianity, traitor to Christ, torturer of Christ, hater of all Christians.

The Gospels carry beautiful stories of Jesus filled with

36

excerpts from Hebrew wisdom literature. But in all these stories the Jew comes out the Devil. All the love in the book is reserved for the Gentiles; for the Jew, only contempt and a curse. The Jew is antichrist.

They want the Jew in the story. He makes it dramatic. Light against darkness. Good against Sin. God's Son against the Devil's Son. The Devil's Son is the Jew (John VIII:44). They need the Jew as the symbol of wickedness. They need anti-Semitism, it is the spice of their catechism.

Christian faith is not anti-Semitic; it is anti-Semitism itself.

And they will not erase it from their text no matter how much misery, suffering and death it may cause the living Jews. Because the living Jews are not their concern. They care only about the Jews of the Gospel; they need them as dramatis personae in their miracle play.

Singing hymns of mystic love, they step over the tortured bodies of ten million Jews whom their anti-Semitism had cut down or burned over the last two thousand years; just as the first Crusaders in the eleventh century drove the Jews of Jerusalem into their great synagogue, set the building afire and marched around the edifice chanting, "Christ, we adore Thee."

CHRISTIAN CAPITALISM

The nineteenth century saw Church anti-Semitism, nurtured for eighteen hundred years on the Gospels as expounded by the Church fathers, seek the new fields of social anti-Semitism. As socialism, Communism and even liberalism openly challenged Christianity, especially the Catholic Church, the priests and ministers naturally set their sights on these ideological rivals.

Instinctively they identified the new enemies with their old hate object, Judaism. Or perhaps their more astute publicists calculated that the Christian masses, imbued since childhood with the Gospel image of the Jew as a hateful

killer, would more readily reject Communism if it were depicted as a Jewish movement. Thus the Church could destroy two enemies with one blow.

Christian capitalism began its campaign in the late nineteenth century by stamping the Protestant convert, Karl Marx, as a Jew, although he himself was a most persistent and brazen anti-Semite. With the zeal characteristic of a convert, in his book, *The World Without Jews* (*Probleme zur Judenfrage*), Marx repeats every possible anti-Semitic shibboleth of the Catholic and Protestant churches, winding up with the hope for a world emancipated from Judaism.

Hitler, as he repeatedly insisted, continued the work of the Catholic Church by letting loose his propaganda against the "Jewish" Communists. The European Christians, especially the Germanic groups, succumbed to his Great Lies concerning the nefarious Jews. They copied old anti-Semitic principles and phraseology. The Jews were conspiring to destroy healthy Christian industry and individuality and replace it with a Jew-controlled Communist society; in this process they, the Jews, naturally would eliminate the Church and all Christian tradition.

Such grotesque accusations fell upon willing ears. For fifteen hundred years the Christians of Europe had been brainwashed—or shall I say brainsoiled?—by anti-Semitic demonology from pulpit and catechism. Now the gory oratory of Jew baiting came from the government itself, the new God. And the Church stood by smiling with sanctimonious satisfaction at the fresh outpouring of its old anti-Semitic hatred.

At this writing the churches have refused to absolve the Jew of God killing, refused to condemn anti-Semitism, refused to admit openly that the sermons were false, that the Jews are not arch-conspirators of Communism.

The Jews have no voice at all in the Red high command; none of the current strategists or theoreticians of the movement is of Jewish origin—yet Church papers continue to smear *the* Jew as the arch-Communist, just as they paint him as the arch-antichrist.

CHRISTIAN CONSCIENCE

occasionally comes to the fore, even in matters pertaining to Jews. In 1948 a Committee for Christian Aid to War Prisoners was formed in Germany, protesting vehemently the Allied war crime trials involving the top Nazi murderers.

Among the most active members and sponsors of said committee were Cardinal Josef Frings of Cologne, Catholic Bishop Johann Neuhäussler of Munich, Lutheran Bishop Theophil Wurm of Stuttgart and Lutheran Bishop Meiser of Munich.

These highly agitated clergymen, who watched the execution of Jewish families with admirable equanimity, could not rest in their efforts to set the Nazi killers free. They were supported by two religious organizations, the Roman Catholic *Caritas* and the Protestant *Evangelisches Hilfswerk*. The German weekly, *Christ und Welt*, led the campaign against Jewish "revenge" seekers.

Cardinal Frings and Bishop Wurm also headed the notorious "Committee for Justice" which became a rallying point for the former Nazi elite. Their Christian Aid Center in Munich supplied indicted Nazi executioners with material aid in escapes abroad and feverishly worked for reduction in sentences of Nazi criminals. Even Ilse Koch, "the Bitch of Buchenwald," she who decorated her lamps with shades made of Jewish skin, was released, though later re-arrested.

CHRISTIAN NAMES

were forbidden to Jews by many Catholic bishops and nobles. In fourteenth-century Spain the Cortes of Toro (1369) and of Burgos (1377) made this prohibition a point of Christian law. Here, too, Hitler revived an old Christian practice.

CHRISTIAN SERVANTS

were prohibited to the Jews by repeated bulls and papal orders. An archbishop in Sardinia, for example, ruled that offenders would be punished by receiving two hundred lashes. The Nazi Germans re-established the ban on employment of Christian servants by Jews.

CHRISTIAN TERMINOLOGY

was extensively used by the Nazi philosophers and political leaders, from Martin Heidegger to Alfred Rosenberg. In his eloquent encyclical *"Mit Brennender Sorge"* Pope Pius XI made reference to the many expressions taken from Christian theology by the Nazis.

Similar plagiarism is practiced by most anti-Semitic groups, who take advantage of latent as well as explicit anti-Semitism in Christian canon and liturgy simply by prefixing their movements with such adjectives as "Christian," "Crusader," "Evangelic," etc.

CHRISTIAN UNIVERSITIES

in Europe did not admit Jews to teaching positions until the late nineteenth century, in many instances not until the twentieth century. Throughout Catholic history Jewish students were handicapped in gaining admission or totally excluded. Hitler's expulsion of all Jews from the academic world, teachers as well as students, was only a variation of a thousand-year-old Catholic policy.

CHRISTIAN WOMEN

In reaction to the multiple suffering of the contemporary Hebrews: "They [the Jews] are receiving just what they measured out to Christians." (Protestant *Women's Voice*, March 26, 1953.)

Aren't these gentle Christian women like the nuns of Queen Isabella who carried faggots to the auto-da-fé? Such hostility makes it clear why Christian Europe watched indifferently the burning of the Jews.

CHRISTMAS

During Christmas of 1936 Julius Streicher in *Der Stürmer* called on "all German Christians" to cease doing business with "the killers of our dear Lord Christ."

"To be intimate with Jews is to defend the crucifiers of our Lord."

It almost reads like a quotation from the *Bullarium Romanum* of the Vatican.

At a Christmas celebration for school children the former school teacher, Julius Streicher, asked his audience: "Do you know who is the Devil?"

"The Jew, the Jew," came the response from the lips of all. Some of the older pupils even knew where the quotation came from: the eighth chapter of the Gospel of St. John.

The Church had done a great job of education on the Jewish problem.

Christmas still provides an opportunity to celebrate, not the Advent of Jesus, but *the* Jew as His Adversary.

In 1967 the vice-president of the school board of Wayne Township, New Jersey, issued a public statement urging voters to defeat two Jewish candidates for the board. Most Jews, he said, were liberals and likely to spend too much money on education. Then came the clincher:

"Two more votes and we lose what is left of Christ in our Christmas celebrations in our schools. Think of it."

In the subsequent election the two Jewish candidates were overwhelmingly defeated.

CHRYSOSTOM, SAINT JOHN (345-407)

Patriarch of Constantinople, by far the most influential preacher of his time, referred to in Catholic literature as "the bishop with the golden tongue." Here is some of his gilded rhetoric:

"The Jews are the most worthless of all men. They are lecherous, greedy, rapacious. They are perfidious murderers of Christ. They worship the devil, their religion is a sickness. The Jews are the odious assassins of Christ and for killing God there is no expiation possible, no indulgence or pardon. Christians may never cease vengeance, and the Jew must live in servitude forever. God always hated the Jews. It is incumbent upon all Christians [i.e., their duty] to hate the Jews."

Thus read the homilies of the foremost orator of early Catholicism.

CHUETA

Spanish corruption of *juéut,* diminutive form of the Catalonian word for "Jew"; name given to descendants of Catholic converts on the Spanish island of Majorca, who are still being ostracized by Gentile Catholics because they are of Jewish origin. See *Individuos de la Calle.*

CLEMENT, SAINT

Pope (88-97?), endeavored to blame the Jews for the Neronic persecution of the Christians. One of the earliest such innuendoes in Christian history.

CODEX THEODOSIANUS (438 A.D.)

This master compilation of Christian Romanism limited the Jews to private or secret religious observance. The Jews had become second-class citizens, to remain thus in most Christian lands until the great American and French revo-

lutions. The Codex banned conversion to Judaism, while Catholic proselytism was encouraged. It permitted the conversion of Jewish children, whose parents could not disown them. A Jew was forbidden to acquire a Christian slave. (Similarly Hitler prohibited employment of Christian servants by Jews.)

CONCORDAT OF COLLABORATION

Nazi "legality" was immensely strengthened by the Concordat with the Vatican (July 20, 1933), an agreement which the Catholic Church had refused to grant the previous Weimar Republic. (Concordats did exist with such component German states as Bavaria, Prussia, and Baden.)

Hitler described the Concordat of Collaboration as an "unrestricted acceptance of National Socialism by the Vatican." Indeed it was, since it subordinated all cultural and educational activities of the Church to Nazi ideology and regimen. It began with the placing of Hitler's portrait on the walls of all Catholic parochial and Sunday schools—and ended with the church bells ringing at every Nazi victory, including the arrest and transportation of the last Jew from every town and hamlet in Germany.

The sellout of Catholicism to Hitler began not with the people but with the Vatican Curia. For Rome it was only a repetition of the Concordat it had previously made with Mussolini. The German bishops followed the Vatican, represented by its Secretary of State, Cardinal Pacelli, later Pius XII; the priests obeyed the Bishops, and the parishioners fell in line.

Never, after the signing of the Concordat, did the Church protest against Hitler or his barbarism; never against his satanic system of bloodshed, including the blood of a million Jewish children. When protests came they were invariably concerned with infractions against the interests of the Church. As Bishop Christoph Bernhard von Galen declared in 1935, "It is not my job to mourn past political structures or to criticize the present ones." Adolf Cardinal Bertram in

43

1936 most loyally declared: "Not a single pastoral letter of the German Catholic clergy ever criticized the National Socialist Movement or, God forbid, the *Führer*."

Pater Alfred Delp, one of the few exceptions to the closed ranks of subservient churchmen, bitterly warned before his execution (following the attempt against Hitler's life in July, 1944) : "The future historians of Germany will have to write the bitter chapter about the total failing of the Christian Churches."

CONFISCATION

The Grand Master of the Knights of the Hospital of Saint John in 1305 sent a memorandum to Pope Clement V, suggesting that half of the goods of the Jews be seized by the Church in punishment for Christ's killing. A similar suggestion had been made previously by another great crusading figure, Peter of Cluny.

The good Pope went further, much further, and had all Jews expelled from France, confiscating their goods.

Confiscation of Jewish property was the initial step in Hitler's internal policy, to be followed later by executions. By 1305 France had already had its Jew burnings; Pope Clement's expellees were only a remnant of the once considerable Jewish populace.

CONSTANCE

In 1349 monk-led Flagellants killed the "accursed" Jews of this Swiss town. The tombstones of their cemetery were used to build the great cathedral of the town.

Degrading restrictions burdened the few Jews who drifted back to Constance as late as the middle of the nineteenth century.

The use of consecrated Jewish tombstones as building material for new edifices and fortifications was widely practiced by the German Nazis as a sign of contempt for what

Bishop Luigi Carli, prominent in the Second Ecumenical Council, recently termed the "accursed Jewish religion."

CONSTANTINOPLE

Civil rights of Jews in this great city, which was once Byzantium, were severely curtailed from the time of the first Christian emperor, Constantine. Restrictions and humiliations imposed by the overbearing clergy of the Greek Church were incessant.

A new era came for the much harassed and persecuted Jews with the fall of Constantinople (1453) and extinction of the Byzantine Empire by Mohammed the Conqueror. The Moslems offered the Jews of the Renaissance sanctuary from certain destruction at the hands of the Christians of Western and Southern Europe.

Similarly, the position of the Jews in the Moorish segments of Spain was one of dignity and respect and stands in marked contrast to the vicious, bloody persecutions at the hands of the Catholic Church.

CONVERSION SERMONS

In 1577 Pope Gregory XIII (1572-1585) decreed that all Roman Jews, by pain of death, must listen attentively after their Sabbath services to a Catholic conversion sermon, first in the church San Benedetto alla Regola, later in Sant Angelo in Pescaria.

In 1823 Pope Leo XII re-established the ghetto in Rome, which had been rendered wide open by the victorious French troops of Napoleon; and he ordered the revival of forced conversion sermons on the Jewish Sabbath.

Not until the Garibaldi freedom uprising was the Papal yoke removed from the Jews in the Vatican state. On December 13, 1870, victorious King Victor Emanuel II granted the Jews all civic and political rights. After almost two thousand years the Jews of Rome were free of papal terror.

CORFU

On this Greek island in 1891 the local clergy of the Orthodox Church accused the Jews of having slain a child for its blood. Many Jews had to flee for their lives since the local authorities failed to protect them.

CORPUS JURIS CIVILIS (529-535)

Justinian's definitive Code of Roman law made the already draconic restrictions of the *Codex Theodosianus* still more rigorous. Christian theological considerations dominated all its "Jewish" legislation. Jews were not permitted to testify against a Christian, were barred from public functions, had only limited property rights, and their marriage to Christians was a capital offense. (Cf. the Nuremberg Laws.)

COUGHLIN, FATHER CHARLES EDWARD (1891—)

A blustering American version of the nineteenth-century German anti-Semitic court preacher Stöcker. In the 1930's, from his shrine of The Little Flower in Michigan, Father Coughlin used the new medium of radio to broadcast the same basic message to Depression-ridden America— "Blame the Jews!"—clothed in the same vague context of Christian Socialism. In case his listeners forgot the message, the "Radio Priest" repeated it in his own magazine, *Social Justice.*

In 1966, on the fiftieth anniversary in the priesthood of Father Coughlin, whose anti-Semitic radio chats bewildered America and gave aid and comfort to Hitler, the following eulogy was delivered to the ill-spoken priest:

"Father Coughlin was committed to a better social order, to a world of justice [!]—to a life worthy of man as a child of God—he was a giant in this generation."

Thus spake Mother Church about the man who, more than any other person on this continent, tried to justify

46

Hitler's persecutions of the Jews by smearing the victims with slanderous medieval charges.

COUNCIL OF BASEL (1431-1443)

Invoked by Pope Eugenius IV. Reinforced the familiar restrictions upon Jews—separate quarters from Christians, compulsory attendance at Church sermons, and prohibition of study at universities.

COUNCIL OF PARIS

forbade Christian midwives to attend Jewish women in labor (1212). Those who helped bring the brood of the Devil into this world would be expelled from the Holy Church.

CRETE

The Jews in medieval Crete were compelled by the Orthodox clergy to affix a wooden devil figure to their doors, to warn Christians against entering their homes.

CRUCIFIXION

The Roman leader Varus (139-169) crucified two thousand captive Jews within view of Jerusalem. The Romans were adept in crucifixion; it was their way. Crucifixion was never the Hebrew way. No criminal or rebel was ever crucified by Hebrews. Even the Jew-hating scribes of the Roman bishops blamed the Jews only for instigation, never crucifixion; and this to please their Roman benefactors beginning with Constantine—an opportunistic perversion of history to placate the powerful emperor.

CRUSADERS

on their first rampage took Jerusalem in 1099. The cross-emblazoned knights of Christian love herded all Jews into

the great synagogue and burned them alive, man, woman and child. While the Temple was ablaze they marched around it singing, "Christ, we adore Thee." We even have drawings of this ceremony in contemporary diaries.

The Holy Sepulcher is a symbol that invokes religiosity in many Christians. To the Jews, however, it remains a fearful harbinger of bestial attacks on their people. Anti-Semitic fury preached in the Catholic churches by Crusading monks filled the rivers of France, Germany and Austria with the blood of Israel.

CUBA

The Inquisition was active in this island in the seventeenth and eighteenth centuries. In most cases the Holy Office put only wealthy Jews and Marranos to the torture. After they confessed and went to the pyre, their property was confiscated. Again, greed beclouds the religious issue.

It is reported that Spanish-language antisemitica finds a ready market among certain "right-wing" and "upper-class" Cuban emigrés in the United States. No matter what one's present troubles, it is comforting to blame the scapegoat learned about at mother's knee—Mother Church, that is.

CYPRIAN, SAINT

A third-century Bishop of Carthage, the most outstanding Catholic churchman of that era; demanded that all Jews be expelled at the point of the sword.

CYRIL OF ALEXANDRIA, SAINT (376-444)

This "Doctor of the Church" incited the Greek mobs to kill or expel the Jews (415). Not until the conquest of Egypt by the Moslems did a Jewish community come into its own again in Alexandria.

Cyril was a typical parchment theologian. He, like most

of the other Catholic Fathers, could not see a human soul for the black letter of his dogma. He looked at the massacre of Jews with equanimity; only texts could concern the saint.

CZERNOWITZ

In this Ukrainian town in 1579 the Jewish inhabitants were subjected to brutal and bloody outrage committed by the Voivode, Peter the Lame, a barbarian with two crucifixes on his chest, who proclaimed his determination to "avenge the killing of Christ."

D

DACHAU

On September 15, 1935, the notorious Nazi hate-sheet, *Der Stürmer,* printed a letter from a German girl, who wrote: "The Jew is speaking venomously against Christians; he should therefore be sent to Dachau." A similar reason was given by the Fourth Lateran Council for shutting the Jews up in ghettos.

DAGOBERT

This Frankish king (629-639) sent his royal edict to the Jews: convert or suffer expulsion. The Church was the rigorous host; the king was only the bouncer.

DAMASCUS INCIDENT

In 1840 a Franciscan friar disappeared in the city without trace. The Franciscan Order claimed that the Father was killed for his blood by Jewish Passover celebrants. Under torture, numerous Jews confessed, implicating others; some were executed, others finally released under pressure from humanitarian elements abroad.

DANZIG

In 1723 the Bishop of Danzig, failing to obtain an expulsion order against Jews from the city council, roused the mob against them. Most Jews were beaten to death; only a small number escaped.

DAUPHINE

In this old province of France in 1247 six Jews of Valréas were accused by Franciscan monks of having drunk the blood of a Christian child found dead. The Jews were horribly tortured, then burned. The Bishop of St. Paul-Trois-Châteaux thereupon imprisoned all Jews in his domain and robbed them of their properties.

DEGGENDORF

A Catholic tourist town in Bavaria whose great attraction is a Catholic church where sixteen oil paintings depict Jews in medieval dress desecrating wafers (hosts) with hammers, thorns and fire.

Ten thousand "worshipers" make the pilgrimage to Deggendorf yearly to absorb, along with the Mass, a booster shot of Jew hate.

The events which are commemorated by the Catholic clergy go back to September 30, 1337, when all the Jewish people of the town, including their children, were burned to death for cutting up consecrated wafers. Of course, the homes of the Jews were ransacked by the mob.

Today little Deggendorf still enjoys prosperity because of the armies of pilgrims who come, not to atone for the brutal massacre of innocent Jews, but to bewail the mutilated host.

To make the picture gallery understandable to the German pilgrims, the local padres adorned it with such explanations as: "The Holy Host is being scraped to the very blood by wicked Jews."

Only last year Bishop Rudolf Graber of Regensburg, responsible for Deggendorf, admonished its clergy not to deviate an iota from the "traditional practice."

Graber's General Vicar, Karl B. Hofmann, replied to critics: "We are not the only ones displaying such illustrations." Indeed, the Vicar is right.

Is it surprising that the Germans and Austrians found it easy to carry out Hitler's orders for Jew extermination? The Christian churches had readied twentieth-century Germans for their role in the holocaust.

DEICIDE

Introduced as a running theme of the Gospels to brand the Jew as a scapegoat for a Roman deed. Rome by then (fourth century) was the protector and benefactor of Christianity.

John Chrysostom (fourth century), the most influential Catholic theologian of all time, placed the "God killer" charge at the center of all Christian teachings. A millennium and more before Hitler he propagated an *identical* thesis: "The Jews are the pestilence of the universe."

The mainspring of anti-Semitism has remained, for 1500 years, the Christian accusation flung against the Jews of being the killers of Christ. Such accusation has not been withdrawn by the Vatican Council, but rather re-emphasized by the Schema that the Jewish leaders and the people who followed them pressed for the death of Christ.

Such teaching in all its gruesome detail of the piercing of hands and feet, the cruel demand of the Jews to break the bones of the dying Christ—all that remains and impresses itself indelibly upon the susceptible minds of Christian children.

When the Council, as a considerate afterthought, stated that the Jews of today are not responsible for this murder, and that even the Jews of antiquity were not *all* responsible —this is most generous!

However, the belated qualification has little effect upon

51

the boys and girls who for years are subjected to an obviously anti-Semitic and monstrous murder charge. I pray you, take a look at the Gospel of St. John, which is referred to as "the Spiritual Gospel." Of the 32 references to the Jews in this text, every single one is violently anti-Jewish.

As long as the charges that *the* Jews were the killers of the Christian God are not dropped—straight and unequivocally—the children raised in Christian Sunday schools will grow up in Jew hatred. I regret to say that the Schema of the recent Council, contrary to the wishes of Pope John XXIII—a truly great human being—is not the beginning of a new era in Catholic teaching, but rather a subtle confirmation of the old. Saying that my two-year-old grandson or the Jewish neighbor's wife across the street, is not a killer of Christ—well, no normal Catholic adult thinks differently. Here again we are given something by the Council that we have had for centuries. What we desire, and what all right-thinking people of the world desire, is that the Christian churches stop using the Jew as a scapegoat in their theological drama and once and forever drop the defamatory untruth of the Jews in particular being the killers of Christ.

One thing we know: those who followed Christ were all Jews. How many of those who urged His death were Greeks, Romans, Egyptians, Persians—no one knows. And everybody knows that the Procurator of Judea, Pontius Pilate, was a hard, all-powerful ruler, in behalf of the Roman Caesars, who reduced to ashes not only Alexandria, Athens, Carthage, Syracuse, Corinth, but eventually, Jerusalem. It suited the Bishops of Rome in the 4th century to make the Roman oppressor appear like a powerless, benevolent judge, totally subject to the whim and will of Jewish priests.

It is time that, in the spirit of Pope John XXIII, there be an end made to the deicide charge. There is no beginning or "initial stage" to withdrawing a false accusation. Justice knows only truth or falsehood; justice doesn't creep up on a judgment in multiple stages. The well-meaning people of the world are waiting for the Christian churches, not to

make a beginning of justice, but to make an end to injustice.

And those who wait—after Vatican II, what did they hear?

"In conclusion, I hold it legitimate to be able to affirm that in the time of Jesus *all* the Jewish people were responsible *in solidum* for the crime of deicide, although only the leaders physically consummated the crime.

"It follows that Judaism must be considered as accursed by God." (*Pal. del Clero. XLIV,* April, 1966.)

Such an opinion, expressed by Bishop Luigi Carli, asserting perennial Jewish guilt for an alleged rabbinical judgment at a time when the majority of the Jews lived outside of the borders of Israel, reflects correctly the centuries-old attitude of anti-Semitic Catholicism.

What else could you call a religion that considers today's Jewish children (even new-born babies) *already* guilty of deicide and accursed by God? Only in German Nazism do we find a corresponding judgment of guilt. Hitler, too, theorized that he could gas to death Jewish infants because their grandfathers allegedly opposed Germany's expansionist war machine in World War I.

Catholicism of the Carli kind is kin to Hitlerism. Both condemn Jews, young or old, just because they are Jews, and both consider Jews *"vogelfrei,"* that is, without any legal protection. Of course, some Catholic liberals and pseudo-liberals are embarrassed by their own church's shameful history of anti-Semitic persecutions and are desperately trying to cover the gaping wounds left by the Carlifatti on the conscience of modern humanity.

Mankind has just done away with Hitlerism, without the help of the Christian ministers of Jesus, and now the Catholic Church would put the Jews right back where they were a generation ago, on the sacrificial block of bigotry.

Christian youth will continue to imbibe with their mother's milk Carli's interpretation of the Jew as a descendant of a Devil's brood who accomplished the death of Christ and whose religion is accursed by God forever.

The tragedy here is not just the opinion expressed in

official Catholic "learned" journals by a foxy old bishop with a decades-old background of Jew-baiting. The tragedy is that such a primitivist with his head on backward should be chosen by the Vatican to chair the Ecumenical Curia charged with the job of preparing a new "Declaration on the Jewish Question" that would take the Catholic Church out of the company of Himmler, Hitler and Eichmann and put Rome on the way to redemption and tolerance, as the late John XXIII planned, wished and inaugurated. What happened instead, through the Carlifatti, is that the Ecumenic message extolled by John XXIII died with the great Pontiff. What the world began to hear thereafter were no longer the celestial tones of peace and brotherhood, but the ugly mutters of a bedeviled Curia, taking up the old anti-Semitic chant: *Hep! Hep! Hep!*

We Jews have been betrayed by Vatican II. We have been betrayed by promises that were slowly, deliberately, twisted until we see through the final version of the Schema only the hooked cross of anti-Semitism.

DEMONS

The Jews are demons, proclaimed Pope Innocent III (1198-1217).

DEMONSTRATIO ADVERSUS JUDAEOS (160-235)

A brutal essay in which its author, Saint [*sic*] Hippolytus, "proves" that Jews must always be slaves because they "murdered" the only offspring of their Benefactor. He wishes for them most dire occurrences. Some later-day anti-Semites quote Hippolytus in defense of Nazism as an act of divine punishment upon the Jews.

DERROTA MUNDIAL

or *World Defeat,* a vicious "modern" anti-Semitic work in Spanish by Salvador Borrego, expounding the medieval

Catholic theorem of an international anti-Christian conspiracy by world Jewry.

DEVIL'S ADVOCATE

The Vatican's appointee to oppose beatification and canonization, the stages of raising to sainthood persons who may appear deserving of such recognition. I am not concerned here with errors of judgment in this intricate process of confirmation of holiness, such as elevation of nonexistent individuals or alleged victims of ritual murder who were presumptuously sanctified, as for instance little Simon of Trent.

I am touched by the endeavor to accord to the gentle Pope John XXIII public veneration, as I am shocked by the astonishing efforts of some reactionary Vatican circles to propose the author of the Nazi Concordat of Collaboration, Pope Pius XII, to such high status.

We Jews shudder at the word "saint," since so many of the vitriolic proponents of Jew slaughter, beginning with the early Church Fathers, were "saints." The Orders of Saint Dominic and Saint Francis provided the Inquisition with its bestial specialists for hundreds of years. The saintly friars conducted their interrogations and inevitable executions by tying Jewish men, women and children by their wrists to a stake or to a wall, at the foot of which slow fires burned to extend the agony of the victims.

Indeed, I know of no sainted, beatified or canonized figure in Catholicism that ever put a stop to the incessant War against the Jews. And if those pillars of the Church possess the power of heavenly intervention, God help us, in the light of their ominous darkness. I don't think that Saints who on earth led the war cry against us will be inclined to mercy above.

Will Pius XII now speak up in the heavens? He who stood silent on earth when the diabolical Hitler gassed the kin of Jesus?

DEVILS

In his pamphlet *Von den Juden und ihren Lügen,* Martin Luther declares that one may not mention the Jews in the same sentence with the Papists or even the Moslems, because the Jews were creatures of the Devil, as the Gospel teaches (John 8:44—"You are of your father, the devil.")

In numerous medieval church cartoons and illustrations the Devil carries a Jew-badge on his clothing.

Such barbaric anti-Semitic "religious" sentiment was prevalent, and most strongly so, in Germany, where Hitler found the ground well prepared for his "racial" campaign.

It was only a short step from the Gospel's "Devil Jews" to the Nazi story book quoted at the Nuremberg Trials:

> "The evil devil speaks to us
> Out of the Jewish face;
> The devil who in every land
> Is known as wicked plague."

DIALOGUE WITH TRYPHO

The first "objective" discussion by a Catholic theologian, Saint Justin Martyr (100-165), with an (imagined) rabbi, includes the Saint's opinion that all Jews are damned forever for having "murdered" the Lord.

DICTIONARIES

in Spanish and Portuguese countries still carry a number of objectionable Catholic Church definitions of "Jewish" terms. Jew is often defined as a synonym for "usurer," "swindler," "devil."

The new "revised" edition of the dictionary of the Portuguese language published by the Brazilian Literary Academy (Catholic directed) explains to its readers: "Synagogue: place for illegal business." This definition is remarkably close to Stalin's. Most Spanish and Portuguese and

56

many Italian "imprimatur" dictionaries are shot through with anti-Semitic didactics.

In this connection, it is worth noting a carry-over into a secular American work, Webster's International Dictionary (Third Edition). Among its definitions are: Jew (noun), "a person believed to drive a hard bargain"; Jew (verb), "to cheat by sharp business practice"; Jew down (verb), "to induce (a seller) by haggling to lower his price." The latter two definitions are accompanied by the explanation, "usually taken to be offensive."

None of these definitions were to be found in the previous Second Edition of Webster's. Their appearance now may be attributed to the editors' "pragmatic" approach to the American language, recognizing any and all words now in use, as they are used. Nonetheless, in this case such unqualified recognition serves to dignify and perpetuate the ancient stigma fastened by the Church on the People of the Book.

DIVINE(?) PUNISHMENT

The medieval Church, deep into modern times, was instrumental in depriving the Jew of civil rights, of his property, of his dignity and bodily safety.

The Church then turned around and proclaimed: "Mark the terrible fate of the Jew. This is divine punishment for his deicide! The wealth of the Church and the miserable conditions of the synagogue prove the guilt of the Jews."

DOGMA

If the whole of the four Gospels were to be accepted as absolute and genuine, then the statement of John, chapter 8, paragraph 44, that the (!) Jews were the offspring of the Devil is infallible.

Such an assertion implies that all the family of Jesus, all of them, and their children and their children's children, were the Devil's brood.

I cannot conceive a more monstrous assertion, a more insolent intolerance toward God's Chosen People and Christ's own kin than the above. No semanticism or word play can make this horrid insult to the Holy Family more palatable.

It is understandable why the Nazi hierarchy, from Hitler and Streicher down, quoted so frequently this sick verse of the Gospel of St. John. This gospel was promulgated under the aegis of Roman Bishops who were determined to make the Roman killers of Jesus look like angels and the Jews, who were the only ones whom He made His Apostles, into devils.

DOLLAR ANTI-SEMITES

appear sporadically in all Christian countries, even in the United States, which has an enviable record of fair play toward its Jewish citizens. Hate is a commodity. There always will be those willing to sell it in the manner of the patent medicine peddler. Their spiel, of course, is reversed; they exhort the gullible *not* to buy. Buy not Judaism—it is un-Christian, it is conspiratorial, it is aggressive, it is out to overpower you, and so on.

These hate vendors, cunning in their business, invariably attach the words "Christian," "Cross," "Crusade," or some denominational adjective to the name of their organization. Knowing the value of the traditional attitude of disdain toward Jews embodied in these terms, they start off with the asset of being "Christian gentlemen."

Most of the American and British professional anti-Semitic agitators were ne'er-do-wells with little imagination who hit upon familiar church anti-Semitism as a ready product, adding other borrowed accusations as they went along.

They could never command a notable following since they were uninspired and unconvinced, hence uninspiring and unconvincing. They attracted odd little groups of walking inferiority complexes who yearned for snappy belts and

boots. Occasionally they would persuade some elderly man of wealth to contribute to their support. In the long run, their campaigns dwindle to smearing walls with swastikas, overturning Jewish tombstones, and modeling their operetta uniforms like degenerate exhibitionists.

DOMINICANS

were the most vicious of the Catholic orders. Their privileged position in the Inquisition was only a small part of their war against the Jews.

Consciously or by conditioned reflex, they never failed to include the Jews in their sermons against infidels and heretics.

In 1422, Dominicans led a fierce campaign against the Hussite heresy in Bohemia. They spiced their sermons with deadly accusations against the Jews: drinking blood from Christian corpses, driving nails through consecrated wafers representing the host, and poisoning wine and water. The masses of Christians, having no other tutors but the clergy, were kept in a furious heat against the Christ killers.

The Dominican preachers openly invoked their Christian assemblies to violence and the destruction of Jewish property. Their slogan, deep into the eighteenth century, was: "Why seek for the enemies of Christ if His killers are right among us?"

In similar manner, the Nazi troops en route to fight their traditional enemies in France, Poland and Russia paused to massacre Jews as the absolute enemy of a Christian Germany.

DOMUS CONVERSORUM

A conversion mill established 1232 in London by Henry III. The campaign was of little consequence since in 1290 all Jews were expelled from England.

DREYFUS CASE

The notorious framing of the Jewish Captain Alfred Dreyfus was possible only because of the deep anti-Semitic sentiment of the French clergy (Edouard Drumont, etc.). The Catholic press, and indeed almost all Catholic opinion, was committed to support of the frame-up. Its exposure caused irreparable damage to the political influence of the clergy in France.

DRUMONT, EDOUARD

French anti-Semite who in his *La France Juive* (1886) attributed all ills of Christian France to the Jews. Even rising anticlericalism was "created by Jewish power." His writings, widely distributed by a gullible clergy, helped to create the background for the Dreyfus frame-up.

DU MONTFORT, FATHER (1673-1716)

Influential Catholic priest in Brittany, who wrote and composed a great number of popular religious songs shot through with anti-Semitic offense: "Jewish barbarians broke his limbs, they cut his flesh, they bared his nerves, they . . ."
These pious songs are still being chanted in the French countryside.

DUNS SCOTUS, JOHN (1266-1308)

English Franciscan monk and renowned theologian, who "proved with convincing logic" that not only was it a privilege but a duty of the Catholic Church to take away the children of reluctant Jewish parents and forcibly baptize them. Also, the parents should be compelled by all means to convert. Any such efforts would be true piety—so philosophized "the Doctor Subtilis."

E

ECK, JOHANN VON (1486-1543)

German Catholic theologian and one of the chief opponents of Lutheranism; vehemently attacked all secular authorities that tolerated Jews in their territories.

While Von Eck disagreed with Luther on all major ecclesiastical issues, in matters Judaica they concurred.

An epigone, the Jesuit Adam Contzen (1570-1635) of Mainz, called the Jews "poisonous animals" who should be hounded into oblivion. Contzen was Professor of Moral (*sic!*) Theology at the university.

ECUMENICAL CLIMATE

Pope Paul VI, cunctator of ecumenism, directed the proper Vatican secretariat to cooperate with Protestant translators of the New Testament, and we shall have another English version of the Greek text.

From the efforts of Wycliffe (whose corpse was desecrated by the clergy) and Tyndale (who was burned by the Church) to the Catholic Douai Bible and the King James Version, the differences in the Christian canon and legend are minimal.

The last few decades have burgeoned with philological attempts to interpret the New Testament, by Catholics and Protestants alike. Like their predecessors, the current translators use either the Greek editions or the Vulgata, a Latin text prepared from the Greek.

But neither Jesus, His Apostles nor His followers spoke Greek or Latin—they spoke Hebrew. When speaking of peace, the great ecumenic theme, Jesus said not *"Eirene,"* nor did He say *"Pax."* He said *"Shalom."*

And while the Catholics, true to the doctrine of the "perpetual virginity of Mary," contrary to the Protestant theologians, refer to Christ's brothers as "brethren," Christ's kin were, and because of ecumenic superficiality, still are

subject to derision and hate in the very Gospels that bespeak His love.

No matter in what linguistic or doctrinal detail Catholics and Protestants differ, they all agree to retain in the coming Gospel translation the naming of *"The* Jews" as sons of the Devil, bloodthirsty tormenters and killers of Christ, idolators of a God-accursed religion!

This last curse against the Jews was repeated only months after the end of Vatican II by none other than Bishop Luigi Carli, the appointee of Paul VI to head the Ecumenical Curia dealing with the Jews and Judaism.

As long as the Christian theologians are unwilling to excise these ugly references to the people of Jesus from their canon, it will remain a book of death to the Jews, even if the new translators succeed in recruiting a few "Uncle Tom" Jews to participate in their "ecumenic committee."

There can be no real ecumenism with "sons of the Devil," and so we are described in the New Testament.

Someday, in the distant future, we hope there will arise a true concept of brotherhood even among the Christians and they will cease teaching their young that the Children of Israel are diabolical God killers.

Someday the Christians will learn that if God considered the Jews a devil's brood, He would not have sent His only Son to be born among them, from the womb of a Jewish mother.

Such a canon is not of God; the mark on the forehead of the Jewish nation as it appears in the Gospels was placed there not by Him but by Satan.

EISENMENGER, JOHANN ANDREAS (1654-1704)

Lutheran and anti-Semitic agitator. His book, *Entdecktes Judentum,* has served as an arsenal of anti-Semitic calumny since 1700.

ELVIRA, COUNCIL OF

Banned (306 A.D.) all community contact between Spanish Christians and the evil Hebrews; prohibited marriage of Christians and Jews (cf. racial purity laws of Nazism).

EMANCIPATION

of the Jewish people in Christian countries received its great impetus with the American and French revolutions. America led by a hundred years all other nations. Here is a partial chronology of freedom:

1636, Rhode Island granted religious liberty.
1669, "Jews, heathens and dissenters," granted liberty of conscience in the Carolinas.
1777, Constitution of New York State placed Jews on a status of complete equality with other residents.
1781, Joseph of Austria abolishes poll tax and issues "Toleranz patent."
1786, Religious liberty granted Jews in Hungary.
1788, Poll tax abolished in Prussia.
1790, French National Assembly grants citizenship to Bordeaux Sephardim.
1791, French National Assembly grants equality to the Jews.
1796, Batavian National Assembly grants equality to Netherlands Jews.
1806, Napoleon's Assembly of Jewish notables held.
1807, Session of Napoleon's Sanhedrin.
1808, Jews of Westphalia and of Baden emancipated.
1811, Jews of Hamburg emancipated.
1812, Jews of Mecklenburg-Prussia emancipated.
1830, Abolition of More Judaico (Jewish oath) in France.
1831, Emancipation of Jews of Jamaica.
1833, Emancipation of Jews of Hesse.
1846, "Toleration Tax," abolished in Hungary.

1848, Emancipation of Jews of German States.
1849, Jews of Denmark emancipated.
1858, Jewish disabilities removed in England.
1859, Equality granted in Italy.
1860, Austrian Jews emancipated.
1861. Jewish oath abolished and Jews emancipated in Württemberg.
1865, Disabilities removed in Sweden.
1865, Complete equality granted in Belgium.
1866, Emancipation of Jews in Switzerland.
1867, Emancipation of the Jews in Hungary.
1869, Jews granted political equality in Prussia.
1872, Bavarian Jews emancipated.
1904, More Judaica abolished in Rumania.
1905-6, Jews granted political rights in Russian Empire.
1908, Jews granted political rights in Turkish Empire.
1919, All citizens equalized in U.S.S.R.
1919, Jews granted equality in Rumania, Poland, Latvia, Lithuania, Czechoslovakia, Yugoslavia.
1932. Equality of all citizens granted in Spain.

ENDLOESUNG

"The final solution" of the "Jewish problem," so well known through the Nuremberg and Tel-Aviv trials, never fully materialized for the Hitler-Himmler-Eichmann group, as it did not fully materialize for King Ferdinand and Queen Isabella or the Catholic royalty of Portugal, France and England.

All expelled some Jews and murdered others who stood by Judaism.

Somehow the Jews remained, as Saint Augustinus said, *"necessarii credentibus gentibus,"* historical witness to Christian salvation.

Germany came closest to *Endlösung* under Catholicism after the Black Death era which followed the Crusade massacres, the Rindfleisch butchery, the well-poisoning killings

and the ritual murder bloodbath. By 1500 Catholic Germany was *judenfrei*, as were France and of course England.

The Jews perished by tens of thousands, hundreds of thousands, men, women and children, under the ax and the sword and the torch, drowned, quartered, burned, garroted, knifed and stuck like pigs.

Israel was at the mercy of the Catholic Church and there was no mercy—this was a Christian world and, as Hitler later explained, there was no room for the *"Pariah-volk."*

It was the people of Jesus, His mother's people, Joseph's kin, whom the Catholics murdered. From the Ebro to the Elbe, from the Tiber to the Seine and Thames, all the rivers of Europe received the blood of Israel, of Christ's Israel, His Apostles' Israel—the blood of the direct descendants of all those who erected in the Judean hills the great edifice of Christendom.

Israel had to die because the Romans would not tolerate a king of the Jews. What irony and what tragedy!

And it was the Teutons, Iberians, Gauls and sundry Visigoths who drew the blood of Christ's very kin! The barbarians in bearskins who were living a savage life when the Psalms were written by David, the kingly bard, whose ancestry the evangelists claimed for Jesus—it was these barbarians who won the blessing of the Church as they ripped the holy scrolls of Judea and punished with fire and crimson swords the People of God, the People of the Book, the People of Christ.

The Catholic Church failed to obliterate the perennial seed of the Holy Land, and the Nazi Teutons failed, but Israel was left a much reduced nation.

We cannot deny that the Church and the Nazi Germans have done us grievous and permanent damage. Our children have fallen away in front of our eyes, and our women been tortured to death, even more by the Church than by the modern savages.

It may be thousands of miles away where this happened,

and a thousand years ago. But my kin was thus brutalized by the pretenders to Christ, and there is no example in all history, primitive or civilized, of men doing to men for centuries what Christians have done to Jews.

And there is no end in sight since the Church refuses to change a word of its precious catechisms and codes and dogmas and scripture. To the church the word is sacrosanct, but the life of a Jew is just a Jew's life.

ENGLISH LITERATURE

The Canterbury Tales (1386) by Chaucer is one of many classical literary pieces with a Christian anti-Semitic motif—in this case the depicting of a Jew as a vampire. With typical Christian malevolence of the time, the Jew is styled a member of that "God accursed" race. Such literary pieces, imbued with direct or indirect Jew hatred, have done much to keep anti-Semitism alive by a kind of subliminal effect.

Marlowe joined the same sad literary clique with his play, *The Jew of Malta* (1592). Marlowe's villain is a monstrous Jew who revels in the killing of Christians, by well poisoning or plain murder.

Shakespeare followed the easy road to public appeal in his *Merchant of Venice* (1597) by switching the characters of a Venetian tale. In the Venetian tale the flesh-greedy merchant is a Christian who makes a wager with a Jew against a pound of the Jew's flesh. Shakespeare simply reversed the roles and made the Jew an ogre.

English anti-Semitism was kept alive by a surly clergy. Chaucer, Marlowe and Shakespeare could never have come across a single Jew, since the Jews had been expelled from England in 1290. They were not permitted entry until 1659, by Oliver Cromwell, who got his edict through Parliament in spite of a venomously Jew-hating clergy. The English had forsaken Catholicism, but not its Jew hatred.

Essayists like Charles Lamb (1823) berated the Jews

66

viciously for "killing Christ." Even children's literature has been poisoned by the Gospel image of the Jew as a money-changer and Judas. In Grimm's German *Fairy Tales* a story, "The Jew in the Bush," stars a cheat, thief and scoundrel, a Jew who winds up on the gallows.

Not even the "Mother Goose" verses escaped the Sunday school venom:

"Jack sold his egg to a rogue of a Jew,
Who cheated him out of half his due."

It took the advent of the Giant Killer Hitler to remove these references from the American editions. Other Christian nations still perpetuate them, as British dictionaries still define "Jew" in the old Church manner: a cheat, a disreputable trader.

EPHRAEM, SAINT (306-373)

Highly regarded in the Eastern Church, refers in his hymns to the synagogues as whorehouses.

EPHRAIM OF JERUSALEM

This benign patriarch, passing through Bucharest (1764-66) ordered Prince Alexander Glinka to demolish the synagogue. It was done.

EPIPHANIUS, SAINT (310-403)

In his histories of heresies mentioned dishonesty and indolence as typical Jewish characteristics.

ERFURT

In this German town on June 26, 1221, a band of pilgrims from Friesland bound for the Holy Land stormed the Jewish quarter and killed twenty-six Hebrews. For hundreds of years this pious victory was commemorated. But it was made insignificant by the murder of three thou-

sand Jews in August, 1348, as poisoners of wells. The accusations were spread by Dominican monks of the city.

ERWIG (680-687)

This Spanish King was a most pious ruler who made twenty-eight anti-Jewish regulations into law. The Twelfth Council of Toledo (681) approved all of them. In 694 the Seventeenth Council of Toledo, together with this noble King, reduced all Jews to servitude, prohibiting their religious rites, and ordained that all Jewish children above seven be taken from their parents and converted to the Cross.

ESTELLA

Through this and other Spanish towns bordering France, the Franciscan friar, Peter Olligen, wandered in 1328, preaching in churches against the God killers. Thousands of Jews were martyred.

ETHIOPIA

In the second half of the nineteenth century European missionaries appeared in Addis Ababa and began an intensive campaign against the native Jews (Falashas) who had been living there for more than a thousand years. They failed to break the spirit of the Falashas; however, some of the Ethiopian Jews attempted to flee to Palestine (1868).

EUGENIUS III

Pope (1145-1153) ; offered mercenary Crusaders, as an enlistment inducement, absolution from any debt owed to Jews.

EUSEBIUS

Bishop of Caesarea who flourished around 300, maintained that the Jews in every community crucified a Christian at their Purim festival as a rejection of Jesus. This kindly saint also asserted that during the Roman-Persian war the Jews purchased ninety thousand Christian prisoners merely for the pleasure of killing them. His *Ecclesiastic History* is standard in Catholic libraries.

EVIAN

Site of conference called in 1938 to discuss the problem of Jewish escape from Nazi Germany, attended by representatives from thirty-two countries. No help was given the Jews.

The German Protestant and Catholic Church leaders were rapidly integrating their activities with the newly formed Nazi organizations. To the Jews of Germany all doors of escape were shut, as were all doors of entry in the rest of the world.

EVORA

In this Portuguese city in 1497 the Catholic authorities under King Manuel issued the edict that all Jewish children under fourteen years be taken from their parents and distributed by parish priests among Christian parents.

In April 1506, the only synagogue in town was destroyed. A generation later the Catholic Inquisition of Portugal began its murderous work here.

EXCHEQUER JEWS

A term coined by King Frederick Barbarossa, who placed the Jews of the Rhineland in fortresses to protect them against the Crusaders of the Catholic Church, claiming that the Hebrews belonged to his "private exchequer."

Upon occasion, other rulers of Europe also tried to protect their industrious and skilled Jewish subjects from the fury of the Church.

For example, Philip Augustus of France (1181-1223) fought tooth and nail with his barons for the possession of the Jews—artisans, traders, and manufacturers alike— since, like his royal fellows, he drew great profits from the talent of the Jews.

Unfortunately, monks and priests from the bishops on down, enflamed by their own hateful liturgy and litany, constantly pushed for the death or conversion of Jews. To placate the powerful church, or whenever it suited them, the rulers would drop the Jews. The Church was ever ready to take over and lead the mob against the marked Jews, trapped in their ghettos.

EXISTENTIALISM, CHRISTIAN

has in Martin Heidegger its most influential representative. Catholic and Protestant seminaries alike have adopted the body of thought of this philosopher, making it predominant in their classrooms and manifestos. Here is what the Christian existentialist has to say:

"The Führer himself, and only he, is the current and future reality of Germany, and his word is your law.

"There exists only one single German way of life, a way whose enrichment is being shaped in the National Socialist Revolution. *Heil Hitler.*"

F

FAGIN

The tendency of a popular writer to ingratiate himself with a wide public by pandering to their prejudices is readily discernible in this figure of a wicked "fence" created by Charles Dickens in his novel, *Oliver Twist*. The Christian churches had popularized the image of Judas. The very

70

Gospels, in their Romanized editions, take advantage of the word play that marks the traitor Judas as a Jew, although Jesus and the Apostles also were Jews. In most catechisms the Jewishness of Gospel heroes is ignored and that of Judas stressed.

Prejudice, originally nurtured in the world of the Christian religion, does not end there. Its fictional image becomes imbedded in a secular canon consisting of literary classics and thence finds its way into common speech. Consider the definition of Fagin to be found, a century and more after the publication of *Oliver Twist,* in a current American dictionary: "adult who instructs others in crime, especially one who teaches children to steal."

FAULHABER, CARDINAL MICHAEL VON (1869-1952)

in his notorious Advent sermon of 1933, defended the Old Testament, but attacked the Jews of his day and disavowed any impression that he was pleading their case against the threats of Hitlerism.

A leading article in *Klerusblatt,* organ of the Bavarian Priests Association, followed the "Christian" sermon of Faulhaber by admonishing Catholic teachers to point out to their pupils that the Old Testament, sacred to Christians, was in direct conflict with "current" "Jewish" mentality.

FERRER, SAINT VINCENT

Dominican itinerant preacher (1350-1419) who traveled with a retinue of three hundred Flagellants. In his zeal for the conversion of Jews he was responsible for their incarceration and severe punishment. He whipped up the populace to intense hatred and suspicion of the Jews, which culminated in the promulgation of the Castilian Edict (January 12, 1412), containing twenty-four articles *contra Judaeos,* among them the creation of ghettos in all Spanish towns.

FERRIOL, SAINT

In 561 this Bishop of Uzes, France, gave the Jews a choice: baptism or exile.

FICHTE, JOHANN GOTTLIEB (1762-1814)

German nationalist philosopher and Protestant theologian with strong anti-Semitic tendencies.

"FINAL SOLUTION"

See *Endlösung*

FLAGELLANTS

in fourteenth-century France and Germany were driven by two "religious" motivations: self-abuse and Jew-abuse.

FLEMISH CHURCH SHOWS

in the Middle Ages exhibited a Jew astride a billy goat, the symbol of devilish lechery. Such portrayals have been preserved in church sculpture and pictures.

FOETOR JUDAICUS

or Jewish Satanic stench, widely popularized by priests and monks; can only be washed away by baptism (Convention of Clermont, 576). German Nazis made similar charges of *foetor judaicus*.

FOURIER, CHARLES (1772-1837)

Raised in a Catholic parochial school, the son of one of the very wealthy merchants of France, he managed to dissipate his fortune and spent his life attacking everything mercantile.

His Church-injected Jew hatred made him single out the Hebrew people as devoid of all patriotism and culture. The Jews were traitors because of Judas; they were usurers because of the papal bulls; they were immoral and should be isolated from all Christians (the ghetto).

While Fourier in his mature years lost all interest in Christian theology, the Church anti-Semitism of his childhood continued to pervade his outlook.

FRANCE

First in 1306 and again in 1394 Jews were expelled from France. As in England, the clergy never flagged in its relentless anti-Semitic pressure upon king and counselors.

On May, 1615, the Parliament of Paris, under severe pressure by the Bishop, reinstated the 1394 edict of expulsion of all Jews under pain of death.

FRANKFORT PURIM

Lutheran pogrom, on Purim in 1612, of the Jewish ghetto, led by the fanatical rabble-rouser Fettmilch. He took Luther's anti-Semitic orders literally.

FREDERICK AUGUSTUS I

Saxon King of Poland between 1697 and 1733, permitted the Catholic clergy to enforce the Council of Basel decree that compelled Jews to listen in their synagogues to "conversion sermons." In some instances the Church had to call out the army to enforce attendance (Lvov, 1721). The Catholic Church, with the help of a greedy nobility, instituted most burdensome ordinances and restrictions upon the Jews. In 1720 the Catholic Synod of Lovich prohibited the Jews from building new synagogues or repairing old ones.

Under Frederick Augustus II the Catholic Church went one step further by reissuing at Plozk (1733) the edict:

73

"The Jews should be only tolerated as a reminder of the suffering of Christ and in their position as serfs serve as an example of God's punishment of infidels."

With this horrid upsurge of Catholic anti-Semitism—which, incidentally, never left Poland—accusations against Jews as child murderers, well poisoners, blood drinkers, and host desecraters became a daily occurrence. Hebrew prayer books were confiscated and burned in Kamenetz-Podolsk by the Catholic clergy under the leadership of Archbishop Dembovsky.

FREDERICK THE GREAT (1740-1786)

The philosopher-king of Prussia proved clearly that a man can be a liberal on many levels and still be an anti-Semite.

His rigid Protestant Church school training was not lost on this monarch. He forbade immigration of Jews and restricted Jewish families to one child. He found various pretexts under which to extract protection money from the Jews, such as toll taxes on cattle, etc.

It was only the Napoleonic era that brought the Jews of Germany and Austria a respite from degradation.

FREEMASONRY

In the official *Dictionnaire apologétique de la foi catholique,* now in print, this is written about the Jews under the above heading:

"In the mind of Satan, the synagogue has an immense place. The Devil relies on the Jews to govern Freemasonry. The Jewish brain directs the action against the Church, the Pope, Christ. Crucify Him! Crucify Him!"

The editor of the *Dictionnaire* is Père d'Alès, S.J., professor at the Catholic Institute of Paris.

Julius Streicher in his *Stürmer* used almost identical phraseology.

74

FRENCH CATHOLICISM

Chaplains of the armed forces of Vichy France were prohibited by the Catholic Church from serving in the Partisan forces of the Free French during World War II. Most Catholic bishops remained loyal to the Nazi-supported Pétain "government" and denounced all its opponents as "rebels." The record of Catholic clerical collaboration with Hitlerism was assembled in *The French Catholics Under the Occupation*, a book by the liberal Catholic journalist, Jacques Duquesne.

During the years of the Nazi Occupation, the majority of the French clergy interpreted France's military defeat as "a just punishment" for the country's abandonment to "Jewish Freemasonry." Hitler appears as the punishing arm of the Lord, much like the pagan Emperor Titus of Rome, whose destruction of Jerusalem was interpreted as Divine vengeance for the crucifixion. Especially during Holy Week, the Catholic clergy in France as well as Germany stressed, not the bestiality of Nazism, but rather "the cruelty of the Jews toward the Savior."

FRENCH POLL

of 1966 on anti-Semitism, conducted by the French Institute of Public Opinion, showed that most of French prejudice toward the Jews sprang from early Church teaching and was strongest in communities where no Jews existed at all.

Half of the Frenchmen polled would oppose a Jewish President; one-third would never vote for a Jewish representative. Almost half of the Frenchmen polled consider the participation of Jews in the country's industrial and commercial life as an evil; 20 percent would not consult a Jewish doctor in fear of being poisoned, while more than 33 percent would never work for a Jew.

Needless to say, these prejudices can be traced back to

the thousand-year-old religious instruction in anti-Semitism preached by the Catholic Church and its parochial schools.

FRENCH REVOLUTION

Catholic clergy, through provincial representatives, made strenuous efforts to stop the granting of civil rights to the Jews by the National Assembly.

FRIES, JAKOB FRIEDRICH (1773-1843)

Sentimental German philosopher and theologian who suggested that all new-born Jewish infants be thrown into rivers, as a simple solution to the "Jewish problem."

FUEHRER JESUS

"The Führer of every Christian is Jesus Christ, the Führer of every German is Adolf Hitler."—Society of National Socialist Priests and Ministers, signed: Rev. Paul Fiebig, 1940.

G

GAYRAUD, HIPPOLYTE

Dominican monk, professor of theology, who promoted "Christian anti-Semitism"—as if there were any other. Father Gayraud declared: "A convinced Christian is by nature a practicing anti-Semite." At the first Congress of the Christian Democrats in Lyon (1896), he clamored that the Catholic Church has always been anti-Semitic "on a high moral [!] plane."

GELBE FLECK (Yellow Badge)

The yellow band issued by the Hitler Germans, with or without the Star of David, has its origin in an edict of the

76

Catholic Church. It was promulgated during the Fourth Lateran Council convoked by Pope Innocent III in 1215. The Jews were ordered to wear a distinctive dress. A comparable badge or dress of shame was also prescribed for prostitutes and lepers. Medieval illustrations frequently show the Devil with the Jew badge.

These badges of shame imposed upon Jews by the Vatican took many forms in different lands: hats, armbands, circlets. They made Jewish men, women and children easy marks for attack, under the Nazis as under the Church authorities.

GELEITGELD

"Protection money" which Jews had to pay to the local abbot or noble in Germany. This was paid in addition to the poll tax.

These fees were extracted from the Jews until the end of the eighteenth century, when the French Revolutionary armies arrived and liberated them from this oppression.

GENOCIDE

was preached a thousand years before the Germans ran amuck in their Jew hatred. The Church-inspired Crusaders put to death or caused the suicide of more than one-third of the Hebrew population in Central Europe in the eleventh century. When Emperor Henry IV issued an edict permitting the forcibly converted to return to the faith of their fathers, Pope Clement III forbade, under dire threats, such disregard of holy baptism.

GENUFLECTING

in a manner to ridicule Jesus has been attributed by Catholic liturgy to the Jews. In fact, this was done by the Roman soldiers, not the Jews. (See Matthew 27:27-29.)

GERMAN CATHOLICISM

In a prearranged conference on April 26, 1933, between German Chancellor Adolf Hitler and Catholic Bishop Wilhelm Berning, Hitler stressed the fundamental agreement between National Socialism and Catholicism on the "Jewish question."

At the conference Hitler affirmed that "the Catholic Church had always regarded Jews as evildoers [*Schädlinge*] and had banished them into ghettos. He [Hitler] is only doing what the Church had been doing for fifteen hundred years."

This and a number of other conferences led to the infamous Concordat of Collaboration between Berlin and Rome, a crowning achievement for the Papal Nuncio, Msgr. Pacelli, later Pope Pius XII. The signing of the Concordat gave an imprimatur to Hitler's terror regime.

At a time when the whole civilized world stood aghast at the rising Brown Dragon, the Vatican put its seal of approval on this band of bloodthirsty political adventurers who promised in all their declarations, including *Mein Kampf,* to annihilate every Jewish man, woman and child.

Was not Hitler confirmed, then, in his statement that he was only doing on a systematic scale what the Catholic Church had been doing all along?

Some incidents in the enforcement of Brown Catholicism:

Except in Bishop Konrad von Preysing's See of Berlin, all—but all—Catholic diocesan publications carried Herr Goebbels' propaganda articles, including those of vilest anti-Semitic tone.

The bells of all Catholic churches in Hitler's Germany rang jubilantly at the "annexation" of Austria. In Austria itself Theodor Cardinal Innitzer appealed to the populace to "approve" the union. The Cardinal signed this appeal: "Heil Hitler."

On April 20, 1939, on the occasion of Hitler's fiftieth birthday, all Catholic churches—but all, without exception

—raised the Nazi hooked cross in celebration. This was a voluntary gesture of solidarity accompanied by telegrams of felicitation to "the protector of the Reich" from all but two of the bishops.

Long before, in 1934, Archbishop Gröder ordered that the swastika be raised next to the Church flag on all patriotic occasions.

In October, 1939, Adolf Cardinal Bertram asked all dioceses to ring their church bells at the expected fall of Warsaw. Reverend Hans Kerrl, Minister for Religious Affairs, had given similar instructions to the Protestant clergy.

God was on the side of Hitler; the Christian church leaders placed Him there. Never mind the half-million Jews of Warsaw, the kin of Jesus.

Then, as now, the kin of Jesus were pariahs forever beyond pity, be they women or children or invalids, to be hated, accursed. "They pushed for the death of Christ," as the Vatican Council has so distinctly declared. "They," *the* Jews, pushed for the death of Christ; for Hitler "they," *the* Jews, were the root of all evil.

Hitlerism and Catholicism, two movements that joined so harmoniously in one purpose, both condemned the Jews as such.

Jesus said, "Let the children come unto me," and the Christian churches let a million Jewish children come unto the Devil himself, who choked them to death with his noxious fumes and then burned their pain-twisted bodies like foul meat.

Meanwhile the Christian clerics hailed the antichrist with hymns, blessings and bells from one end of Europe to the other.

The Pope had made a concordat with the Devil, and both kept their bargain.

Hitler is dead, but Catholicism still cries out for the blood of Israel amid its pretentious Ecumenism: The Jews pushed for the death of Christ.

Hitler is dead, but Christian anti-Semitism is very much

alive, and the teachings that nurtured Nazism are still being repeated in Christian churches, and in religious schools. They preach the same old Gospel that the Jews are the sons of the Devil, that the Jews have bloody hands, that the Jews wanted to break the dying Jesus' bones, that the Jews are betrayers of God, that the Jews are accursed by the Lord and that they desecrate the temples.

Nothing has changed to stop another Hitler from rising. The Christians need a Devil for their liturgy, and the Jew suits them well.

GERMAN PROTESTANTISM

Its founder was the rebellious monk, Martin Luther (1483-1546), who gave Hitler his basic program: Get rid of the Jews and take their possessions. In Luther's words: "Take all their coins and jewels, silver and gold . . . [let] their synagogues and schools be set afire, their houses be broken up—[let] them be put under a roof or stable like gypsies."

It is noteworthy that Hitler followed these directions implicitly, even including the gypsies in his master plan.

The Protestant clergy in Germany welcomed and supported National Socialism. After Hitler's election a new Protestant Reich Church was formed. The German Protestants made Hitler's confidant, Chaplain Ludwig Mueller, the new head of their church. In July, 1935, Hitler appointed Hans Kerrl to be Minister for Church Affairs. With very few exceptions the Protestant pastors fell in line. Anti-Semitism, a traditional Lutheran tenet enlarged only in detail by Hitler, won their overwhelming support.

In the ten long years of dominant National Socialism, which of the ten thousand German churches, chapels, Sunday schools, and meeting houses, heard an appeal from the Protestant clergy to stop the torture and suffocation of Jewish children, women and unarmed men?

It is wrong, it is false history, to lay the blame for criminal indifference to the slaughter of Jews only upon

Catholics and their stony Pope. The Protestant church of Germany was thoroughly Lutheran in its anti-Semitism. When the Nazis placed the Jews in ghetto stables and camps, they only followed Luther's precept; when they burned Jewish synagogues, homes and schools, they only carried out Luther's will; when the Germans robbed the Jews of their possessions and heritage, they only did Luther's bidding; when the Germans reduced Jews to concentration camp slavery, they merely followed the teaching of Luther: Make the Hebrews slaves of the serfs!

There was no anti-Semitic crime prescribed by Luther that the Germans failed to carry out, and there was no crime perpetrated by the Nazis that Luther had not ordered in his book, *Die Juden und ihre Lügen*.

GERMAN THEOLOGIANS

Protestant as well as Catholic, they were almost to a man vociferously anti-Semitic: Schleiermacher, Hegel, Herder and Harnack are just a few of those who held the libel of the Jews as God killer to be Gospel truth.

GHETTO

For a Jew to leave the ghetto was punishable by death under Hans Frank, Nazi Governor of Poland. This, of course, was only a repetition of a similar papal ruling of 1215. How time crawls!

GLYATOVSKY, JANNIKI (d. 1668)

Russian Orthodox cleric who wrote a widely publicized pamphlet, *Messia Pravdivi*, against Judaism.

GOBINEAU, ARTHUR (1816-1882)

Early French racialist and anti-Semite, who took his main concept from the Catholic blood-purists of fifteenth-

century Spain (Alfonso de Spina). Gobineau's *Essay on the Inequality of Human Races* greatly stimulated Alfred Rosenberg.

GOD IS DEAD

The basic and most fundamental dogma of all Christianity.

God died and left His Son's Testament in a Greek translation (no Hebrew text has ever been found, yet neither Jesus nor the Apostles wrote or spoke anything but Hebrew), to be followed implicitly.

If the New Testament states that the Jews are the Sons of the Devil and are bloodthirsty, treacherous, the killers of God and thus forever accursed, this is Gospel truth, the Word of God.

The dogma of the Jews' deviltry is incontestable since God Himself no longer makes changes; indeed, He is dead and left the Gospels as His heritage to the Christian churches.

No group or nation or alliance of nations in all known history has ever perpetrated on a hapless minority such sadistic atrocities over so long a time as the Christians have on the Jews.

Not one denomination or another, but *all* did, and especially those of the Catholic faith: They have choked to death little children in the presence of their parents to make them denounce their fathers and mothers as well poisoners, as blood drinkers, as plague carriers. They have shriveled the naked breasts of women with hot irons to make them betray their husbands as breakers of holy wafers. They have stretched the bodies of fathers on the rack to make them denounce their own flesh and blood as false converts.

What the Germans did to six million Jews in the Second World War is only a continuation of long-established Christian bestiality toward the Jewish people, practiced by European Christians and especially the Catholic Church

every decade of every century for the last two thousand years.

If the Christians believed in God, they could never have perpetrated or tolerated the monstrous deeds they did to the Jews. But they think God dead. Neither do they believe in the resurrection. They believe only in the Greek book put together in the fourth century, from some fragmentary scrolls, by a church made dominant in the Roman Empire by the pagan king, Constantine, who in all his days never accepted their faith for himself.

If they believed in the resurrection, how could they face the returned Jesus after all the unspeakable cruelties they inflicted on his people? Jesus had brothers and sisters, cousins and uncles, distant kin and friends who remained Jews in the land of Israel. What became of their descendants? They left for many lands as did their Apostolic brethren—to Iberia, to Gaul, to Germany, to the north and the west. What did the Christians do to them? The Christians tormented them during the Crusades, the Inquisition, and a thousand times in a thousand towns and villages.

How could the Christians face Jesus after what they did to his kin and the kin of the Holy Mother Mary and the kin of Joseph?

But the Christians did what they did because they believed neither in God nor in His Son. They thought Him dead, and the Holy Spirit a mere dream.

What they have left is a Greek book, and the best part of it, in which they all take delight no matter how they may disagree on details of liturgy, is: The Jews be damned! The choice part about the Jew as Devil, no one can take that out of their Greek book. That is Gospel truth, that is divine inspiration, that is God's word!

You can't question a dogma, they say, and the hate passages in the New Testament are God's word. They have to stay there, these poisonous little accusations, and innuendoes: Jews are Sons of the Devil, Jews are bloody killers of Christ, Jews are betrayers of God, Jews are condemned forever, Jews are spitters on God, torturers of

God, breakers of God's dying bones! Even the youngest infant born yesterday in a Jewish home is accursed forever. *Pereat Judea!*

GOD'S SPY

On February 15, 1898, the *Civiltà Cattolica* had written that "the Jew was created by God to serve as a spy wherever treason is brewing. First economic, anti-Semitism will become what it must be, political and national."

GOOD FRIDAY

is the unholiest day of the Christian calendar: it serves not to commemorate the Hebraic message of Love as expressed by the gentle Jew of Nazareth, but rather the Roman Church philosophy of vindictive and hateful revenge on the descendants of an ancient nation where an alleged jury of a few elders "ordered" a man—and Jesus was a man then—to be tried by the local Roman security chief on the charge of impersonating Caesar.

Good Friday is the day when Christians in sermons, lectures and "passion plays," berate and befoul everything Jewish. With devious art and cunning, the agonies of crucifixion are again described, depicted and relived— although the Christians themselves in the centuries of their history have tortured to death not one Hebrew, but ten million of them, including at least a million infants and children who were of the same flesh and blood as the noble Jesus ben Joseph.

It is not the Roman-style execution which Jesus suffered, together with thousands of other Jews, at the hands of the conquerors of Israel that is worthy of remembrance after all these centuries, but rather the Hebraic precept of Love of Man, even Man the Stranger and Man the Enemy.

Is it not time to cease the sanctimonious dramatizing of one man's pain, to drop the hypocritical self-righteousness

and smug "empathy" with the Son of God, whose Hebrew mother and father-in-flesh are still subject to vile hate and vituperation in their surviving kinfolk?

It seems these militant Christians want forever to strut the broad parade-ground of hate rather than seek the narrow path of love.

GOUGENOT DES MOUSSEUX, HENRI

French anti-Semite of the late nineteenth century, author of *Le Juif, le judaisme et la judaisation des peuples chrétiens,* published on the eve of the Vatican Council (1870). Gougenot was a most influential Catholic lay leader, a daily (!) communicant, whose malevolent book was prefaced by Father Voisin, director of the Catholic Foreign Mission in Paris. Pope Pius IX gave author and book his blessing.

Gougenot blamed the defeat of Catholic Austria by the Protestant Prussians on the Jews, an example Hitler followed by blaming the Jews for Germany's defeat in World War I.

GREGORY I (540-604)

This anti-Semitic Pope has been referred to by many as "the Great." He called Judaism a superstitious, perfidious and depraved belief. He praised the Visigothic King Reccared for his severity in anti-Semitic regulations. He proposed many cruel edicts against the Jews, depriving them of their civil rights.

GREGORY XIII (1502-1585)

Among the bulls of this Pope: compelled the Jews of Rome to maintain a house of conversion (1578); prohibited Jewish physicians from attending Christian patients (1581); appropriated from the Jews all their canon litera-

ture (1581); ordered Jews to listen to abusive anti-Semitic conversion sermons every Saturday in their own synagogues (1584).

GREGORY OF NYSSA, SAINT (331-396)

called the Jews assassins of the prophets, companions of the Devil, a race of vipers, a sanhedrin of demons, enemies of all that is beautiful, and more—not all of it printable.

He and Saint John Chrysostom, who in loving brotherliness styled the Jews "hogs and goats in their lewd grossness," are the most outstanding of the Byzantine Church anti-Semites, who were largely responsible for the fear and disdain in which the Jews were held in the Russian Empire.

GROEBER, ARCHBISHOP KONRAD

of the German Rhine provinces, in his pastoral letter of March, 1941, to the clergy in his diocese, attacked the Jews along simple Nazi propaganda lines, winding up with a reference to Christ killers and adding that whatever happens to the Jews is only the fulfillment of God's vengeance —making Hitler the right arm of the Lord.

GRODNO

In this Polish (now Russian) town Jesuits arrived in 1616, with wild anti-Semitic accusations of host desecration and blood orgies. The last ritual-murder scare in this town, inspired as always by the low clergy, occurred in 1820.

GUI, BERNARD (d. 1331)

Author of one of the many "manuals of inquisition" which gave hints on how to spot a Jew or a "backsliding" convert and how to extend and intensify the suffering of the interrogated by flame, garrote, rack, whip and needle.

A number of priests were always present, crucifix in hand, to take down the "confessions" of the agonized Jews. Children were customarily martyred in front of their fettered parents.

Cardinal Francisco Jiménez de Cisneros and Cardinal Juan de Torquemada, who burned nine thousand Jews in Queen Isabella's Spain in order to get their wealth for Spain's American empire-building, developed cruelty to an art that left Heydrich and Eichmann little to add.

Inquisitional tortures continued well into the eighteenth century.

Neither illness nor pregnancy could spare a woman from the bite of the Inquisition instruments wielded by the protectors of loving Christ. Since all the property of the convicted fell to the Inquisition corporation, to be shared equally by their majesties, there was an added incentive to intensify the Inquisition. Denouncers were well rewarded, and a person denounced was a person indicted and convicted, since no living creature could withstand the refined methods of punishment the clerics had devised. Every single part of the human anatomy had been carefully studied and experimented upon to find those most sensitive to pain.

Scarcely ever since has excruciating maltreatment been refined as it was by the Dominicans and other practitioners of the Holy Office of the Inquisition.

Gui's manual tells the Inquisition staff and their spies how to discover "Jewish practices" among "converts" and Marranos:

"Putting on clean or festive clothes, clean and washed shirts and hairdress; arranging and cleaning their house on Friday afternoon, and in the evening lighting new candles, with new tapers and torches, earlier than on other days of the week; cooking on the said Fridays such food as is required for the Saturday, and on the latter eating the meat thus cooked on the Friday, as is the manner of the Jews; keeping the Jewish fasts, not touching food the whole day until nightfall, and especially the Fast of

Queen Esther, and the chief fast of Cinquepur (Yom Kippur), and other Jewish fasts, laid down by their law . . . and on the said fast days asking pardon of one another in the Jewish manner, the younger ones to the elder, the latter placing their hands on the heads of the former, but without signing them with the sign of the cross . . . Saying Jewish prayers . . . with the face turned to the wall, moving the head backwards and forwards as the Jews do; cutting the nails and keeping, burning or burying the parings; cleaning or causing meat to be cleaned, cutting away from it all fat and grease, and cutting away the nerve of the sinew of the leg . . . killing oxen as the Jews do, covering the blood with cinders or with earth; giving the Jewish blessing before eating, called the *baraha;* reciting words over the cup or vase of wine, after which each person sips a little, according to the custom of the Jews; not eating pork, hare, rabbit, strangled birds, conger-eel, cuttle fish, nor eels or other scaleless fish, as laid down in Jewish law . . . pouring water from jars and pitchers when someone has died . . . making divinations for children born to them, on the seventh day; not baptizing them, and when they have been baptized scraping off the Chrism put on them in the sacrament of baptism. . . . If they give Old Testament names to the children, or bless them by the laying of hands; if women do not attend church within forty days after confinement; if the dying turn towards the wall; if they wash a corpse with warm water; if they recite the Psalms without adding the *Gloria Patri* at the close; who say that the dead Law of Moses is good, and can bring about their salvation, and perform other rites and ceremonies of the same."

GUILDS

of craftsmen throughout the Christian territories of Europe up to the eighteenth century rejected Jews as members. If any Jewish craftsman succeeded in joining a local unit, the other members relentlessly pressured for his expul-

sion. The Church-based anti-Semitic homiletics had taken their effect.

In the earlier years of Hitlerism the Catholic and Protestant exclusion tactics were adopted by the Nazified guilds and societies and all Jews were expelled. The expellees, of course, were later systematically executed; the persecution of Jews by the churches in previous centuries, while equally hateful, was less efficient.

GUILT

Hitler finding the Jews guilty of Germany's defeat in the First World War is the same as the Bishop of Orleans blaming the Jews for the destruction of the Church of the Holy Sepulcher in Jerusalem, or the Bishop of Rome condemning the Jews for an earthquake that disturbed the Easter procession in 1020.

Jew hatred has its own logic.

GUILT (COLLECTIVE)

During the slave revolt of August, 1791, in Santo Domingo, mobs of Negroes carried a giant crucifix through the streets, howling:"The whites have killed Jesus! Kill all the whites!" This ironic parallel to the Church's blanket indictment of the Jews was recorded by Heinrich Heine.

GUILT BY RELATION

is a variation of the judicial malpractice of guilt by association. During the McCarthy era in the United States thinking people, Protestants and Catholics alike, abhorred the idea that a man might be punished because his brother was an alleged or proven defector, or a woman subjected to criminal investigation because her mother was suspect.

It is astonishing to see the very same Catholic or Protestant theologians, teachers and clerics, who vociferously protested "guilt by relation" as a perversion of

justice, accept with equanimity the condemnation of the Jewish people as a whole because some few members of their race thousands of years ago allegedly voted for the execution of one of their clan.

H

HEIDAMAKS

Ukrainian mercenary bands under the leadership of Cossack hetmen who roved Eastern Europe in the seventeenth century. The priests of the Greek Orthodox Church relentlessly incited them to destroy the accursed enemies of Christ. It took little fresh indoctrination to convert the Cossacks into a snarling pack of Jew-hounds.

HEP! HEP!

Anti-Semitic riot slogan, first shouted by the Crusaders; derived from the initials of the Latin phrase, *Hierosylma est perdita* ("Jerusalem is lost"). The cry was taken over by Hitler's storm troopers.

HERDER, JOHANN GOTTFRIED VON (1744-1803)

German Protestant theologian, court preacher at Weimar; an inspiration to the philosophical and theological faculties of Hitler Germany, Herder spoke thus of the people of God:

"The Jew is a parasite growing on the branches of other nations."

"Together with Fichte and Hegel, he placed the crown of 'Chosen People' on the Teutonic Nation."

HERR

The Nazi practice never to address a Jew with the usual *Herr* (Mister) had its origin in the Papal Bull of

90

July 12, 1555, issued by Pope Paul IV (1555-1559) entitled *Nimis absurdum*, wherein it is distinctly prohibited for Jews to refer to any of their race as "Mister" (*Herr*).

On April 10, 1566, Pope Pius V renewed all orders of this Bull with his own *Romanus Pontifex*.

HILARY OF POITIERS, SAINT (d. 367)

marked the Jews as a perverse people, forever accursed by God.

HIPPOLYTUS

Third-century exegete of Catholicism. Like the generality of Church Fathers, he attacked the Jews on all grounds and no ground. He gloated over their sufferings because "they" were descendants of a race that rejected the Lord. He became one of the schismatic Bishops of Rome.

HITLER'S BIRTHDAY

On Hitler's fiftieth birthday, April 20, 1939, Protestant and Catholic bishops of all but two dioceses in Germany urged the following prayer in pastoral letters to the faithful:

"Remember O Lord our Führer, whose secret wishes Thou knowest. Protect him with Thy inexhaustible kindness. Give him the victory of heaven for him and his folk." (*Katholische Monatsschrift*, May, 1939)

HOMO DIABOLICUS

Nowhere outside Hitler's salons and meeting halls was the Jew so often referred to as "diabolical" as in the Christian churches. Time and time again in the Gospels, in Church edicts, catechisms and literature, Judaism is depicted as devilish and Jews as the Devil's brood.

The language used by the early Church Fathers, and

91

later by the Popes, in referring to Jews, resembles in coarseness and brutality, the style of Streicher rather than Hitler.

From Pope Innocent III, throughout the history of the Vatican, the Torah was called "vomit." If a forcibly "converted" Jew "relapsed" into the faith of his ancestors, the faith of Jesus and Joseph, the solemn word from the Chair of St. Peter was: The dog returns to his vomit.

The most colorful gutter descriptions of the Jews, however, were offered by Martin Luther, who wanted the lot of them wiped off the face of the earth. Common decency forbids the repetition of Luther's barnyard black-humor in this book. Those interested can find it in Streicher's *Stürmer*, where Luther is often quoted word for word, dirt for dirt.

HORNED HAT

The Catholic Council of Vienna decreed in 1267 that all Jews had to wear horned hats (*pileum cornutum*) to indicate that they were the offspring of the Devil.

HOST DESECRATION

In 1215 Pope Innocent III declared the consecrated wafer offered in communion to be the real body of Christ (doctrine of transubstantiation). After this date nothing was easier than for the generally anti-Semitic Catholic clergy to claim that Jews had nailed, cut or otherwise defamed the holy wafer—which meant Christ Himself.

Underlying the "host desecration" phobia was the idea expressed by the renowned Catholic preacher, Berthold of Regensburg, that Christ *physically* was present in every wafer. The Jews, by mutilating a consecrated wafer, could therefore kill Christ again and again.

In 1243, at Berlin, all Jews of the suburb Bernau were burned for host desecration. In 1510 twenty-six Jews were burned alive for piercing the Eucharist.

HUGH OF LINCOLN

In the year 1255, an English boy of that name was found dead in a well. Scores of Jews were apprehended and under unspeakable tortures all confessed to having crucified the child.

Such ritual murder trials were monstrosities, yet the Catholic Church has publicly denounced only the one held in the Italian city of Trent.

HUSSITES

Followers of the reforming Czech priest, John Huss (1369-1415). The Mother Church began its bloody war against them, as it did its similar campaigns against the Albigensians, Waldensians and other "heretics," with a massacre of Jews. This was an obvious political maneuver on the part of the Church to identify their current religious enemy with the traditional Devil's offspring, the Jew.

Hitler similarly accused the Communists, the Americans —indeed, all his adversaries—of being inspired, directed or allied with Jews.

HYMN BOOKS

"God has built His Church in spite of envious Jews." This is a quote offered by the great essayist Oliver Wendell Holmes in discussing the evil of anti-Semitic phrases in Protestant liturgy.

Holmes suggested the removal of all such offensive lines from Hymns, prayers and catechisms, since their repetition creates in the worshiper's mind a pattern of the Jew as an accursed killer.

An example taken from *The Child's Scripture* (Presbyterian) used in Sunday schools:

Question: "Who put Jesus to death?" Answer: "The wicked Jews."

Question: "How did they put him to death?" Answer: "On the cross."

The effect, of course, of such "teachings" on the child's soul is traumatic.

I

IGNATIEV, NIKOLAI PAVLOVICH (b. 1832)

Author of the notorious "May Laws" of Russia promoting anti-Semitic legislation. Direct organizer of pogroms by his "barefoot brigades." The Orthodox clergy were his most ardent collaborators.

IGNATUS III

Jacobite Patriarch, who declared in November, 1965: "It is a dogma of the Church that the guilt of the crucifixion of Christ must fall upon the Jews to the end of the world."

It appears that Pope Paul VI agrees, to judge by his outburst in March of that year, in which he scorned *the* Jews for "killing the Lord."

IMPRIMATUR BY THE VATICAN

Recently The Church published a new catechism for distribution to the school children in Italy. The Pope himself gave it his personal imprimatur. This book, which the present Pope endorsed, is entitled "Message of the Gospel." ("Il Messaggia Degli Evangli.") The author is Professor Don Angeli Alberti. Quoting from the text: "How much shame the Jews must feel when they see that The Devil, whom they prefer as their Leader, is defeated. And the Jews, like The Devil, will forever crawl round the world, defeated—reduced to a society of money-grubbers. God's Curse is reserved exclusively for them, and they will forever wander the earth. This is their Eternal Punishment for refusing to accept Jesus Christ."

INDIVIDUOS DE LA CALLE

Ghetto people of Palma on the island of Majorca, also known as "Chuetas." They are descendants of Jewish converts, Marranos, who ate pork in public to prove their Catholic faith. In 1591 more than fifty of them who tried to escape from the island were caught and burned at the stake.

The local Dominican monastery published in 1755 a complete list of Chuetas condemned to the "purifying flames."

The Chuetas are still pariah among the pure-blooded Catholics, who will neither associate nor intermarry with them.

INNOCENT III (1161-1216)

This most cruel of the cruel Popes threatened Alfonso the Noble of Castile with excommunication if he continued to treat the Jews like people. The gentle Vicar wrote: "The Jewish vagabonds are to be treated as serfs."

INSOLENCE

A repeated charge made by clerics against the Jews. Wherever and whenever secular authorities found room for the Jew in government or official enterprise, the ecclesiastics would raise a spiteful cry: "Insolence!"

The Church could not rest with a Jew in office anywhere. In 1081 Pope Gregory VII wrote to Alphonso VI of Castile: "We must warn Your Highness that the Crown cease to permit Jews to rule over Christians. To permit Jews to have authority over Christians is the same as to oppress the Church and elevate the synagogue."

INTIMACY

From the early Church Fathers to the end of the Papal States in 1870 the faithful were ordered by the hierarchy

to avoid any intimacy or social intercourse with the Jews.

In the March, 1936, No. 10, issue of *Der Stürmer*, Julius Streicher severely reprimanded a member of the Nazi party for having called a Jew his friend: "A German who fraternizes with a Jew is calling the Devil his brother."

Streicher was only quoting from the *Bullum Romanum*.

ISIDOR OF SEVILLE, SAINT (560-636)

He, too, wrote a tract *Contra Judaeos*. It seems that all the loving saints of the first Christian millennium had an uncontrollable urge to say something nasty about the Jews. Insecurity? Fear of a vigorous rival faith? Rejection of their spiritual parents? A fawning need to absolve their adopted father, the Roman Emperor? Perhaps we should leave the question to the practitioners of pathological psychology.

J

JEROME, SAINT (d. 420)

Translator of the Vulgata, who proves in his *Tractate Against the Jews* that they are congenital liars who lure Christians into heresy. They should therefore be punished until they confess. With Saint Augustine he can be called the spiritual father of the Inquisition.

JESUITS

In their periodical, *Voce della Verità*, the Jesuits in 1873 forecast: "In case of reconciliation between the Pope and the Kingdom of Italy, the Jews will have to return to the ghetto."

Jesuits were the most anti-Semitic segment of the Polish clergy in the seventeenth century. Until quite recently, they also excluded all Catholics of Jewish blood from their society—a racialism practiced far more widely in Catholic circles than is generally known. The similarity to notorious modern racist ideologies is inescapable.

JESUS

While living on earth not only was He a Jew, He was the Jew of Jews, faithful to the Law of Moses, which, as He said, He came to fulfill, not to destroy. Without the Law of Moses, there could be no Christ, no Messiah. Jesus was circumcized, wore the long-falling earlocks of the Hebrews, keeping His hair uncut at the corners, would touch no flesh of the pig, would fast on the day of repentance, would eat no leavened bread at Passover time, would wash His hands before partaking of food while murmuring the prescribed blessing, would wear the ritualistic garment adorned with Tzitzin.

Jesus was a Jew among Jews, yet so has the Christian Gospel twisted truth and history that most of its readers identify only Judas with the Jews and Jesus with the "Gentiles," whatever that may mean, since neither Greeks nor Romans, Persians nor Syrians, expected a Messiah; and Jesus could neither speak in their alien tongues nor pray in accord with their alien paganisms.

When Jesus spoke, only Hebrews could and would listen; when he sent out His Apostles, only Jews were selected; and when He gave up His Soul, it were daughters of Israel who wept for Him.

JEW

Hitler used only the singular for the Jewish people, never the plural. Whatever displeased him he would blame on *"Der Jud."*

Nazis referred to "the banker Jew," although of the nine million Jews of Europe, six million lived in the slums of Russia, Poland and the Balkans, many existing from hand to mouth in an almost beggarly manner.

The Christian Gospels and theologians similarly refer always to "the Jews" as a generalization, a generic term. They do not say some Jews voted against Jesus; they say "the Jews."

The Christian theologians call "the Jews" killers of Christ. although only a few hundred could possibly have voted before Pilatus to find Jesus guilty; most of the Jews in Palestine could not even have known of whatever trial there may have been, while the majority of Jews had long before left their homeland for Alexandria, Babylon, Rome and other cities.

Yet such is the nature of Christian "reasoning" that their theologians, like Hitler, hold all Jews responsible for what one or a few of them might have done thousands of years ago.

It was all the easier for Hitler to sway the Christian Germans and Austrians and much of the rest of Catholic Europe to his anti-Semitic philosophy because the Christians of Europe had for thousands of years been Church-trained to hold all Jews guilty of the failings of even one.

Church anti-Semitism fitted Nazi anti-Semitism hand in glove; as Hitler said, "I am only continuing the work of the Catholic Church in my fight against the Jews."

JEWISH DOCTORS

"Avoid seeking a Jewish physician and take no remedy from Jewish chemists." Time and time again did the Vatican repeat this admonition coupled with threats of severe punishment.

In 1934 the devout Christian, Julius Streicher, Gauleiter of Nuremberg, proclaimed: "Avoid the pernicious teachings of Pasteur, *'Judenstämmling.'* Avoid the charlatan Robert Koch and his nefarious tuberculin. Avoid Paul Ehrlich, the Jew, and his Salvarsan; he drove millions of Germans to certain death in order to enrich himself."

Streicher only elaborated on the old Catholic edict. He also repeated the warning against Jewish doctors having intimacy with Christian virgins.

For a Protestant precedent in the identical vein, listen to Martin Luther, shortly before his death: "The Jews re-

vile our Lord every day. If they had the power, they would kill us all. Indeed, their physicians often do it."

Five hundred years later Josef Stalin, a theology seminarian of the Orthodox school, repeated the charge against Jewish doctors in Soviet Russia.

JEWISH MATERIALISM

In 1592 Pope Clement VIII wrote: "The world suffers from Jewish monopolies and their deceitful actions. The Jews have caused poverty especially to farmers and working-class people and the very poor."

The grammar is faulty even in the original Latin, but the text is a ready model for *Mein Kampf*. And, for a more recent reminder, the Nazi theorists had only to consult the encyclicals of Pope Leo XIII (*Tametsi,* 1900) and Pope Pius XI (*Quas Primas,* 1925) which warned the Christian world against "Jewish materialism."

JEWISH WORLD CONSPIRACY

The myth of the above, culminating in the long uncovered forgery, "The Protocols of Zion," was nourished by the Catholic hierarchy beginning in the early medieval centuries. In its more modern form it appears in the "Mémoire pour servir à l'histoire du Jacobinisme" by the French Jesuit, the Abbé Barruel in 1797.

Barruel describes the French Revolution as the planned culmination of secret societies directly inspired by the devilish Jews. In similar manner of reasoning Streicher traced the origin of Communism to Jewish planning of world conquest. Both the Catholic Church and the National Socialist Party condemn Freemasonry, an offshoot of French Revolutionary thinking, as a creation of Jewish planning to undermine "Christian" morality. To the Catholic Church even today Masonry is anathema and off limits on pain of excommunication. To Abbé Barruel the sinister head of the

99

conspiracy was Adam Weishaupt, a Bavarian Jew, one of the "Sons of Satan."

In 1806 Abbé Barruel presented to influential circles in Catholic France a letter allegedly received from an army officer, J. B. Simonini, whose identity the Abbé failed to establish, claiming to "have knowledge" that the Jews had already established cells in all towns and villages of Christian Europe in order to take over the western world including the Catholic Church. All churches would be turned into synagogues and all Christians reduced to slavery.

The Holy Synod of the Orthodox Russian Church jumped into the fray stamping Napoleon Bonaparte as the Anti-Christ, since he offered the Jews of Europe the civil rights they were utterly deprived of by the Christian churches (October 1806, Moscow).

Together with a fellow Jesuit, Father Grivel, Barruel wrote expanding papers on the structure of the Secret International whose Jewish Grand Master "had power over life and death of all Freemasons, including members of the Inner Council." "The purpose of this world-wide conspiracy is the creation of revolutions, upheavals, unrest and assassinations."

It almost seems that Hitler took whole paragraphs of his "Mein Kampf" from the zealous Jesuits.

The French Catholic Gougenot des Mousseaux belabored at great length the issue of Jewish-Freemasonry Conspiracy in his anti-Semitic text "Le Juif, le Judaisme et la judaisation des peuples chrétiens" (Paris, 1869). His book, widely publicized by the Hitler elite, had been enthusiastically prefaced by the head of the Foreign Missions Catholic Seminary in Paris, and the author received special blessings by Pope Pius IX for his Christian coinage.

An epigone of both Barruel and Mousseaux was the Abbé Chabauty, curé of Saint-André at Mirebeau in Poitou.

In his work "Les France-Macons et les Juifs" he reasoned that Satan himself masterminded the Jewish-Masonic plot to dominate the world.

100

"The Protocols of Zion," forgeries from Alpha to Omega, the last chapter in the anti-Semitic phantasy of the Christian Jew-baiters, at this writing is distributed in all Catholic republics of Latin America with headquarters in Mexico City. Even in New York City and Miami Beach the "book" enjoys unrestricted sales in foreign language and "Spanish" liturgical shops.

In the eighties of the last century Pope Leo XIII himself deemed it not below his dignity to encourage attacks against the Jews as Masonic conspirators. Father R. Ballerini and Father F. S. Rondina, affiliated with the Jesuit "La civiltà cattolica," depicted the Jews much in the manner of Streicher, as a giant octopus holding the Christian world in their grip.

Catholic papers throughout Europe called for a repeal of Jewish emancipation and sequestering of Jewish holdings.

It is such an arena that Hitler stepped into a generation later; the ground was well prepared, by the Christian churches of all denominations.

No adventurer was reckless enough, no schemer low enough, no politician cheap enough not to find support of the Christian churches in their effort to malign, vilify or slander the Jews. The Jew was *vogelfrei,* outside the protection of the law.

In 1893, in his book "La Franc-Maçonnerie, Synagogue de Satan" Monsignor Meurin, Archbishop of Port-Louis, Mauritius, declared that all Freemasonry was Jewish, exclusively Jewish. The bishop's congenial Léo Taxil, a sage to the French village priests, confided that the American Freemasons had a central telephone in New York operated by the Devil himself, who keeps in touch with his subordinates in this manner.

The Archbishop called on all rulers of the world to remove the Jews from places of writing, banking, teaching, medicine and all other communications in order to save the Church.

Hitler abided by this call, and the European Churches abided by Hitler.

101

JEWS' ISLE

Not until the middle of the eighteenth century did the clergy of Switzerland permit the Jews to bury their dead in Swiss soil. The Jews had to use as their burial ground a little river island beyond the borders.

JOHN I

King of England who in 1210 arrested all Jews in his domain and "fined" them whatever they possessed. Since Abraham of Bristol was unable to satisfy the greed of the King and his prelates, his teeth were pulled out one at a time.

JOHN XXII (1316-1334)

By far the wealthiest man of his time, this Pope was a far-planning financial genius. Simony within the church was so great that it became the focal point of Protestant attack. Yet the high clergy of this very era accused the Jews of being money-minded.

A prototype of the twentieth-century steel magnates and bank-Junkers of Germany, who joined the Nazi outcry against Jewish greed.

JOHN XXIII (1881-1963)

The one and only Pope ever to speak out in behalf of the Jews had, before his death, composed a *Prayer of Repentance* in which this true vicar of Christ begged God's forgiveness for the untold suffering brought upon the Jewish nation by the members of the Catholic Church. On his deathbed the Pontiff urged that this prayer be said in all Catholic places of worship. Up to now, this has not been done; the good Pope's wish should be neglected no longer.

Quoting from Pope John's *Prayer of Repentance*:

102

"We admit that over hundreds of years our eyes were blinded, so as not to see the Beauty of Thy Chosen People and not to recognize the features of our firstborn brother. We admit that the sign of Cain is upon our forehead. For centuries Abel was lying in blood and tears while we had forgotten Thy love. Forgive us, O Lord, the curse we unjustly spoke out over the people of Israel. Forgive us, that in their flesh we crucified You the second time! We did not know what we were doing. . . ."

JOHN, GOSPEL OF

is the most anti-Semitic Gospel of the four. It calls the Jews children of the Devil (VIII:44). Here are some other quotes from this tract of spiritual love:

"The Jews kept persecuting Jesus." (V:16)

"The Jews kept murmuring about Him." (VI:41)

"Jesus did not want to go to Judea because the Jews were seeking to put Him to death." (VII:1)

"Jesus asked the Jews, Why do you wish to kill me?" (VII:20)

"You children of Abraham are desirous of murdering me." (VIII:40)

"The Jews picked up stones to throw at Jesus, but He hid." (VIII:59)

"The Jews decided anybody who would accept Jesus would be expelled from the Synagogue." (IX:22)

"The Jews went out to seize Him but Jesus slipped through their hands." (X:39)

"Jesus did not dare to walk about openly; He withdrew with His disciples near the desert." (XI:54).

"The High Priests planned to kill Lazarus because he made others believe in Jesus." (XII:9)

"The Roman cohorts and the Jewish guards of the High Priest took Jesus into custody and bound Him." (XVIII:12)

"Jesus said: I might not be delivered to the Jews." (XVIII:36)

"Pilatus told the Jews again and again, Jesus is innocent. But the Jews cried: Do not set Him free." (XVIII: 38-40)

"Pilatus went out again where the Jews were and said: Jesus is innocent. But the High Priests and their guards cried out: Crucify Him!" (XIX:4-6)

"Pilatus was looking for a way to release Jesus, but the Jews shouted: If you release Jesus you are not loyal to Caesar." (XIX:12)

"Pilatus hesitated: Shall I crucify your King? And the High Priests answered: We have no King but Caesar." (XIX:15)

"The Jews pleaded with Pilatus to break the legs of the dying Jesus to hasten his death." (XIX:31)

"The disciples of Jesus gathered behind closed doors in fear of the Jews." (XX:19)

The above are verbatim quotations from the Gospel of St. John as it is taught to Christian children and adults in the Western world. Thus the scribes of the Bishops of Rome turned the simple Gospels of the Hebrew—and only—followers of the living Jesus into a totally perverted historiographic document that was designed to absolve the Caesars and their governors from all responsibility in the thousand-fold massacres of the witnesses of Christ—to make these masters of the bloody coliseum charitable judges and to stamp the Jewish victims—of whom Jesus was just another example—as perpetrators of deicide.

Racial Christianity as practiced in Nazi Germany had its origins deep in the Gospel of St. John. This particular Gospel, more than the Synoptics, creates the impression that Christianity found its first followers among people fundamentally different from the Jews.

Jesus, His family and His friends are referred to as if they were gentiles, alien and inimical to the Jews, who are lurking in the background, ready and eager to destroy them. Concurrently, all mention of the Hebrews is defamatory and hostile: The Jews have no knowledge of God (8:19); The

104

Jews are imitators of the Devil, who is their father (8:44) ; The Jews are forever in sin and are doomed to die thus (8:21).

No wonder that among unbiased Christian historians, as well as Jewish scholars, the Evangelist John is known as "the father of anti-Semitism."

Not once—but not once—does the word "Jew" appear in the Gospel of St. John except in derisive manner. The Gospel has without question served as a foundation of Jew hatred and contempt throughout the Middle Ages right up to the days of Streicher, who never tired of quoting from "his Bible."

To cleanse this Gospel of its malevolence would be a service not only to Jews in the modern community but also to the consciences of all liberal-minded Christians.

JOHN OF DIRPHEIM

This Bishop of Strasbourg demanded and received from King Henry VII of Germany in 1308 the Jews of Rufach and Sulzmatt. A few were thrown into dungeons, the majority burned alive. The charge was "desecrating" holy wafers.

In 1338 another group of Jews was massacred by the Bishop on the anniversary of the conversion of St. Paul.

JOHN OF EPHESUS (516-585)

claimed the honor of having destroyed seven Jewish temples and turned them into churches, an example that guided Christian rulers for a thousand years. The destruction of synagogues was carried to its ultimate on November 10, 1938, when the Nazis destroyed all Jewish houses of worship in Germany and Austria.

JUDAS

A device of the Roman Gospel writers to stamp Iscariot, the alleged betrayer of Jesus with the surname of "Judean" (Jew).

As Pope Gelasius I (492-496) philosophized: "In the Bible the whole is often named after the part; as Judas was called a devil and the devil's workman, he gives his name to the whole race."

In similar vein, modern anti-Semites stigmatize one Jew and involve the whole nation as his identicals. Rothschild is a capitalist—all Jews are capitalists. Trotsky is a Communist—all Jews are Communists.

Recent sociological polls show that almost half of the Catholics in this country believe Judas, the traitor, was a Jew and that barely ten per cent realize that all the Apostles of Christ were Jews. Only five per cent of the Catholics were aware that St. Paul was actually Saul, a Jewish rabbinical student.

All without exception considered the Catholic faithful as having taken the divine prerogative of being "God's Chosen People."

JUDE

This German word for Jew became a term of opprobrium, especially in the Hitler era.

Here, again, the German Nazis harked back to the hissing hate of the early Church Fathers.

Eusebius of Caesarea, the Church historian, used the term "Jew" only in reproach or derogation, as did Justin Martyr, Clement of Alexandria, Origen of Caesarea, Ephraem, Jerome, Augustinus, etc.

JUDENBLICK

was introduced into the German language by wandering monks as a synonym for "evil eye." A favorite expression of Streicher.

JUDEN-NASE

or "Jew-nose," mocking German reference to Jews as characterized by hooked or bent noses; widely used by Nazi propagandists, it originated in the church decoration and liturgical illustrations of medieval Catholicism.

Medieval religious art abounds with examples. To mention only a few—

—In the Berner Chronicle of 1474-1483, Picture No. 13 depicts Jewish ritual murderers (*Kindfresser*) with *"Krumme Nasen"*;

—The Florentine Chronicle of Giovanni Villani marks the Jewish "torturer" of a blessed wafer with an exaggerated nose;

—A French chronicle of 1321, illustrating the expulsion of the Jews by Philip Augustus, shows his victims with ugly bent noses;

—In the Rhein Codex Balduini of 1330 the leader of a Jewish deputation seeking audience with Heinrich VII appears endowed with a *Juden-Nase* that would have done credit to *Der Stürmer*.

The origin of most such Nazi Antisemitica can easily be traced to medieval Christian liturgy and art in which the Jew is portrayed not only as spiritually deformed, but as a physically ugly monster.

The medieval horned hat forced upon Jews derives from the gospel reference to Hebrews as Devil's offspring. Conversely, the Devil is often depicted in medieval church art with "Jewish" attributes, such as a hooked nose, Star-of-David badge, and the like.

JUDENREIN

"Clean of Jews." This term, widely used in the Hitler era, was coined in the middle of the fourteenth century in Germany by the Catholic clergy, who incited the faithful to exterminate the Sons of the Devil on the charge of well poisoning. Within two years nearly 350 Jewish communities were tortured into confessions and then "drowned, burned, hanged or burned alive," as contemporary chronicles report.

Germany was *"judenrein,"* to be made so once again by German Christians raised on the same hate theology.

Hans Frank, the infamous Nazi Governor of Poland, stated on August 1, 1942, in Cracow: "No Jew will ever see Germany." Similar statements were uttered scores of times by bishops, cardinals and popes alike when they expelled or martyred Jews in France, England, Spain and Portugal.

JUDENSAU

"Jew Pig," a cartoon-symbol of a pig giving milk to piglets and Jews which decorates choir stalls, pillars and eaves of Protestant churches in Wittenberg, Regensburg, Basel and elsewhere.

In the cathedral of Wittenberg a rabbi stands behind the sow, holding up its tail. As Luther describes this bit of art: "The Rabbi looks into—the Talmud."

Streicher reproduced some of these examples of religious aesthetics.

JUDENSTEIN

This rock in Rinn, Austria, where allegedly on July 12, 1462, Jews murdered a Christian child to drink its blood, was until recently visited by devout pilgrims who promised themselves miracles. An ugly anti-Semitic reference had been engraved there by the Church.

JUDENZOLL

"Cattle tax" imposed upon Jews in Central Europe when traveling from one town to another. Existed up to the eighteenth century.

Toll charges were often designed to humiliate the Jew. Philip V, the Catholic monarch of Spain (1703), fixed the toll at one head of cattle for one Jew. In other places Jews were ordered to cast dice as a reminder of Golgotha, though even the Gospels record that it was Pilate's Roman soldiers who gambled for Jesus' raiment. In most Christian countries the Jews had to pay a head tax.

In Salzburg the Catholic Bishop retained the Jew tax until 1791. As elsewhere, the change was brought by the French Revolution, whose adherents considered the cattle taxes abhorrent and inhuman.

JUSTINIAN'S CODE—See *Corpus Juris Civilis*

JUSTITIA ET MISERICORDIA

"Justice and Charity" was the inscription on the banners of the Inquisition. The chief question which concerned the charitable judges of holy law was whether the convicted should die by fire. Guilt could always be proven by torture.

The question has never been answered: Which was the deeper motivation of these heartless holy men—greed for the property of the condemned, or religious fanaticism?

K

KATHOLISCHE JUGENDGRUPPE

This nationwide Catholic youth organization of Germany was combined with the Hitler *Jungvolk* following the Concordat of Collaboration sponsored by Msgr. Pacelli, later Pope Pius XII. Together, they sang the *Horstwessel Lied* in the church vestries: *"Wenn das Judenblut vom Messer*

spritzed . . ." (When the blood of the Jews runs off the dagger).

KINDFRESSERBRUNNEN

The "fountain of the child devourer," erected in 1540 in Bern, depicting a Jew with a sackful of infants and swallowing one of them. In 1294 all Jews of this Swiss town were either killed or expelled because of an alleged "ritual murder."

KISHINEV

City in Bessarabia; while under Czarist Russian rule, scene of a severe pogrom in April, 1903, which began with a Church-inspired ritual murder accusation. Orthodox seminarians had a heavy hand in the murder of the Jews.

Under Soviet rule the traditional attitude toward the Jew is maintained: F. Mayatsky, author of the anti-Semitic tract *Contemporary Judaism and Zionism* in 1965 was appointed full professor of philosophy at the State University of Kishinev.

KREMS

A town in Austria where, in 1349, all Jews were driven into their houses and burned alive on the charge of having brought the Asian plague. Similar outrages were committed in Germany and Switzerland by a population incited to Jew hatred by a fanatical Christian clergy.

L

LA CIVILTA CATTOLICA

Official Jesuit journal, published in Rome, which supported with vehemence the anti-Semitic attacks on Alfred Dreyfus, even after his innocence was proven in the French

military courts. Agreeing with Bismarck's statement that "The Jews were created by God to act as spies," the journal suggests that Jews be deprived of citizenship and remain in the land only as "alien guests."

A generation later, in 1936, *Civiltà Cattolica* took the same medieval stance in an article on Nazi anti-Semitism. The editor explained that the Christian world (Germany) must defend itself ("without unchristian hate of course") against the Jewish danger by withdrawing all civil rights from Jews and placing them in ghettos.

LA CROIX

Daily French paper edited and published by the Fathers of the Assumption during the latter part of the nineteenth century, which supported strenuously the anti-Semitic journalism of Edouard Drumont, most vicious Jew baiter of France.

Like Hitler, Drumont maintained proudly, "I am guarding the Christian world against the Jews. I am defending the creation of the Lord."

The clergy of France stood behind Drumont, as the clergy of Germany stood behind Hitler. *Le Monde,* the unofficial organ of the French Catholic hierarchy, put itself completely at the disposal of Drumont. Monsignor d'Hulst introduced Drumont as "Sergeant of Christ."

In another paper, *L'Univers* (May, 1886), a missionary priest interpreted Drumontism as the "expropriation of Jewish property." Here, too, Hitler found a page to borrow from Catholic text.

LAGARDE, PAUL ANTON DE (1827-1891)

Prominent German Protestant theologian of Göttingen, specializing in ethics, who referred to the Jews as fungus. This influential teacher of Protestant seminarians rejected the "humanist" idea of dealing with the Jews as people. "They are *Bacillen* and should be exterminated, not saved."

111

A few generations later, Hitler used the very same term concerning the Jews—*"Bacillen"*—and the many Protestant students of Lagarde kept a reverent silence when the extermination began.

LAMENNAIS, FELICITE ROBERT DE (1782-1854)

French priest and social philosopher who considered the Jews lower than slaves: "Indeed, even slaves have to stoop in order to see them."

Such an assertion, of course, only repeated the beliefs of the early Church Fathers, but this was written after the French Revolution. The Nazi Alfred Rosenberg shared Lamennais' "thinking."

LAND

The refusal to sell land to a Jew has been for fifteen hundred years official policy of the Church. As late as 1893 the Catholic Diet of Cracow (Poland) declared: The Jews are our enemies; who sells a piece of land to a Jew or leases it to him is undermining the welfare of our nation. A generation later Hitler incorporated this stricture in his Nazi platform.

No state is more devotedly dedicated to agriculture than Israel, yet for centuries the Christian clergy, from Martin Luther and Saint (!) Vincente Ferrer of Inquisition fame, repeated the fatuous charge that Jews refused to work the land.

To begin with, except in the free States of America, up to the late eighteenth century the tillers of the Christian world were little more than serfs, villeins or slaves. In Russia they remained so until 1861. Furthermore, the Christian churches had, since the days of the Jew-hating Church Fathers, constantly exhorted, admonished, and ukased both Christian land-owners and serfs to shun association with Jews.

Thirdly, the Jew could hardly acquire land in Christian

112

Europe where, as late as 1869, countries such as Switzerland, northern Italy, Bavaria, and Prussia refused to grant him civil rights and permanent residence. The Jew, therefore, had to resort to artisanship and other professions which he could ply while on the run. The Germans referred to the Jews as *Packjuden* because the Jews carried packs on their shoulders like the Wandering Jew, Ahasuerus, of medieval legend. The Jew was the gypsy of Christian Europe, forever on the run, driven out of one town, looking for work in the next. Many towns limited his stay to months, weeks or even days. And behind this unrelenting pressure from his Church-inspired Christian neighbors was the threat of another horrible pogrom.

So the Jew of the Middle Ages became an artisan or petty trader in the service of villages or small cities, living his fearful ghetto existence at the end of town. The Jew was often the poorest of the poor, but the churches managed, as did the Nazis later with the fictional Süss, to build up a singularly wealthy Jew as the prototype of all Jews.

Hitler successfully inflated the canard of Jewish capitalism to fantastic proportions, although of the nine million Jews of pre-war Europe, nine-tenths lived from hand to mouth in pogrom-ridden Eastern Europe.

It was easy for Hitler; the Church had portrayed the Jews for centuries in the Gospel image of "moneychangers."

LAODICEA, COUNCIL OF

Fourth-century assembly of church leaders; forbade Christians to respect the Jewish Sabbath.

LEO VII

This good Pope of the tenth century suggested that the Jews be given the Gospel to hear, and if they rejected it, that they be expelled.

LES JUIFS DEVANT L'EGLISE ET L'HISTOIRE

In this standard work of the Dominican doctor of canonical law, Pater Constant (1897), the following is stated about the Jews:

"In the heart of every Jew flows a traitor's blood."

"A Jewish child over the age of seven can be baptized against its parents' will."

"No Christian may be in the service of a Jew."

"No Christian woman may nurse a Jewish infant; this would appear to the Church an outrage; it means bringing the Devil into contact with the Holy Ghost." [The Devil, of course, is the Jewish child.]

"A Christian may not eat with a Jew."

"Even in a prayer the Jew must be referred to as 'perfidious.'"

"A Jew may not instruct a Christian, in science or out."

"A Jew may not occupy a position of honor or a public office."

"A Jewish physician may not attend a sick Christian."

"A Jew may not be a magistrate because of his perfidy."

"A Jew may not be a soldier; he may only be an old clothes dealer, a ragman, a peddler or a moneylender."

So reads the treatise on justice of the distinguished Dominican, written at the turn of this century. Such, historically, are the wishes and often the ordinances of the Church in relation to the Jews. Modifications occur only insofar as the Church lacks power of enforcement. Was Hitler wrong in stating, "I am only continuing the work of the Catholic Church"?

LIMPIEZA DE SANGRE

Spanish term, meaning "purity of blood." Much of the time of the church functionaries of the Spanish Inquisition was taken up with examination of the racial background of the accused. Dissidents, heretics or suspects with even a trace of Jewish blood were foredoomed.

The concept of *limpieza* had begun to poison Spain before the Inquisition was established in 1478. In June, 1449, "Aryan" Catholics in the town of Villa Real fell upon the Semitic Christians (Marranos), mutilating and murdering the lot of them. They spared only those who could claim blood-pure Christian descent for three generations. Similar outrages occurred in the fourteenth and fifteenth centuries throughout Spain.

We note that Hitler's blood-purity rule, recognizing as Germans only "Aryan" people of the third generation, was clearly formulated by Catholic fanatics in Spain five hundred years before.

LONDON

In the early Middle Ages ecclesiastical pressure upon the Jews of England never ceased. Mobs were driven to riot, kings to confiscation.

In 1262 in the city of London fifteen hundred Jews were butchered. In 1279, 280 more were executed at the behest of the Catholic Church, and the rest driven from the city. Their possessions fell to the crown. In 1290 King Edward I, on All Saints' Day, ordered that all Jews be shipped out of his kingdom on hired boats. Perverse captains drowned many a Jew for his remaining belongings.

The early kings of England played a sinister game in collaboration with the bishops: The bishops got the Jews killed or exiled, the kings got their property.

LUBLIN

In this Polish city in 1648 Jesuits led a mob into the ghetto where they cut down eight Jews. For this pogrom they were publicly brought to account by King Ladislaus IV. Their influence, however, continued to make itself felt through anti-Semitic sermons and pamphlets. They were also responsible for the ban against Jews serving as pharmacists.

LUCERNE

From this Swiss city the Jews were expelled in 1401 by direct pressure from the Church and not permitted to settle again until 1869.

LUEGER, KARL (1844-1910)

Leading anti-Semitic politician of late nineteenth-century Austria, who propagated "Christian Socialism." As Mayor of Vienna, he was strongly supported by clerical elements. The rabble he roused from among the Austrian lower middle-class included an unknown young man named Adolf Hitler.

LUTHER, MARTIN (1481-1545)

This terrible man was a predecessor of Hitler. He demanded that all Jews not only become slaves, as Saint Augustine ordained, but be made slaves of the serfs, so they might never touch the hand of a Christian German.

In his tract *Schem Hamphoresh* (1544) Luther referred to the Jews as ritual murderers, poisoners of wells and, since they were worse than devils, demanded the burning of "all their synagogues and talmuds."

Here is what the foremost Protestant leader recommends for the Jews:

"They should be forced to hardest labor as handymen of serfs only; they should not be permitted to hold services; every Christian should be admonished to deal with them in a merciless manner; if you suffer, strike them in the jaw; if I had the power, I would assemble them to prove to us that we Christians do not worship God, under penalty of having their tongues cut out through the backs of their necks."

Luther's references to the Jews in his pamphlet *Die Juden und ihre Lügen* (*About the Jews and Their Lies*) are not repeatable. They are coarse, vile, vicious and vulgar.

Luther had spewed forth enough seed for the fresh growth of anti-Semitism in its most atrocious forms.

LWOW

In this Polish town severe persecution of the Jews commenced September 1, 1592 when Archbishop Salikowski ordered the Jews to erect a church. In rapid succession followed accusations of blood drinking and host desecration. In 1603 the Jesuits closed the synagogue. Only by paying heavy ransom could the Jews rededicate their temple in 1609.

LYON

Copies of tax records indicate that by order of the archbishop of this city (1340) a Jew who passed through Lyon had to pay 12 deniers as tariff or else receive a blow.

LYUTOSTANSKY, HIPPOLYTE

Catholic priest who was converted to the Russian Orthodox Church, and in 1869 distributed a booklet on *The Use of Christian Blood by Jews in Their Rituals*. He was one of the molders of the anti-Semitic mind of Czar Nicholas II.

M

MAGDEBURG

Archbishop Robert of this German city in 1261 seized all the property of "his" Jews and held the influential ones for ransom by "foreign" relatives.

An inspiration to Adolf Eichmann, who offered Jews for a ransom of trucks.

MAINZ

In this medieval trade center of the German Rhineland, hundreds of Jews were massacred by Crusaders infuriated by a fanatical Catholic clergy; only a few chose baptism before death.

MALA SANGRE

"Bad blood" was attributed to the Jews in fifteenth-century Spain by the Franciscan friar, Alphonso de Spina, in his book *Fortalitium Fidei*. He accused even the Marranos and conversos (converts) of being defiled forever by their Jewish blood. He appealed for a pure-blooded Christian Spain and the destruction of all racial Jews, professing or converted. His exhortations found willing listeners among the Catholic faithful. See *Limpieza de Sangre*.

MARIE THERESE (1717-1780)

Catholic Empress of Austria, strongly anti-Semitic, who decreed the yellow badge for Jews and endeavored to drive them from Bohemia.

MARRANOS

Spanish word meaning "pig," probably adapted from the Arabic word *mahram* which meant "something prohibited"; commonly used as a term for Jews or Moors who had been converted to Christianity, especially those suspected of accepting the Christian religion only to escape persecution. To prove their "sincerity," such converts might be called upon to eat pork in public.

Marranos were often treated by the Catholic authorities like common Jews who had to be obliterated. Hitler adopted the same attitude toward the European Catholics of Jewish origin. See also *Chueta*.

MARTINEZ, FERNANDO

was one of the Spanish Dominican friars who in 1369 exerted pressure on Henry II, King of Leon and Castile, to demand such exorbitant taxes of the Jews that many had to sell themselves into slavery in order to escape death by burning.

In his fanatical preaching Martinez "proved" that the Jews were responsible for the Black Plague because of their uncleanliness and malodor. (The latter charge often was repeated by Julius Streicher, arch-publicist of Nazi anti-Semitism!)

Martinez inflamed the populace of Seville into anti-Jewish riots. Jews were ordered into *juderías,* and the homes as well as the synagogues of the unfortunate were burned. (Here, too, the National Socialists of Germany followed the Catholic example: All synagogues were put to the torch by the German Neo-Inquisitionists.)

Martinez compelled the Hebrews to wear badges of recognition and forbade them to ride horseback. He prohibited sexual intercourse between Jews and Iberians, even prostitutes, and debarred them from all licensed professions. (Hitler emulated the Dominican, adopting all of his strictures, even the prohibition against riding horseback.)

The Dominicans, however, extended special leniency to Jewish children—if they informed on their parents. You can imagine the fate of the luckless parents!

MARX, KARL (1818-1883)

A childhood convert to Protestantism, he adopted Lutheran anti-Semitism. In his pamphlet, *Zur Judenfrage,* he charges that the basis of Judaism is greed; the Jew's God is money. Marx demanded the emancipation of the world from Jewish usury and money, a slogan readily taken over by Hitler.

MECKLENBURG

On October 24, 1492, twenty-four Jews, two of them women, were burned alive in this German city after a priest charged that they had impaled a consecrated wafer. The place of the pyre is still called *Judenberg*.

MEMORBUCH

A book to commemorate the names and events of the martyrdom of the Jewish people at the hands of the Christian clergy and their helpers.

MEXICO

From 1536 (the first auto-da-fé) until 1820 (close of the Holy Office) hundreds of Jews, Judaizers and Marranos were indicted and burned by the Catholic hierarchy.

The Catholic clergy in Mexico has written its own special chapter in anti-Semitism. Numerous Marranos were put to torture and "confessed," involving their own kin and friends. Francisca Nuñez de Carabajal was kept in dungeons for over three years, living from one excruciating torture to another, always in the presence of Catholic priests with Christ on their lips and venom in their hearts. She was finally burned alive on February 24, 1590. So monstrous was her agony during her confinement that she implicated her own children in fantastic evil deeds.

Even after a half-century of revolutionary secularization and disestablishment of the Catholic Church, Mexico City today is the source of thousands of copies of anti-Semitic works, including the infamous "Protocols of the Elders of Zion," reprinted in the Spanish language. These new bottlings of an old poison are widely distributed in Central and South America. Mysterious subsidies have brought more thousands of these works to bookstores in

the United States which are patronized by Spanish-speaking Americans and Cuban refugees.

MISCEGENATION

The "Seven Part Code" of King Alfonso X (1252-1284) proposed by the Castilian clergy stipulated (Law IX): "Jews who have carnal relations with Christian women are guilty of criminal insolence and shall be put to death."

Hitler adopted this law for Germany.

Like the Church, however, Nazi Germany "tolerated" the "use" of Jewish women by Christians; in fact, the Nazi troops, who, let us recall, were blessed enthusiastically by both Protestant and Catholic clergy, had their military bordellos stocked with Jewish virgins taken from their families during the extermination roundup.

Many of the basic statutes of the Nuremberg Law can be found in the Code of the Roman Emperor Constantine I (306-337), who adopted the cross as a symbol of imperial rule. Constantine, who murdered his wife and son, ordained: No Jew may marry a Christian; no Jew may fraternize with a Christian; no Jew may hold an office reserved for Christians.

MONEYCHANGERS

The traditional identification of this Gospel reference with "*the* Jews"—as if the other attendants at the Temple were "Gentiles"—was frequently used by Hitler and Stalin. In one of his speeches Hitler compared himself to Jesus Christ and stated that like Him he would drive out the Jewish moneychangers, "a brood of vipers and adders from the temple of purity."

Indeed, no modern literature is as full of Gospel citations as that of the great anti-Semites of France, Germany, Spain and Russia.

121

The Gospel of St. John contains thirty-two references to "the Jews," all associating them with hateful actions from blood greed to sadism and foul betrayal.

The Gospel of St. John reads as if Jesus were living in a Gentile world, brutally interfered with by Jews, "whom He fled and avoided." How is the lay Christian to know that Jesus grew up in a Jewish home, observed all the rituals so often ridiculed by outsiders, spoke only Hebrew and its vernacular Aramaic, preached only to Jews in their synagogues or assemblies, was followed only by Hebrews, all his Apostles and those who loved Him and believed in Him being Jews?

The whole advent of Christianity was a Jewish drama, from alpha to omega, except the crucifixion, which was pure Roman. The Romans tolerated no king but Caesar, no God but Caesar.

It suited the Catholic Bishops of Rome, given supreme pontificate over the Empire, to show their gratitude to Emperor Constantine by "rehabilitating" the Roman police chief, the Procurator of Judaea, as a noble judge and blaming Jesus' agony on the ancestors of the obdurate Jews who would not bend their knees to the Bishop of Rome.

The Jews were the makers of Christianity, from Jesus to Paul, and not its destroyers.

MONGOLS

Their invasion of Eastern Europe in the Middle Ages was also blamed on the Jews by an ever eager clergy, claiming they were the "lost ten tribes of Israel," and that "the Jews are in league with the Mongols to kill the Christians as they killed Christ."

MONIEUX

A walled town in France near the Italian border where the armies of the First Crusade in 1095 put to death all Jewish inhabitants. A Hebrew chronicle of the day, set

down by a Jewish woman who escaped as by a miracle, gives the details of this home-front heroism by the soldiers of the Cross, hundreds of miles from the Holy Land.

MONKS

and the lower Catholic clergy were among the worst inciters of anti-Semitic riots right up to the eighteenth century. Lack of substantial education left them little above the man of the plow or the man of the street. However, "the cloth" gave them enough protection and respect to allow them to rave and riot against "the killers of Christ."

In 1350 in the Bohemian town of Eger a "preaching monk" raised the mob and all Jews were massacred, their houses plundered, their books sent to the Bishop of Prague.

Similar incidents occurred a thousand times over in a Europe darkened by Catholicism for eighteen hundred years.

MORE JUDAICO

The Jewish oath was based upon the Christian church concept that Hebrews were, by definition, deceptors and enemies of truth. In practice, while the Church was dominant, the Jew's word was never taken against a Christian, and contrariwise, the Christian's oath on the New Testament was nearly always taken against a Jew.

The German Catholic Church authorities produced in the thirteenth century a widely popular form of Jewish oath: the Jew had to stand on the raw hide of a sow, facing an open Torah. He still was scarcely ever believed, of course, but the ceremony produced a double insult to the Jew, his faith, and his belief in his own dignity.

With the rise of worldly jurisprudence the Jewish oath became modified. The churches, however, while losing ground to the state jurists, retained their spiritual hold on both judges and juries, and the Jew avoided whenever possible the frustration of going to court against a Christian.

More judaico was abolished in Western Europe during the first half of the nineteenth century; in Rumania not until 1914.

MORTARA AFFAIR

As late as 1850 in Italy a bigot nurse secretly had a sickly Jewish infant baptized to "assure its recovery." In 1858 the Church authorities kidnaped the child and by order of Pope Pius IX refused to return it to its parents unless they themselves would convert. Three hundred years earlier this sort of crime was commonplace; in the nineteenth century it caused quite a stir in the Western world, but to no avail.

MOSCOW

Under Ivan III (1440-1505) a council of the Eastern Orthodox Church was convoked which accused Jews of slandering God's Son. A number of Jews were burned alive, others perished in the dungeons.

MOSLEMS

If not for the hospitality extended by Sultan Bayazid II of Turkey and other Moslem rulers, the Jews of Western and Southern Europe would have perished in the Inquisition era.

MUELLER, LUDWIG

On July 23, 1933, a group of National Socialist Protestant ministers, among whose "honorary" members were Frick and Göring, won a clear majority among the Lutheran clergy of Germany and elected Reverend Ludwig Mueller their *Reichsbischof*. Ludwig Mueller, a rabid anti-Semite, met Hitler in 1926. They compared their respective views most favorably.

124

MUFTI, THE

Haj Amin el-Husseini, Palestinian Arab leader, designated Mufti, or chief counselor in Koranic law, of Jerusalem during British rule of the Holy Land. Instigator of anti-Jewish demonstrations and riots; after outbreak of World War II, fled to Nazi Germany. There he endorsed Hitler's anti-Semitic program, his logic being that if the Jews were exterminated in Europe, there would be no further Jewish immigration to Palestine. He attempted to win recruits for Hitler's armies among the Moslem population of the occupied Balkan countries. Proclaimed a war criminal after Allied victory, he found refuge in Cairo, Egypt.

N

NANCY

The bishop of Nancy spoke at the French National Assembly in Paris on December 23, 1789: "The Christian people regard the Jews with abhorrence; to grant them rights as citizens would set all France aflame."

Adolf Hitler concurred a century and a half later, and one of his first deeds of statecraft was to abolish the civil rights of Jews.

NARBONNE

In 897 the bishop of this French town appropriated all the Jewish lands in his diocese with the help of the feeble King Charles the Simple. Appropriation of Jewish property has been widely practiced in our time by professional anti-Semitic governments.

NAZI VATICANISM

Despite all the enthusiastic ringing of church bells at Hitler visits, Hitler victory celebrations, *Dritte Reich* festivals, parties, and shows, I do not claim that all the Vatican

hierarchy was Nazi-minded; but under Pope Pius XII the Vatican hoped for, fervently hoped for, Nazi victory and not that of the Allied cause.

In Rome itself the Pope, Pius XII, stood quietly at the window when Jewish women and children were seized at whip point and loaded into extermination buses.

There is one thing, however, that bothered the Vicar of Christ—namely, "What will become of Italy if the forces of Germany withdraw and we will be left at the mercy of the Allies? Freemasonry is already coming more and more to the fore!"

With great emotion the Pontiff then said:

"We empower you to state explicitly, to everyone, that the German people, in particular, have always been clasped in Our heart and that the German people, who are now being so sorely tried, are, more than any other nation, the object of Our very special concern. We have always given outward, as well as other, expression to our great sympathy for Germany, by interrupting Our private audiences so that members of the German Armed Forces who wished to visit Us might not have to wait unnecessarily.

"We make unceasing efforts to help, and especially to relieve the German people from the pressure of the dreadful terror attacks. Let everyone be convinced that, where the situation permits, we do everything that possibly can be done."

Even when Rome was in Allied hands, in 1944, the Germanophile Pope refused to raise even his voice in protest against the Himmler-Eichmann butchering of Hungarian Jews. He explained later, much later, that he did not want to give the thirty million Catholic Germans pangs of conscience about their wartime duties.

What nobility of motive lay behind his silence in the face of outrages committed on the children of the One Whose vicar he professed to be!

Following is an appeal of the cornered women, children and unarmed civilians of Jewish faith to the Catholic conscience:

126

"To the Christians of Hungary:

"In this final hour of their tragic destiny, the Jews of Hungary turn imploringly to the Christians of Hungary. They address their words to those whose existence they have shared for a thousand years, in good times and bad, on soil in which their ancestors are at rest.

"We kept silent when we were robbed of our possessions, when we lost our human dignity, and our status as citizens. We did not decide upon this extreme step even when we were driven from our homes. But now our very lives are at stake. And this we write in pain: that the lives involved are those, alas, of but a fraction of Hungary's Jews . . .

"In the name of our children, our aged, and our defenseless women, in the name of us all as we face certain death, a frightful death, we address this prayer to the Christian community of Hungary . . . ."

The answer of Pope Pius XII, already witnessing the collapse of Hitlerism, mind you, and living under the unwelcome but full protection of the Allied armed forces, was: *Silence*.

What lay behind his silence? Eugenio Cardinal Pacelli, from the spring of 1939 Pope Pius XII, former Nuncio in Berlin, always was unduly sympathetic to the German cause. To the worldwide appeal on behalf of the tortured Jewish women and children, he replied that he wished to remain "neutral" in this conflict.

This Pope was never neutral. He repeatedly damned the Russians for alleged "pagan" brutalities and attacked the British and Americans for endangering Rome and bombarding his beloved Monte Cassino, but he steadfastly remained "neutral" in the face of wanton atrocities perpetrated on a million Jewish children, proving the total indifference of this Vicar of Christ toward the suffering of Jews because they were Jews. In front of his very window Jewish families were dragged off to extermination camps, but the Vicar turned the other way. He had just appointed Franz von Papen, who had held the stirrup for Hitler, Councilor of the Holy See.

127

One cannot serve two masters and Pacelli opted for the one below, not above. Pius XII was certain Hitler would win the war; all his actions were based on this premise. Thus the Vicar of Christ became the chaplain of the Third Reich.

NEO-CATHOLICISM

In January of 1967 Pope Paul VI appointed the German Duke Karl Friedrich zu Lowenstein to the twelve-member International Council of the Church. Radio Vatican made a special announcement of this, the greatest honor the Holy See can bestow upon a layman.

In 1933, the Year of the Wolf in Germany, the Duke took over leadership of the Catholic student society *Unitas*, and from then on during the crucial Hitler decade, served as a fountain of National Socialist pronouncements and affirmations. From this *Unitas* came the utterance, "Catholic thought and the essence of German Fascism are self-identical." He denounced his own cousin for lecturing abroad before a Jewish audience.

The Brown Princeling was a protégé of the pathetic Cardinal Faulhaber who blew first hot then cold as the Swastika rose in the German heavens.

His appointment prompts the question—just how "new" is the "new era" of present-day Catholicism?

NEOFITA, CASA DEI

The House of Catechumens was established in Rome on March 21, 1548, by the Vatican for the specific purpose of compelling conversion of Jews. The house was supported by oppressive taxation of Jews. Popes Pius V and Gregory XIII were especially active in the business of compulsory conversion of Hebrews.

In November, 1604, the chief rabbi of Rome, Joshua Assouth, and his four children were dragged into the house of conversion.

For all practical purposes the house was abolished in 1810, at the time of the French occupation. In the Nazi era the chief rabbi of Rome was driven into the hands of the Church by more subtle means.

NEO-NATIONALISM

in Germany can count heavily on the support of the nostalgic clergy. A leader of this group is Josef Cardinal Frings who has become a vociferous apologist for the rise of the brown-shirted heroes of the Hitler decade.

This Archbishop of Cologne blames not the red-handed Germans for the KZ massacres, but rather the Jews themselves. In an extensive interview reported in a West German newspaper, the prelate explained that the Jews of Germany were capitalists who flaunted their immense wealth during the 1920's. The Cardinal also criticized the Jews for their intellectual and cultural influence.

The Cardinal did not even hesitate to question the fact that six million Jews had been most cruelly done to death by his countrymen. He was not sure, he said, that the total was "six million."

For the record it should be stated that Cardinal Frings has always been a man of great compassion. In the early years after Hitler's defeat he helped organize a campaign to prevent "acts of revenge"—Jewish, of course—against "German nationals," even though these "German nationals" were charged before the whole civilized world with the most dastardly crimes against humanity.

NEO-THOMISM

On August 7, 1941, Marshal Pétain sent an inquiry regarding the Vatican's attitude toward the possibility of anti-Jewish measures in Vichy France to the distinguished Catholic leader, Léon Bérard, French Ambassador to the Holy See. The Ambassador replied, after close consultation with the staff of Pius XII, with quotations from Saint

Thomas Aquinas, who, living in the dark ages, held that Jews were destined to be slaves of the Christian rulers, and therefore be barred from all government activity and limited in the professions. The Ambassador also cited the Vatican as not wishing to quarrel with the Vichy Nazi regime over "the Jewish issue."

NEUTRALITY

Would Pope Pius XII have proclaimed neutrality if, instead of a million Jewish children, an equal number of French or Dutch youth had been choked to death by German poison gas? I wonder. I wonder.

NEW TESTAMENT

An anthology of twenty-seven pieces finally constituted in 382 by the Council of Rome as the canon of the Church.

The Synoptics and John were included, but other fragmentary gospels eliminated, such as the Gospel of Peter. Many other "gospels" were circulated in the early centuries, which also purported to be the sayings of Jesus and epistles of evangelists. "The Epistle of Barnabas," "The Shepherd" of Hermas, "The Gospel of the Ebionites" are just a few of the early endeavors of Christian followers to express the prevalent attitudes and beliefs of the early centuries.

The truly verifiable Jesus tradition of the first and second centuries lacks the anti-Semitic interpolations that desecrate the Roman New Testament sponsored by the later Bishops of Rome.

The New Testament is, next to *Mein Kampf*, the most influential anti-Semitic book in print. Both books mention the Jew only in the most derogatory manner: as a traitor, a bloodthirsty murderer, a defiler of temples, a money-changer full of greed, a pitiless enemy of the divine and noble, a scurrilous hater of the divine, a devilish schemer to deprive mankind of salvation.

130

Both books consider the Jew accursed forever and pitilessly hold *the* Jew responsible for what *a* Jew may or may not have done.

Both books are responsible for the systematic execution not only of millions of men and women but also of children who were guilty of nothing but being born Jews.

Both books have created such hate of the Jew that their readers felt satisfaction in putting even these Jewish children to death in most cruel and torturous ways.

As King Philip II of Spain, defender of Catholicism, ordered: "Do not garrote them before burning; let them feel the full pain of the flames."

Both books have inspired charges against the Jews of conspiring to gain world-wide power over the Christians.

Both books brought Jew hatred to such a pitch that even the dead were not given to relatives to be buried. The persecutors burned the bodies of their Jewish victims as they would foul flesh and dumped their ashes into sewers.

To the Christian churchman the lines above may sound offensive, but the offense is theirs. Ours is only the grief that almost ten million of our kinsmen, among them a million of our little children, were dealt with so bestially.

If the Christians love to drink of the Hebrew wisdom in the New Testament, as it was uttered by the gentle Jew Jeshu and his gentle Jewish Apostles, let them also drink of our tears and our blood, which have flowed freely for two thousand years, because of what the Roman Bishops added to the *Verba Christi* to denigrate the Jew. They have not ceased torturing us.

While *Mein Kampf* is responsible for a greater total of wanton executions than the Catholic churchmen of the New Testament, the Catholic clergy was even more cruel than the Nazis and preceded most burnings with cunning tortures.

Hitler repeatedly pointed out during his successful conference with the representatives of Cardinal Pacelli (later Pope Pius XII) in connection with the Concordat of Col-

laboration that he was only continuing the fifteen-hundred-year-old "work" of the Catholic Church—namely, to confine and destroy Judaism.

While Nazism may be moribund, anti-Semitic Catholicism is in full bloom. As recently as April, 1966, Bishop Luigi Carli of Segni, who was appointed by the Vatican to head the four-man Ecumenical Curia formulating the "Jewish Declaration," wrote in the clerical review, *Palestro del Clero:* "Judaism carries by its very nature the judgment of condemnation by God."

Mein Kampf is dead, but the New Testament, with its over one hundred anti-Semitic references to the Jews, interpolated by Roman Bishops of the fourth century, lives on to stigmatize, segregate and sting the Jews.

The Jew continues to be depicted as killer and torturer of Christ and greedy defamer of the Temple. In the words of Luigi Carli, the spokesman and head of the Ecumenical Curia, anti-Semitism is not condemned by the Catholic Church, but Judaism is!

NICHOLAS III

This Pope in 1278 made it obligatory for Jews to attend Church sermons in which the Jewish people were described as treacherous God killers. Vincent Ferrer and Raymund of Penaforte, both saints and luminaries of the Catholic Church, also practiced this form of psychological sadism.

Not until 1870 was the monstrous ritual abolished.

NICHOLAS OF CUSA (1401-1464)

This learned Cardinal of Germany traveled in the fifteenth century as a personal delegate of Pope Nicholas V, expressing at all meetings and councils his fanatical hatred of the "God killers." He ordered clerics and civilians alike either to convert Jews or expel them.

NORWICH

In this English town in 1276 a Jew was burned alive for refusing to admit that Jesus was God.

NUMERUS CLAUSUS

or student quota system was practiced in Church schools before it reached the secular institutions. The Jew, ghetto-ized by the popes and restricted by the bishops, had only rare opportunities for study since education was in large part directed or influenced by clergymen. Here, too, an anti-Semitic measure of the secular modern world finds its early origin in the Church.

O

OATH

On August 12, 1942, the Ministry of Justice of Germany ruled that an oath given by a Jew had no legal validity.

Such a "judicial" attitude was only a resurrection of the medieval Church attitude, which lingered on in the Western world up to the American and French revolutions.

OBERAMMERGAU

This Bavarian town continues, every decade, to stage performances of an anti-Semitic Passion play depicting the suffering of Jesus "at the hands of the perfidious Jews." The play draws an immense tourist crowd that watches the coarse re-enactment of gospel legends in which Judas and the other Jews appear as a fiendish, shaggy, bloodthirsty lot who subject the gentle-looking savior to thorning, beat-ing, spitting, kicking and other abuse.

Christ's Apostles and followers, of course, are played by refined-looking Bavarians whose countenances display Ger-man gentility and compassion.

133

Passion plays derive, in corrupted form, from the "miracle" plays of the Middle Ages. The Oberammergau performance is said to date from a vow undertaken by the community in 1634 to escape the plague. The vicious text of the present Passion Play was written by a local Catholic priest in 1860 and has never failed to arouse peasants as well as city visitors to resentment against the diabolical Jews who were plaguing the Aryan Jesus.

Despite world-wide protests and threats of boycott, the village declared in 1966 that no changes would be made in the text for the performance scheduled in 1970.

OBSCURANTS

Christian writers of catechisms and histories, especially for the young, have managed successfully to veil the totally Jewish milieu of the life of Jesus so that the majority of Christians are not aware of the fact that all—but all—of the people who surrounded and supported Jesus in his lifetime were Hebrews.

These educators in religion describe the mother of Jesus as a "young woman espoused to a man Joseph," who lived "in the country of the Jews." The Apostles are referred to in these school texts as "twelve men chosen by Jesus."

The word "Jew" is used only for an enemy or a bloodthirsty disbeliever.

OLD WINE IN NEW BOTTLES

In the introduction of a revised edition of the New Testament, published in 1959 by "Ars Sacra," the Catholic Professor of Theology Otto Karrer interprets the Jews as a people forever accursed.

In another New Testament "revised" by Father Werner Becker, published in 1962 by Kösel Verlag, the Jews are introduced as "people given to lies and viciousness."

In a 1964 Catholic edition (one million copies) of Holy Scripture, recommended by the Bishop of Rothenburg, Carl

Joseph Leiprecht, the Catholic theologian Peter Ketter writes: "The Jewish people are accursed because they listened to unscrupulous inciters."

All of these "new" editions are still being distributed.

OPPENHEIM

In this German town in the fourteenth century the Jewish population withdrew into their ghetto, set it afire and perished in the flames. The Christians of the town were on the march to kill them for "poisoning" their wells.

In numerous other German towns the Jews were put to death on the same charge. The carnage was horrible in Cologne, Worms, Frankfurt, Erfurt, Colmar—often incited by wandering Catholic "Flagellants."

ORDER OF THE SKULL

The romanticized title of the German *Schutzstaffel*, better known as the SS. The "elite" of the SS, membership in which was rather difficult to attain (therefore alibis of "compulsion" are suspect), were in charge of all concentration camps and their institutional atrocities. It is worth noting that as late as 1946 Archbishop Gröber, later Cardinal Gröber by the grace of "God's Vicar," stated: *"Die SS in Freiburg sind die anständigste* [nicest] *Organization der Partei."*

ORIENTALIZATION

of the Jewish image in Church art and manuscript illumination was of the caricature variety which began in the "Dark Ages" and culminated in the cartoons of *Der Stürmer*.

For example, when the Jew was not portrayed in the horned hat favored by the ecclesiastical law-givers of the Middle Ages, he was usually shown wearing a Saracen turban—although Jews had become "Westernized" in dress

during their centuries of domicile in Europe. The artistic repetition of turbans and suchlike exotic props identified Jews, in the minds of the largely illiterate populace, with the Moors, Saracens, Turks, Mongols and other "Asians" who threatened Christian Europe.

OSSERVATORE ROMANO

The official Vatican newspaper that, throughout the Nazi alliance with Mussolini—until the very last day, and beyond—manifested an undaunted spirit of collaboration with the fascist elements, refused to print any news of the horrible atrocities perpetrated upon the hapless Jews and kept even the mass kidnapping in Rome itself of Jewish women and children, destined for execution at Auschwitz, from its readers.

Pope Pius XII, whose grandfather, Marcantonio Pacelli, founded the paper, often read the galley proofs of his chosen news vehicle and would on occasion telephone his criticisms and corrections.

At the height of barbaric brutality by the Gestapo occupation forces in Italy, culminating in the infamous massacre of seventy Jews and hundreds of "other criminals" in the Ardeatine Caves of Rome, Pius XII wrote a personal editorial in *Osservatore Romano* in which he pleaded for *"carita civile"*—"civil compassion"—not by the Nazis, but by the Italian population toward their hard-pressed overlords!

Because of the Pope's admonition, the Italian press refrained for weeks from reporting the latest Nazi *Blutbad* within the confines of the Imperial City. The big news of that day in the press was: "The Pope Enjoys Good Health."

In the evening *Osservatore Romano* repeated again and again the Pope's call for self-control and undiminished succor to the German forces. Not a single word of pity could be spared for the machine-gunned "Jews and other criminals."

The bodies of the slaughtered rotted for months in the

136

foul cave until the stench drove civilians of the neighborhood to give the dead a decent burial.

Monsignor Montini, the present Pope Paul VI, a devoted adviser of the Vicar of Christ, was, like his superior, concerned only with the safety of the Vatican. He complained bitterly to the American representative at the Holy See, Harold H. Tittmann, that the Pope's prestige would suffer were the Allies to bombard Rome.

While the men of the Vatican, and, especially, Pope Pius XII, refused to raise their voices in behalf of the Ardeatine victims, they got religion again when one of the leading anti-Semites of Rome, ex-*Questore* Pietro Caruso, was apprehended for trial after the expulsion of Nazi troops. The Vatican sent no less than a bishop to the trial of the mass-murderer to testify as to Caruso's "good character and fine Catholic background."

It is reminiscent of the German Cardinal Frings' intervention after the war in behalf of elite Nazis. Religion will out: whenever the Jew killings were over, the Christian clergy inveighed against "revengeful Jews."

P

PACEM IN TERRIS

The magnificent spirit of Pope John XXIII in this encyclical moved to strike the accusation of deicide from the pages of Catholic history, but was completely stymied by the "conservative" element of the Vatican commission during the first session of the Ecumenical Council (1961). They could not even muster enough Christian unity to condemn anti-Semitism.

In 1963 a completely watered-down draft of an Ecumenic schema was finally offered under the sponsorship of none less than Pope Paul VI. Archbishop Heenan of Westminster characterized it as totally unrecognizable compared to the text originally shaped in the spirit of John XXIII.

137

This bastardized schema was fully approved by Pope Paul VI. It omitted Pope John's denial that the Jews were Christ killers; it omitted the point that Christ willed to die and that, if anybody denied him, it was all the people of the world except a small flock of Hebrews. In other words, Jews were the only ones who accepted Christ in his earthly lifetime; no one else did. Therefore the general charge against the Jews as God killers was historically false and theologically biased. Anti-Semitism based on the charge of deicide was to be condemned.

Pope Paul VI, by sponsoring the anti-Semitic schema of the reactionary prelates, placed himself at the head of the inveterate Jew haters in the Church. Equally so, by appointing the blatantly anti-Semitic Bishop Luigi Carli as the head of his Curia to solve the "Jewish Problem," he made a wolf the shepherd.

Just for the record, there is no Jewish problem—the Jews have not persecuted the Catholic churches nor butchered, boiled or beheaded Catholic priests—but there *is* a Catholic problem: Catholic priests and their agents have burned and tortured to death an untold number of Jews.

PAPAL SOLICITUDE

During Charlemagne's reign, Pope Stephen III lodged a sharp complaint with the Bishop of Narbonne "that Jewish people on French soil enjoy full equality with Christians and that Christian men and women defile their souls by living under the same roof with the traitors of Christ."

Under Louis the Pious, Charlemagne's successor, the Bishop of Lyon addressed a note to the prelate of Narbonne, expressing great concern "because I see the virgin bride of Christ [Gentile girls] sit down to eat in the company of whores [Jewish girls]."

Almost the identical words were used by the Brown Shirts to condemn Judaeo-Christian fraternizing.

Pope Benedict XIV (*A Quo Primum*, 1751) warned against any intimacy with the Hebrews, referring obviously

to Pope Innocent II (1198-1216), who wrote in an encyclical: "Jews are like a rat in the sack or a snake in the bosom. Christians therefore may not enter the service of Jews; no public position may be bestowed upon Jews; no Christian may seek the cure of a Jewish physician."

All this and more Brown Shirt Vaticanism may be found in the *Bullarum Romanum* under the headings of the Popes Nicholas IV, Paul IV, Pius V, Gregory XIII, Clement VIII.

Indeed, there is not a single Pope on record who was not anti-Semitic in deed, word, or implication except good Pope John XXIII.

PARIS

Upon the orders of Pope Gregory IX (1242) to destroy all Hebrew literature, twenty-four cartloads of Hebrew sacred books were burned in Paris.

PASSAU

In this Bavarian town in 1478 a local priest charged Jews with breaking a holy wafer (host). The accused were tortured and burned. The synagogue was "converted" into a church, which still publicizes the "desecration"—of the host, of course.

PASSION PLAYS

because of their Christological character invariably depicted the Jewish characters as killers or traitors (e.g., Judas). Those still to be seen today, of which the most famous is performed at the Bavarian town of Oberammergau, are no different in their insistent denigration of the Jews.

For example, a Passion play which has been presented for more than fifty years in a Catholic church in Union City, New Jersey, was recently analyzed by the American Jewish Congress in these terms:

"In the play, Judas is presented as a caricature identical with Julius Streicher's stereotype of a Jew in *Der Stürmer*. . . .

"The Jewish priests are depicted as brutish louts, cunning and corrupt. . . .

"The climax is the Crucifixion, accompanied by an electrical storm whose terrible lightning and rolling thunder constitute a magnificent spectacle—and which reduced many of the children in the audience to hysteria. . . .

"The entire production is a searing, hate-filled indictment of Jewry. The Jews are satanic; the Christians are divine disciples of the Lord Jesus."

Thus Union City's Passion play lives up to its advance billing as "America's Oberammergau"—indeed, it goes Oberammergau one better: the Bavarian Passion play is only staged every ten years, while Union City's extravaganza of Jew-hate is given weekly performances every year during the Lenten season!

PASTORAL ANTI-SEMITISM

"Degenerate Judaism together with Freemasonry is the carrier of mammoth capitalism. To fight the evil influence of Judaism is not only the privilege but the duty of every good Christian. . . . A dam should be erected against spiritual dirt and immorality which threatens the world from the Jews."—Gföllner, Bishop of Linz (Austria) : Pastoral Letter of January 21, 1933.

PASTORELLI

A shepherds' Crusade in 1320 led by a berserk parish priest and a fanatical Benedictine monk. It began and ended with the massacre of French Jews, and was widely favored by the Church.

On the road to Carcassonne five hundred Jews took refuge from the Pastorelli in a fortification where, after their

140

food gave out, they killed their children and women, themselves perishing sword in hand.

The siege near Carcassonne, six centuries before the bombardment of the Warsaw ghetto, reminds us that the history of Jewish resistance to Christian savagery has been perforce a long one.

PAUL IV (1555-1559)

This Pope instigated the burning alive of sixty convert Jews for "pretense." He enforced the ghetto rules in Rome and the wearing of the yellow leper badge; excluded Jews from all professions and trades except manual work; destroyed all but one synagogue in his domain; banned all contact of Jews with Christians, as well as the reading of the Talmud.

He appointed the sadistic Cesare Galúaba "commissioner of faith" for the Italian town of Ancona. Galúaba terrorized sixty-three Jews into conversion. Twenty-three other men and women, whose names are handed down to us in contemporary chronicles, refused baptism; they were all hanged and then burned on the Piazza della Mostra.

Only some Turkish Jews escaped the holocaust. Sultain Suleiman II obtained their release by threatening the Pope with retribution.

Not until French occupation of Ancona did the Jews obtain security in the city. Even then, in 1797, a fanatical clergy incited the populace to sack the ghetto. In 1826 Pope Leo XII re-established in Ancona the ghetto that had been eliminated by Napoleon Bonaparte.

Finally the Revolution of 1848 brought full freedom from Catholic persecution to the Jews of Ancona.

PERDITIO

"Disaster" is the name Pope Gregory I (590-604), the father of the "Historic Church," assigned to Judaism, a

faith he stigmatized as shot through with perfidy. This great Pope spewed out a colorful stream of gutter-abuse against the Jews. He cursed them as "wild asses" and "dragons of poison" with "their hearts a den of beasts."

PERFIDY

of the Jews was included in the Catholic Good Friday liturgy: *"Oremus et pro perfidis Judaeis."* This has been omitted recently. Christian liturgy abounds in negative references to the Jews.

PERU

In 1639 twelve Portuguese Jews were burned at the stake by the Inquisition.

PETER OF BLOIS

Archdeacon at the English town of Bath in the twelfth century, who wrote *Against the Perfidious Jews*. He took the title for his tract from a Good Friday prayer of the Catholic liturgy. His conclusions: "The Jews are beasts. You can see it on their faces."

The gentle deacon was often quoted by Sir Oswald Mosley, British sympathizer with the Nazi movement.

PETER OF CLUNY

One of the highly revered figures in Catholic history, who, during the Second Crusade, implored King Louis VII of France to punish the Jews since they were worse than the Saracens. They defiled Christ and robbed the Christians. They should be forced to pay for the Crusade, yet they should not be killed immediately—rather, they should be made to live under constant torture.

We have here a striking similarity with Hitler's depriving all European Jews of their funds to help finance his

wars, and then letting them suffer a painful degradation and captivity before extermination.

PETER THE HERMIT (b. 1050)

A French monk of Amiens with a venomous tongue, who was the most ferocious anti-Semitic Crusader of the Catholic clergy.

PETER THE VENERABLE

Abbot of Cluny, who admonished the Crusaders: "What does it profit to persecute enemies of Christianity outside when evil Jews in our midst deface Christ with impunity?"

An almost identical appeal was made by Reinhard Heydrich to the Germans not to wait for attacks on France and England, but to destroy first the Jew, the enemy within their borders.

PHILIP III (1245-1285)

upon repeated urging of the clergy required the Jews of France to attach a horn-shaped figure to their badge. Even Michelangelo accepted the Vatican suggestion that he crown his "Moses" with Devil's horns.

PIUS V

in 1569 expelled the Jews from the Papal States except for Rome (the Bull *Hebraeorum gens*).

PIUS VI

As late as 1775 this pope issued an edict compelling the Jews in the Papal States to listen, after their Sabbath services, to anti-Semitic "conversion" harangues delivered in the synagogues by unscrupulous clerics.

It was only a year before America's Declaration of

Independence, yet the Pope's bull reiterated the most severe restrictions upon Jewish life, from ghettoism to the yellow badge of the Middle Ages.

With the rising spirit of revolution in America and France, freedom riots occurred in Rome in 1793. The Vatican blamed these riots on the Jews as enemies of the old order, and a vicious pogrom followed in the Roman ghetto.

In 1798 French Revolutionary armies occupied Rome, and for the first time in over fifteen hundred years the Jews of Rome could breathe freely.

PIUS VII

This pope demanded in 1815 that all Jews, who had been given civil rights under the French occupation, be removed from all public offices in the Papal State.

His successor, Pope Leo XII, asked that the Jews be punished since "they had tortured and murdered Jesus."

Incidentally, this last quotation was repeated verbatim in public during "Holy Week" of 1965 by Pope Paul VI, the Ecumenist.

PIUS IX

As late as 1870 this Pope rejected a petition of Jewish inhabitants of Rome to abolish the ghetto. A year later King Victor Emmanuel, disregarding the Pope, had the gates removed.

PIUS XII

See Nazi Vaticanism; *Osservatore Romano; Stellvertreter.*

POBIEDONOSTZEV, KONSTANTIN PETROVICH

Procurator of the Russian Orthodox "Holy Synod," who proposed an *"Endlösung"* of the Jewish problem in the latter nineteenth century: the expulsion of one-third of the Jews, forcible conversion of the "better" third, and starvation by internment of the last third.

After the assassination by radicals of Czar Alexander II (1881) the slogan of the Russian Orthodoxy was: Kill the Jews who killed Jesus and the Czar. Great pogroms, inspired by the clergy, swept Russia. They began with Easter Sunday church assemblies and Jews in 160 towns were attacked, mutilated and killed. Only through the intervention of foreign governments, especially the United States of America, were the hapless victims permitted to leave Russian territory.

POGROM

Russian word meaning "devastation," an apt name, indeed, for the officially directed attacks against the Jewish communities of Russia. Pogroms in Russia were too numerous even to list. In a single week during October, 1905, 670 pogroms took place, encouraged if not invoked by the Orthodox clergy, leaving thousands of Jewish men, women and children dead or mutilated.

The United States, as it had after previous pogroms, prevailed upon the Czarist government to permit emigration of the Jews to its shores. Czar Nicholas II protested loudly to intercessors from abroad: "But they are Christ killers!"

POLAND

Major anti-Semitic activity began with the Council of Breslau (now Wroclaw) in 1267, which advocated the Jew badge and the ghetto. With the rise to power of the

Catholic Church under the Jagiello dynasty, the lot of the Jews became unbearable.

The Catholic Church charged ritual murder and desecration of holy wafers to arouse the populace. In 1399 thirteen Jews were burned alive in Posen for "breaking the host."

Incited by clergy of the Eastern Orthodox Church, hordes of Cossacks under their hetman, Bogdan Chmielnicki, fell upon Poland (1648-1658), massacring over one hundred thousand Jews in the most cruel manner to protect Christianity from "the Jewish devils." Victims were mutilated by Ukrainians and Tartars alike. Infants were slit alive, women were ripped open and then sewn together with live rats in their bowels.

In 1664 Catholic seminary students attacked the Jews in Lemberg after a ritual murder charge.

Attacks and pogroms continued well into the twentieth century. During the German siege of the Warsaw Ghetto in the Second World War, Poles rendered no aid to the Jews; there are on record numerous cases of denunciation of Jews in hiding to the Gestapo in Warsaw.

In 1946, a year after the war, inhabitants of the town of Kielce massacred half of their Jewish population— over forty—who had escaped the German concentration camps. The Polish archbishop saw this as a proper occasion to make vicious remarks about the Christ killers.

POLISH CATHOLICS

Hitler declared: "I as a German Catholic ask only what is permitted to Polish Catholics. To be anti-Semitic is not to be anti-Catholic."

"In Rome, under the dominion of the Church, the Jews occupied a position that we should be satisfied to see restored. The Church used every weapon against the Jews, even the Inquisition. Christ Himself was a pioneer in the fight against Judaism."

Thus spake Hitler.

And soon after these words he adopted the Catholic

146

Church's *"Endlösung"* of the Jewish problem: extermination of the Hebrews themselves, men, women and children.

POLISH CHARTER

of protection was granted to the Jews in 1264 by Boleslaw the Pious, King of Poland. Jews were given, as *servi camerae* or "servants of the Court," a guarantee of personal freedom and professional security. Religious as well as physical inviolability was assured.

In 1267 the Church Council at Breslau protested these "outrageous" privileges with which the Jews had been endowed by the gentry of Poland. The Council demanded segregation of Jews into ghettos, the wearing of leper badges, and discrimination against Jews in trade.

King Casimir the Great (1333-1370) strengthened the Charter but the Catholic Church did not cease its relentless anti-Semitism. Charges of ritual murder, well poisoning and host desecration were raised again and again.

In the fifteenth century the Papal Inquisitory Delegate, St. John Capistrano, roused the low clergy of Poland to a high pitch of anti-Semitic frenzy. Jews in Cracow and Lwow were massacred. Small Unitarian groups that appealed in the sixteenth and seventeenth centuries for religious tolerance were soon suppressed by the Catholic hierarchy.

The Jesuits in Poland were particularly aggressive in their anti-Jewish hostility which has persisted until this very day.

POLNA

In this Bohemian town in 1900 local Jews were accused by the clergy of drinking the blood of Christian children. Professor Thomas Masaryk, later President of Czechoslovakia, defended them.

PORTUGUESE INQUISITION

was, if such a monstrosity is conceivable, more cruel than the Spanish. The unfortunate Jews, and Marranos who had been indicted for "Judaizing" (relapsing), languished in filthy dungeons, chained by both hands with their backs to the wall, beaten and otherwise molested by fanatical guards. To narrate the rest would not be helpful since no pen can amply describe the bestiality of the Catholic persecutors.

The Inquisition slogan *Justitia et Misericordia* is characteristic of Christian Jew-hatred: the words of angels, on the fiery tongue of the Devil. Some Popes—for example, Nicolas V, Clement VI and Innocent VI—exhorted inquisitors to be especially severe.

POSEN

The Archbishop of this Polish city, after the death of the benevolent King Casimir the Great (1333-1370), charged the local rabbi and thirteen elders of the temple with having "bloodied" three consecrated wafers belonging to the Dominican Church.

All the accused were burned over a slow fire. The property of all was "sequestered" by the Dominican Order.

POTOCKI, VALENTIN

A Polish count who became a convert to Judaism. He was apprehended at the behest of the Catholic clergy, condemned by the ecclesiastical court, and burned at the stake in the city of Vilna in front of the cathedral (May, 1749).

PRAGUE

In 1389 a Catholic priest in Prague accused Jewish children at play of having thrown sand on his sacred host.

When he incited the mob to a riot, over three thousand Jews became its victims and the synagogue was burned. Some of the unfortunate were tied to the stake by their feet, "so as to quicker reach their Devil's abode."

Prague was one of the many cities along the route of the crusading protectors of the Grail to have its Jewish citizens put to the cross or the sword.

PRANAITIS, JUSTIN

A Catholic priest, who published in 1893 a pamphlet entitled *The Christian in the Jewish Talmud* in the Russian capital of St. Petersburg, "proving" among other things that the Jews were using the blood of Christian children in the baking of matzoth.

He became in 1911 the "expert" witness for the prosecution at the notorious Beiliss trial. His colleague in defamation was Archimandrite Ambrosius of the Russian Orthodox Church.

PRIVILEGIA ODIOSA

Restrictive legislation reducing the civil status of Jews —for instance, in the Christian Codex Theodosianus, the prohibition of "mixed marriages" under penalty of death and disbarment from all official positions in the government, military, judiciary. (Cf. The National Socialist regime in Hitler's Germany.) Thus the canonical as well as imperial laws of Christian Rome and Constantinople were basically anti-Semitic.

PROPAGANDA

of an anti-Semitic nature up to the nineteenth century was primarily in the hands of clerics. They did the preaching, writing, and producing of plays and festivals. There was no way of reaching the masses except through the

149

Church, and the Church was vividly anti-Semitic. Even where schools were not entirely in the hands of the clergy, the latter had sole jurisdiction over classes in religion.

Against this massive one-way tirade hardly a voice could be raised even by well-wishers for reason, tolerance and justice; not until the American and French revolutions had broken the back of despotically entrenched churchism, and separated Church from State.

PROTECTORS OF JEWS

Throughout World War II Italy's armed forces successfully resisted all German efforts to apprehend and deport Jews, Italian or alien. They did not permit the arrest of Jews in territories under their protection, African or European. On many occasions they freed Jewish internees from the hand of the French Vichy police.

The Rumanian general, Antonescu, was able to protect most of the Jewish citizens in Old Rumania, as General Mannerheim saved the Jews of Finland, and King Christian X those of Denmark.

However, Pope Pius XII was determined in his infinite Christian charity to remain "neutral" in the war of ten million Nazi killers against a million Jewish infants and children.

Incidentally, all the generals and the noble Danish king remained unmolested, except for a few letters of protest from Berlin. But Pope Pius XII prayed often and publicly for the victory of the forces of liberation from atheism and socialism.

PROTOCOLS OF THE LEARNED ELDERS OF ZION

One of the many anti-Semitic pamphlets prepared and distributed by the Czarist government after Russia's defeat at the hands of the Japanese (1905). The Jew was to be the scapegoat for a corrupt and discredited government.

Similar pamphlets for a similar purpose were concocted by the National Socialists after Germany's defeat by the Allies. The Jews had caused the defeat. The Jews are at the bottom of any and all Christian misfortune.

In 1921 a correspondent of the London *Times* uncovered the plagiarism of half the *Protocols* from a satire on Napoleon III written by Maurice Joly, a French attorney. Other portions were plagiarized from a story by Hermann Goedsche and other fictional sources.

The forgery of the *Protocols* gives a clear insight into the sickeningly dishonest mentality of anti-Semites.

PROUDHON, PIERRE-JOSEPH (1809-1865)

A French typesetter with little education but a flair for socialist bravado, who found the Jews an easy target for popular libel: "The Jews are stupid and politically inept. Otherwise they would have accepted Jesus as God instead of opposing him. With their messianic stubbornness they placed themselves outside the pale of mankind."

Everything else Proudhon said about the Jews stems from the altar-born hate of his childhood, which he never overcame. And this in spite of his turning in later years against the Church! With him it is the same as with all the other socialist anti-Semites, from Marx to Stalin: they turned away from the Church, even against it, but they remained steadfast in Jew hate.

PRYNNE, WILLIAM (1600-1669)

A Puritan divine who called upon Heaven and Hell to stop Oliver Cromwell's decision to readmit Jews to England (1659). He quoted other objecting voices as saying, "We must now all turn Jews."

This fanatical pamphleteer actually prevented, single-handed, the official return of the Jews; Cromwell's government admitted them only unofficially. Prynne's pamphlet,

A Short Demurrer to the Jews' Long Discontinued Remitter into England, was distributed in church and school throughout the island.

R

RADULPH

A French monk of the Second Crusade who wandered about Europe preaching violence against the killers of Christ. Without exception the doors of the churches were opened to his homily of hate. The mobs attacked the Jews with the cry, "Hep! Hep!—an easy abbreviation for the illiterate of *Hiersolyma est perdita*—"Jerusalem is lost").

RAMERU

In this French town at the time of the Second Crusade (1147-1149) Rabbi Jacob Tam was stabbed five times in the head by a clergy-led mob as punishment for the "five injuries inflicted" upon Jesus. Church-instigated pogroms also occurred in the German towns of Würzburg, Speyer, and so on.

RATISBON

A town in Germany where in the crusading era all Jews were led to the Danube. Those who refused baptism were drowned in the blue waters.

RECESWINTH (649-672)

This Spanish king appeared in person before the Eighth Council of Toledo (653) to denounce the Jews as wormy Christ killers. With the full consent of the assembled clergy he stripped the Jews of all civil rights. He imposed, among other things, relentless floggings and hair extraction for

any sign of "anti-Christian" behavior. All Jews had to sign an order of obedience that prohibited the observance of their religious rituals. Violators were to be burned alive.

RELIGIO LICITA

Judaism was protected under pagan Rome as *religio licita,* a lawful or permitted religion. Pagan Rome treated the Jews no differently than its other subject nations, respecting in general their distinctive religious observances. Emperor worship was rarely enforced in synagogues throughout the Empire. Jews had been traveling, working, settling and trading in Roman lands for many centuries before Jesus. Dispersion was voluntary and wide.

With the rise of dominant Christianity, Judaism became illicit; the only question remaining was how severely it would be oppressed by the Christian authorities.

After fifteen centuries this judgment still stands: "Present-day Judaism is illegal before God and as a religion carries by its very nature the judgment of condemnation by God."

These are the exact words written by Bishop Luigi Carli, whom Pope Paul VI chose, of all prelates, to head the Curia committee charged by Vatican II with preparation of the official "Declaration on the Jewish problem."

Carli's insolent and vicious attack on the Jews appeared near the close of the Ecumenical Council in the Vatican review, *Palestro del Clero.*

Pope Paul VI has not only endorsed Carli's promulgation, but sponsored it and thereby identified himself with traditional Vatican anti-Semitism. Paul VI, unlike the late Pope John XXIII, whose nobility transcended the Dark Ages, embodies the Catholic motto: *"Semper idem*—Always the same."

RELIGIOUS LIBERTY

"Unfettered liberty of religious thought and freedom of speech are the worst plagues of all." So declared Pope Gregory XVI (d. 1846) in the encyclical *Mirari Vos.*

Another Vatican luminary, Pope Leo XII, wrote in 1885: "The equal toleration of all religions is nothing but atheism."

RENAN, ERNEST (1823-1892)

French historian, originally trained for the Catholic priesthood, who can be regarded as the father of anti-Semitic anthropology. He considered the Jew a cunning Semite who endeavors to master "the honest Aryan." The Jew is cancer eating into the flesh of Christian Aryans. The Jew does not work, he only exploits. The Jew is selfish and cowardly, while the Aryan is given to self-sacrifice.

Alfred Rosenberg, Hitler's personal anthropologist, called Renan "the man who discovered the soul of the German."

RESPECT

Some have said I should be more respectful writing about the Christian Bishops since they were men of God.

Perhaps they were.

How shall I speak of the men who preach that my little grandchildren are the poisonous seed of the Devil?

How shall I speak of the men who call my faith accursed by God?

How shall I speak of the men who refuse to condemn the vile hate against my nation, indeed teach it?

How shall I speak of the men who have a history of ripping open the throats of my ancestors like leopards?

They are men of books, you say. But in their books, old and new, from the beginning of time as they count it, my

154

people are depicted with the horns of Satan, with the fangs of Beelzebub, with the greed of Lucifer and the lust of Lilith. All that is evil in their minds they attribute to us, until we appear to the whole Christian world as an apparition from hell.

I shall speak of the Christian Bishops as men of God when they throw off the old clothes of malice and cleanse their Gospels and catechisms and prayers of the infamies with which they have besmirched us. If they do that, there will be a great rejoicing on earth and in heaven.

In spite of the presumption of two thousand clerics and clerks in Rome, the Chosen People are my people. We are still here after two thousand years of the bishops' exhortation, "Burn the Jews!" We feel chosen to stand for the word of God, which they have made a heavy task indeed, an almost unbearably costly privilege.

The Roman Bishops think that they have lifted from our shoulders the mantle of being God's own people and appropriated it for themselves. This is no better than Hitler's claiming that Christ was a Teuton. No one can steer the hand of God—perhaps they indeed think that God is dead and that His Vicar has taken over.

RIBEAUVILLE

In this French town were lodged a score of Jews who in 1331 had been turned over by Louis of Bavaria to the Sieur de Ribeaupierre as surety for a loan of 400 marks in silver. All the Jews were garroted for being poisoners of wells.

RIGORD, PHILIP AUGUSTUS

This monk of twelfth-century France was one of the many medieval clerics who gave "eyewitness" accounts of Jewish murders of Christians. He reports in his *Gesta Philippi Augusti:* "The Jews who dwelt in Paris were wont

155

every year on Easter Day to go down secretly into underground vaults and kill a Christian as a sacrifice in contempt of the Christian faith."

RINDFLEISCH

A devout German nobleman who in 1298 spread word through the town of Rottingen that Jews had spit out a blessed wafer (host) that a group of churchgoers tried to force upon them. Herr Rindfleisch and the infuriated mob set upon the Jewish families of the town and dragged them to the stake. All were burned alive.

This Church-supported *Judenschächter* took his followers through Germany and Austria, murdering the Jewish population. Over one hundred thousand became victims of their wanton atrocities.

The role of individual priests in the ravaged towns during the pogroms is sickening to report.

RITUAL MURDER

This libel, which stamps the Jew a vampire, has been so attractive to Christian anti-Semites that even modern theologians have often hesitated to denounce it. Churches in Austria, for instance, still carry "memorial" tablets depicting the Jew as a ritual killer.

In all cases of ritual murder during Holy Week, the Christian clergy was the accuser. In 1171 in Blois, France, forty Jews were tortured and burned for crucifying and bleeding a child. As late as the eighteenth century Pope Benedict XIV issued a bull blessing an alleged ritual victim, Andrew of Rinn (1755). In this bull the Pope expressed his strong conviction that Jews would murder Christian children because of their "hate of Jesus."

The Catholic Church has not only acquiesced in the veneration of "victims of Jewish calumny" but sponsored the apotheosis of the little corpses through beatification, canonization and sanctification. See also *Vampires*.

ROHLING, AUGUST (Father)

Professor of Catholic theology at the University of Vienna, author of *The Talmud Jew* (1871), a scurrilous "Hep! Hep!" attack on the Jewish people. With Wilhelm Marr—another precursor of Josef Goebbels—the coiner of the term "anti-Semite."

ROME

The first expulsion of Jews from Rome was directed by Pope John XXII, but curtailed by King Robert of Sicily (1321).

The second expulsion occurred in 1944 by order of the Gestapo and with the silent consent of Pope Pius XII.

ROUEN

In this French town the Crusaders of the eleventh century fell upon the Jews and murdered all who refused baptism.

RUMANIA

The Orthodox Church here made numerous ritual murder charges against the Jews as late as the nineteenth century. Medieval anti-Semitic measures forced upon a weak government by the clergy brought about foreign intervention. The Berlin Congress of 1878 ordered the Rumanian government to grant the Jews civil rights. Failure of Rumania to comply brought about large Jewish emigration, mainly to the United States.

The Rumanian clergy gave strong support to the World War II alliance with the German Nazi government.

SALE OF JEWS

was widely practiced by secular as well as ecclesiastic authorities in Catholic Europe up to the eighteenth century, when the French revolution breached the traditional status of the Jew as a serf or *"Kammerknecht"* of the king or bishop.

In the doctrine of Saint (*sic!*) Augustinus and Saint (*sic!*) Thomas Aquinas, the Jew must forever be a slave of the ruling Lord; in the doctrine of Martin Luther, the Jew has to be reduced to the status of a slave of the serfs, otherwise his deviltry might contaminate *"den deutschen Bürger."*

Catholic rulers used to demand ransom from Jewish communities for the privilege of leaving their domain alive. The alternative, of course, was certain death on the pyre. Jewish communities in neighboring and even faraway lands had to raise funds to buy off the Christian rulers of their brethren.

The cynical and barbaric maneuver by which Hitler's agent, Eichmann, endeavored to sell one million Jews for the equivalent of ten thousand trucks was only a modern version of the extortion widely practiced in the past by Catholic regents.

SALVATION

An academic survey of Catholics and Protestants in Germany indicates that 86 percent of those questioned hold that members of the Hebrew faith are beyond the bounds of salvation.

We Jews desire no other salvation but from the Christians. The Devil himself could do no worse to us than have the churches.

SCHIRACH, BALDUR VON (b. 1907)

Convicted Nazi war criminal who was entrusted by the Catholic Church in the Pacelli Concordat of Collaboration with the mobilization of Germany's Catholic youth groups. The Lutheran bishops' conference had already given its consent to Protestant youth being enlisted in official units, which, like all Nazi organizations, were shock-troops in the war against the Jews.

SCHOENERER, GEORG VON

Professional anti-Semite of that unsavory variety that has neither conviction nor faith, but takes advantage of an existing trend and makes the most outrageous statements to place itself "on the crest of the wave." In the late nineteenth century Schönerer rode the ground-swell of Jew hate maintained by Austrian and German clergy.

Wherever the anti-Semitic "surf's up," Schönerers will be found.

SEGREGATION

In a decree of 1442 Pope Eugenius IV proclaimed: "We order that henceforth Christians may not eat or drink with Jews, not bathe or cohabit with them. They may not hold public office nor receive civic honors."

The zealous Pontiff never saw his decree take full effect in Europe. Hitler did.

SEMI-JUDAEUS

Derogatory reference to Christians of Semitic birth commonly applied by zealous Catholic protagonists during the Middle Ages and the Renaissance. The comparable term of *Halb-Juden* was adopted by the Nazi "blood purists."

159

SERFS

During the Middle Ages many rulers of Europe adopted the social reforms proposed by the Catholic Church Fathers and reduced the Jews in their domains to *servi camerae* (servants of the court). As recommended by the saintly Thomas Aquinas, illustrious philosopher of Catholicism, Jews were treated as cattle. They were bought and sold in deals between nobles and kings. On this issue Luther did not differ from the Vatican: the Jew was rightless, a means of exchange.

Pope Innocent III (1198-1216) declared that the Jews are to live in "perpetual servitude." The Third Lateran Council (1179) emphasized that the Jews were "subjects" of the Christians.

SEVILLE

Fernando Martinez, archdeacon of this town in 1391 mobilized the populace in a pogrom against the Jewish quarter. Four thousand Jews were killed; the rest were forcibly enrolled in the religion of love.

From Seville the Church-inspired pogroms spread to Spanish towns everywhere—except, of course, in Moorish territory. Synagogues were converted, together with pitifully few Jewish survivors, to the "True Faith." In some ghettos not a single Jew survived, and the local Christians had their new "House of God" to themselves.

SHYLOCK

The well-known dramatic figure of a vengeful, merciless Jew, brimful of hate for Christians, appears like the materialization of a chimera from the mind of one of the anti-Semitic Fathers of the early Church. Shakespeare, who never saw any Jews in his lifetime, since all Jews had been deported from England in 1290, created this *dramatis*

persona from a story by Gregorio Leti, biographer of Pope Sixtus V, which was published in Venice in 1587.

There is only one difference: The flesh-greedy merchant in Leti's story is Paul Secchi, a Christian, who wagers a pound of flesh from the body of the Jew (Sampson Ceneda) against the Jew's thousand crowns. The Pope intervenes and both pay a fine.

Shakespeare, employing an old trick of the writer's trade, merely switched roles and made the Jew the villain, which gave him a wide-open opportunity to paint vividly a monstrous Hebrew with all the failings and devilishness the populace loved to hate.

The Church of England, by appropriate sermon, prayer and catechism, kept fresh the image of the treacherous Jew. It was this monstrous image which Shakespeare tried to imitate at the expense of twisting an old Venetian story.

SIEGBURG

In this little German town in 1287 all Jewish inhabitants were accused of killing a Christian boy, Johänneken, and draining his blood. All the Jews were burned. Later the Church sanctified the child.

This sort of deliberate beatification or canonization of little corpses lent credibility to the preposterous tales of blood-drinking Hebrews, which even then were rejected as stupid superstition by enlightened men.

SION, SISTERS OF

Catholic religious order founded in 1844 to accomplish the conversion of the children of Jews to Christianity. One means adopted by the order was the establishing of schools where Jewish (and Moslem) pupils were welcome, as well as Christian children. Conversion was disowned as a goal during the 1930's in favor of a policy of fostering under-

standing and recognition of Judaism among Catholics, and of succor to Jews during World War II. In 1967 the Sisters of Sion began publication of a journal, *Sidic*, which aims to record, criticize and advance progress toward Catholic acceptance of Jews and Judaism. A little candle in the still-darkened world of age-old condemnation by the Christian Churches!

SISEBUT (612-621)

This Spanish King, who preceded Ferdinand and Isabella by almost nine hundred years, demanded that Jews convert or leave the country. The Church used every means, such as the secret conversion of children, to force the cross upon the harassed Jewish people.

SOCIAL JUSTICE

An anti-Semitic publication sponsored during the 1930's by Father Charles E. Coughlin of the Shrine of the Little Flower in Michigan. This radio priest was Hitler's most effective public relations man in the United States through his virulent, libelous attacks upon the "international Jewish banker."

The magazine reached a circulation of one million before it was banned from the mails during World War II. Much of the material published by the cunning priest was reprinted from Nazi news services. The good Father also ran serially the fraudulent, plagiarized *Protocols of Zion*.

SPINOZA, BARUCH (1632-1677)

Brilliant Jewish philosopher living in Holland among Portuguese Marranos. For his humanistic attitude he was attacked by both Protestants and Catholics alike. His books were on the Index of the Vatican and were burned by Protestants.

To avoid disaster for their whole community, after re-

peated warnings and admonitions to cease, the elders and the rabbis of the great Amsterdam synagogue expelled Spinoza from their house of worship. Spinoza continued to live in Amsterdam, in later years in Rijnsberg and The Hague, but no longer could the hard-pressed Jews be held responsible for the anticlericalism found in his noble writings.

On his grave, a year after his burial in The Hague, the Dutch Protestant minister, Rev. Carolus Tuinman, had a stone placed, engraved: "Here lies B.D.S. Spit on his grave. Would that his word were buried with him. His pestilence would not devour any more! Renegade Jew!"

STAMFORD

In this English town in the thirteenth century a ghoulish peasant, out plundering Jewish victims, was killed by another marauder. He was immediately canonized by request of the Bishop of Lincoln. This brought a great influx of pilgrims to the town, since the corpse of the bandit performed healing miracles. The desire to create a pilgrim attraction was a major factor in Christian ritual trials.

STANGL, PAUL

SS—Hauptsturmführer and Commander of Nazi extermination camps Solibar and Treblinka. With the help of Austrian clergy escaped his just prosecutors in 1948 into Italy, where the Catholic Bishop Hudal, by Stangl's own assertion, supplied false paper to Brazil.

Stangl was only one of many of the Hitler elite whose flight from justice was made possible by an anti-Semitic clergy.

STATUTES OF VALLADOLID

warned Spanish Christians against food-poisoning by Jewish merchants (1412).

STELLVERTRETER

This German translation of "the Vicar" has become a personal cognomen for Pius XII, the Pope who refused to lend his high office and supreme moral authority over all Roman Catholics in defense of the one million children and five million adults being scientifically exterminated in German ghetto camps. He was the first to know of the immensity of the crime since more than one third of the German officers, Gestapo and SS men involved in the apprehending, transportation and gassing were, like Hitler himself, of the Catholic faith.

When Catholic clergymen, officers and high-ranking civilians in the east of Europe reported the gruesome details of German anti-Semitic atrocities, such as choking Jewish women and children to death in sealed cattle cars, Pope Pius XII refused to see the bearers of such news and brushed aside pleas from Italian friends of the Vatican and some of his conscience-stricken cardinals and bishops.

He, the Vicar of Christ, would not even allow Church periodicals to report the deeds of the Nazis in their ghetto camps. (He did, however, throughout the same period permit the publication of vile anti-Semitic essays on "Jewish decadence" by Catholic Nazi writers.)

He would not ask German Catholics to refrain from bayoneting or gassing Jewish women and children because —mark the Vicar's pastoral tact!—any such admonition "could create in the German Catholic soldier pangs of conscience that might interfere with the war effort."

He would not make an appeal to Chancellor Hitler for pity because "that might worsen the position of the Jews." (How the position of a Jewish woman or child being asphyxiated in a gas chamber could be worsened is beyond any man's imagination.)

Finally, any public or private remonstrances expressed to the German Ambassador in Rome would mean a breach of Vatican neutrality in the war!

This Pope, on repeated occasions breached Vatican

neutrality, but always in protest against the Allies, never against Hitler.

The Pope did intervene directly through his German bishops, and successfully so, to save the lives of thousands of mentally and physically disabled Catholics who had been doomed to a "mercy death" by Nazi decree. He was also instrumental in saving the lives of thousands of Catholics of Jewish origin, converts who were already in the hands of the Gestapo.

But he would not cry out in behalf of a Jewish Jew, even if such persons were taken in front of his very eyes, from the Jewish ghetto in Rome. The majority of Jewish victims taken by the Germans in Rome were women and children. The men joined the partisans in the hills; the old and the women remained with their children, certain that the saintly men of the Vatican, at whose very steps they cowered, would prevent the garroting of the helpless.

Monstrous conquerors of history, hot with the fury of war, have disdained murdering women and children. But the Germans did not. And the hand of the Pope was raised, not to stop the butchery of the innocent, but to bless the German Ambassador, Weizsäcker, who was leaving the Holy See to report gleefully to Herr Ribbentrop: "Although under pressure from all sides, the Pope has not let himself be drawn into any censure of the deportation of Jews from Rome."

Such is the tragic role played by the Vicar of Christ. Yet let not Protestants turn away, satisfied that history chose the guilty one outside their ranks. The Protestant bishops bore no lighter a mark of Cain than the Vatican. They were no less prompt to ring their churchbells when the last Jew in their see was dragged away to oblivion. They, too, glorified Hitlerism at its festivals and victory celebrations.

Look at the photographs of their participation and note the cheerful expressions on their faces! They enjoyed the Hitler happenings and still keep their memory fresh. Faces don't lie, and the faces of Protestant as well as

Catholic clergymen of the Brown Decade display not the benign smile of the gentle Jew Jesus but the arrogant grin of Lucifer.

STOECKER, ADOLF (b. 1835)

Demagogical court preacher of Kaiser Wilhelm I at Berlin, member of the Prussian Diet, and professed "Christian Socialist." He successfully used Lutheran as well as Catholic teachings to direct the German workingman's resentment of the rising power of industry and capitalism against the Jew.

The bankers and industrial Junkers were more than pleased to find in the peddler or storekeeper Jew of Prussia and Bavaria a ready-made scapegoat for their own immensely grown money power.

Pastor Stoecker, with a few well-placed references to the Jewish "moneychangers" of the Gospels and the "thirty pieces of silver" paid to Judas, and the occasional naming of a few known Jewish bankers (e.g., the Rothschilds), knew how to gull a populace apprehensive of the new industrial revolution, to make the average German feel that he needed protection, not from the unnamed new class of money barons and steel magnates, but rather from the "international banker Jew."

Two renowned historians of Stoecker's time, taking a leaf from the pastor's homily, provided detailed dissertations on his simple logic: "The Jew be burned." They were Heinrich von Treitschke and Theodor Mommsen.

In the footsteps of the professors followed thousands of eager students, who made a veritable science out of anti-Semitism. When Adolf Hitler came to power in 1933, the university libraries of Germany could boast of over two thousand volumes on the exciting subject of "Jew Hatred: Why and How." Even foreign countries were affected by this sinful pseudo-historicism, pseudo-economics and pseudo-literature.

While the anti-Semitic passion originated in the Church,

166

as time went on, propagandists, teachers, artists, and writers, who had not been in a church since baptism joined in lambasting the Jewish character. Many had left their churches long ago, rejecting both the ritual and teaching, but one thing ecclesiastic remained with them: anti-Semitism. They could no longer say the Paternoster, but the hundred anti-Jewish sentences from the New Testament stuck in their minds like sharp nails. Of the dogma of their church they retained little, if anything, except a feeling: The Jew is evil, bloodthirsty, God-killing, money-changing, deceitful (Judas).

Little did they know or care, including the ever-lying clerics, that this brew of hate they were stirring would poison the hearts of their people and one day lead them to massacre a million little children and five million hapless adults of the faith that was holy to Jesus, His mother and father.

In America the billionaire Henry Ford complained that the Jews were money-minded. In England the Cliveden set, which lived in the company of call girls, horse races and night clubs, criticized the Jews for being parasites. In France General Pétain, who betrayed the arms and very soul of his fatherland, attacked the Jews for being internationalists. In Russia Stalin, who drank blood brotherhood with Ribbentrop and Hitler, killed the Jews by the thousands for planning to sell out Communism. In Italy Mussolini, whose titled bankers controlled 90 percent of industry and land holdings, raged against the Jews monopolizing industry. And in Austria Cardinal Innitzer stated with the whole weight of his office as a prince of the Church that the Jews were not to be regarded as citizens of the state.

It seems that every anti-Semite attacks the Jews for his own worldly failings.

STRASBOURG

On St. Valentine's Day (1349) all the Jews in this town were burned alive on their cemetery grounds. The charge, propagated by the clergy, was poisoning Christian wells.

STREET CLEANING

and stable cleaning by Jews on certain days of the month, made compulsory by the ecclesiastical government in Mazara and other cities of Sicily, was discontinued on May 22, 1327, with the abolition of ecclesiastic rule on the island.

Again, the Nazi Germans took an old page from Catholic practice in compelling Jewish citizens, including war veterans and invalid women, to scrub streets and sidewalks with their bare hands.

STUYVESANT, PETER (1592-1672)

Dutch colonial Governor of New Amsterdam, who tried to deport Jewish refugees from the terrors of the Brazilian Inquisition back whence they came because "They are hateful enemies and blasphemous of the name of Christ." (Letter to the West India Company, September 22, 1654.)

SUAREZ, FRANCISCO (1548-1617)

Foremost Spanish Jesuit theologian, who placed "any familiarity with Jews" under strict prohibition; that it should be forbidden to enter a Jewish home; that no Jewish physician might be consulted; that Christians might not bathe with Jews; and that Christian women might not nurse Jewish infants. He also advocated that the Jews should be prohibited from erecting synagogues; that at Passover time they should not be permitted to leave their homes; that the books of the Talmud should be banned.

Suárez was greatly encouraged by Pope Paul V. His influence among Catholic seminarians of the Old and New Worlds is still immense.

SUNDAY SCHOOL

is the fountainhead of the flow of anti-Semitic sentiment. From a current children's text widely used by a major Christian denomination:

"Do not use the expression: "Wicked soldiers with ill-treating Jesus.' Children might identify soldier with wicked. The teacher should not talk of 'wicked soldiers' but 'wicked Jews.' " (*Christian Beliefs and Anti-Semitism*, Glock and Stark.)

From the Sunday school test of the Lutheran Church, Missouri Synod, U.S.A., 1955:

"Give proof that the curse which the Jews called upon their nation still rests on them *and their children* to this very day."

These are just two examples of numerous statements of similar and worse character.

T

TALMUD

The banning of Talmudic literature in the Justinian Christian Code (sixth century) served as a precedent for later accusations by anti-Semites against the "malicious" canon of the Jew.

TECUARA

Anti-Semitic youth group in present-day Argentina, "operating" with strong support of local Catholic clergy.

169

TISO, MSGR. JOZEF (1887-1947)

Catholic priest, leader of the Slovak Nationalist movement. After Munich, Msgr. Tiso became Premier of autonomous Slovakia. A year later, when the Nazis occupied the truncated shell of the Czechoslovak state, he became President of the "independent" Slovak Republic—"independent" by the grace of Hitler. In emulation of his master, the Monsignor promptly inaugurated a vehement anti-Semitic program in his puppet domain.

TISZA ESZLAR

In this Hungarian town in 1882 a Catholic priest instigated a trial of Jews for ritual blood drinking. This time the prosecution failed; Christianity could no longer employ torture.

TOLEDO

The third council convened in this Spanish city in 589 prohibited Jews from owning Christian slaves, marrying Christian women, or holding any public office. Gregory (saint), the reigning pope, congratulated the assembly on its holy stand against "Jewish perfidy." (Nuremberg Law in its first form.)

TOLLS

See *Judenzoll.*

TOMBSTONES

Jewish cemeteries in Germany, Austria and Poland were ripped off the consecrated grounds and used for military construction as well as for paving streets by the Nazi authorities.

As with many other outrages, the National Socialists

170

had a precedent in the action of Pope Urban VIII (1623-1644) who forbade the Jews to place tombstones on the graves of their beloved. The Pope also ordered all Jewish gravestones ripped out and used in the erection of a city wall.

TORDESILLAS, JUAN DE

This Bishop of Segovia in Spain in 1410 had scores of Jews arrested and executed for breaking consecrated wafers. His vindictiveness knew no bounds. The beautiful synagogue was finally "transformed" into the church of Corpus Christi.

Christians have a talent for creating houses of worship by putting the flock with the Star of David underground and sprinkling holy water on the altar. The latest such transformation occurred in 1966 in Coesfeld, Germany. The synagogue, which escaped Nazi arson during the *Kristallnacht,* has become "Christuskirche" as of this writing.

TORQUEMADA, TOMAS

Dominican confessor of Queen Isabella, who was appointed Inquisitor General of Spain in 1483. Pope Sixtus IV granted permission for secular trials with two Dominicans in charge. The Spanish Inquisition was perhaps the most cynical plot in the black history of Catholicism, aimed at expropriating the property of well-to-do Jews and converts in Spain, for the benefit of the royal court and the Church. Even dead "suspects" had their bones dug up for "trial" so estates could be confiscated from their heirs.

TORTOSA

Site of the most spectacular dialogue, in 1413, between papal representatives and selected rabbis, where the Church held all the aces, including torture screws, the garrote and

the torch, with the Jews facing the alternative of either dying spiritually through conversion by an abominable religious clique or dying physically on the pyre.

TOULOUSE

In this French town during the Middle Ages the Jews received a blow on the face each "Good Friday" for killing Jesus. In some other towns special mallets were distributed by the worshipers as a Holy Week ritual signifying the need for punishing the Jewish God killers.

For centuries the local clergy considered this a good way for their flocks to work off "understandable anger." The practice of Good Friday beatings persisted in smaller communities of Europe unti! the nineteenth century.

TOUSSENEL, ALPHONSE (1803-1885)

Like Karl Marx and Charles Fourier, a "socialist" anti-Semite, he built his case against the Jews on the little legend in the Gospels which depicts the Jews as moneychangers in the Temple.

The Christian churches had so belabored this point, that while nine out of ten Jews were little more than penniless laborers, artisans or peddlers in East Europe, North Africa and the Middle East, Toussenel, like Karl Marx, steadfastly repeated the Christian theme that the Jews were a grasping international group of Christ killers, bent on world hegemony, and therefore each and every one responsible for the sins of all, in space as well as time.

Toussenel noted that the admitted persecution and execution of Jews and their families was to be accepted with satisfaction as just punishment for their unredeemable guilt and as revenge for their arrogant hate of Christian mankind.

He only voiced what had been the Christian attitude from Chrysostom to Pius XII, from Luther to the German Conference of Protestant Bishops.

172

TOYNBEE, ARNOLD J.

Contemporary English High Church historian, who finds comfort in declaring Jewish martyrdom to be the "deadly recoil on Jewish heads of the shedding of Jesus' blood." The gassing of a million Jewish children in the twentieth century is a "just historic consequence" of an ancestral "crime" of the first century!

Hitler, like the Emperor Titus, appears as the avenging angel of the Lord.

A similar theme is to be found in *A Classical Dictionary* by John Lemprière, D.D., first published in 1788. Here is what the English Doctor of Divinity has to say about the Roman Emperor's destruction of Jerusalem:

"Some authors have reflected with severity upon the cruelties which Titus exercised against the Jews; but though certainly a disgrace to the benevolent features of his character, we must consider him as an instrument in the hands of Providence, exerted for the punishment of a wicked and infatuated people."

Lemprière's dictionary ran through many editions and was widely used in English schools well into the twentieth century, so it may be that Professor Toynbee came upon his deadly cliché ready-made.

TREITSCHKE, HEINRICH VON

Demagogue of nineteenth century Germany, who directed deep-set religious anti-Semitic tendencies into social and economic channels by clever journalistic appeals. He was a pre-Hitler protagonist of the Big Lie. Whatever problem he discussed, Treitschke ended his essays with: "The Jews are our trouble."

TRENT

A famous ritual murder case took place in this Italian town in 1473. A three-year-old boy, Simon, was found dead

in the Adige River during Holy Week. The Franciscan friar Bernardinus (sanctified, of course, by the Vatican), a follower of another saint, Bernardinus of Siena, who had warned that the Jews were planning to destroy Christianity through their physicians, incited the mob to bloody excesses after having *predicted* the murder. The Jews of Trent were tried by the bishop. All were burned.

A few years ago the present Bishop of Trent, after having the case thoroughly studied and examined by a legate, publicly admitted the grievous error of the Church in convicting the Jews of Trent. The two murderous Franciscans are still on the holy roster with the rest of the unholy brothers.

We have had in modern times a recurrence of the physician phobia of Saint Bernardinus. Stalin, a former theology student, accused Jewish doctors of planning to destroy Communism by poisoning its leaders.

The Trent trial gave a great impetus to scores of equally false accusations throughout Europe. See also *Vampires*.

TRZECIAK, STANISLAS

Originally professor at the *Catholic Academy of St. Petersburg* during the Nazi era in Warsaw. A malevolent anti-Semite, he pointed out to the Polish clergy the importance of the Jew-baiting encyclical letter of Pope Benedict XIV, who in the eighteenth century enforced Medieval restrictions on the God killers. Prelate Trzeciak in a pastoral letter exclaimed that to fight the Jews was not only a privilege but the duty of every Catholic. Hitler quoted this letter repeatedly.

U

UKRAINIAN ANTI-SEMITISM

in modern years found its theoretician in the executive member of the Communist Academy of Sciences of Kiev, Profim K. Kichko. In his book, *Judaism Without Embellishment,* published by the Academy of Sciences, Kichko, draw-

174

ing all his arguments from the vast reservoir of Eastern Orthodoxy, declared the Jews to be morally inferior (they betrayed Christ), politically unreliable (they hate the Christian environment) and aiming for control over their Christian comrades.

Significantly, Kichko illustrated his work with anti-Semitic cartoons taken from Church literature of the Czarist period. Kichko has never been removed from his academic position as directing anthropologist at the Kiev University.

UNITED STATES OF AMERICA

is the only one of the Christian nations that never tolerated the torturing, burning, decapitating or hanging of Jews because of their faith. This is simply because the Christian churches in this country never had a right over the life and limb of any resident. Where the Christian churches have wielded power and authority, the Jew has lived under a never-ending threat of religious aggression.

A great number of American colleges are "church-affiliated," however, and therefore prone to anti-Semitism. They refuse to accept Jewish teachers, while employing Christians of any and all denominations. For instance, Agnes Scott College of Atlanta, Georgia, has never in its 78-year history had a Jewish person on its faculty, a record which this Presbyterian institution blandly acknowledges.

This personnel policy, like that of Nazi Germany, is drawn from the rich source of traditional Christian anti-Semitism. I suppose Christ would be rejected as a faculty member, should he apply to the good Presbyters.

The exclusion which has its origin in doctrinal intolerance has also spread to social institutions. A checkup conducted by the Anti-Defamation League in 1966 brought to light that of 505 American country clubs interrogated, 498 would not accept Jewish members—this, after a year of "ecumenism."

USURY

It has been the calculated practice of anti-Semites to charge the Jews with exactly the deed or misdeed they were themselves perpetrating.

Hitler, who sought and almost gained world conquest, charged the Jews with a conspiracy for world control; Henry Ford, who amassed the largest fortune one man has ever possessed, charged the Jews with being money-mad; Queen Isabella of Spain and her consort, who clutched all Spain and more lands than they could manage to their insatiable bosoms, accused the Jews of greed; and Stalin, who spread his spider fingers over the whole globe, denounced the Jewish people for "internationalism."

Who charged the Jews with usury? Let's look at the record.

First, the Catholic Church.

By adopting the legal code of the Hebrews prohibiting any charge for the use of money, Pope Leo I in 443 made the Torah part of the Catholic canon. The ancient Hebrews —shepherds, peasants and fishermen—considered any loan an act of charity, and you don't charge for charity.

The Catholic authorities dominant in all countries prior to the American and French revolutions, tried vainly to apply this Hebrew rule of neighborly generosity to a growing commercial economy, and failed.

In their dilemma the secular rulers of Europe hit upon an obvious way around the prohibition of "interest": "Let the Jews act as the interest brokers; they are not bound by the Catholic canon, neither are they bound by the Hebrew canon in dealing with Christians."

So the Jews became the funnel through which the small but important trade and financial operations were carried on through the Middle Ages. The word "usury" was only used when the Christian creditor, invariably a noble or court personage, was in financial distress and wanted an out. Then king, queen, and feudal lord deserted their "court

Jew" and sacrificed him to the mob, with the clergy sounding the necessary anti-Semitic "slogans." It was easy at such times to raise the cry of "Defamer of the host! Vampire, feeding on Christian children's blood! Poisoners of wells! Bringer of the plague! Friend of the Mongols and Saracens! Spitter on the crucifix!"—once the monks and priests began their baying, the pack broke loose.

"Usurer!" was only a minor charge in the hunting call. The word "usurer" meant little to the common man. Up to the era of the French Revolution, the average European was a serf. He had nothing but his hands and, as a pair of hands, was fed enough to keep body and soul together and raise more hands. That ugly expression is still a leftover in our language: a farm hand, a mill hand. Nobody would lend anything to a farmer or artisan or laborer or miner or soldier or clerk. They had nothing, and were nothing until the French Revolution but a chattel of the lord.

However, the lords could profit from trade and manufacturing, and for these operations they needed literate people, people who could write and count; they themselves could not. And they needed men who would do their bidding as tax planners and tax collectors in trade and industry.

They needed more Jews. And they recruited more of them—until the next disaster. Of course, they charged interest for the use of money. The interest was large as the risk was large. In a way, the so-called "usurers" were actually "insurers" of the merchandise, ships and caravans. Since at least one out of every five ships or caravans would fail to return, because of piracy, brigandage, untamed waves or winds, the rates of the lenders were "usurious" by our standards.

Whatever they were, it was the lord's money and the lord's rate. The Jew was only his counselor, his financial adviser, his tax collector, his court Jew.

It is significant that in all the thousandfold expulsions and killings of Jews in the thousand years of the Middle

Ages it was the clergy that inspired the violence and vindictiveness, hardly ever the secular authorities.

And after the expulsion, whatever Jews were found wandering over the dirt roads of Christian Europe were desperately called back by the lords and mayors; they could not manage without the knowledge and planning of the Jews.

The Jew of the Middle Ages was always like a gypsy, close to his wagon. He never knew when some fanatical monk would raise the old cry: "Burn the Christ killers!"

If one town expelled the Jews, they thanked the Lord for the blessing of their life. They pushed on in the darkness of the night, in the ruts of the little-used roads, using their skills whenever and wherever a town or village permitted.

The guilds would not admit them. The Church prohibited all personal contact. Yet the Jews were the artisans of the Middle Ages.

The Jews made horseshoes, nails and plows for the peasants.

The Jews made pots and pans for the women. They made cloaks and doublets for the men. They brewed beer and distilled brandy.

The Jews were dyers and weavers, furriers and stonecutters, engravers and glaziers, shoemakers and saddlers.

They were illuminators of books, armorers and calligraphers.

The Jews lived in small towns where they could serve the people and be out of the eye of the Church hierarchy. And still they could not escape the wrath of the black-clothed ministers of Christ.

The Jew and his pack became proverbial, the wandering Jew a legend. But not a legend of the glory of God, a legend of the vindictiveness in man.

VAMPIRES

The Jews as vampires, ritually ingesting the blood of Christian children, is a lurid image strenuously publicized in the past as well as in the present by the Catholic Church.

Vampire accusations against the Jews were first made at the behest of the early Church Fathers in the fourth century, a take-off from a Roman accusation against the early Christians, based on their claim that the Sacrament of the Holy Eucharist involved the real blood of Christ. The charge was repeated for the next fifteen hundred years, leading to ritual-murder trials, torture confessions and the burning of Jews.

Numerous pogroms took place in nineteenth century Russia because the Orthodox clergy accused Jews of blood drinking. Large-scale trials were instigated by the Church in Saratov (1857) and Kutais (1878). The last (Beiliss) trial took place in 1911 at Kiev.

As late as 1881 the official Jesuit journal, *La Civiltà Cattolica,* published a series of articles impugning Jews as vampires: "Such atrocious Hebrew deeds must be founded on some fact, because they excited so much anger of the people."

In an issue of 1892 (No. 8434), joining *Civiltà Cattolica* and other leading Catholic periodicals, the official Vatican newspaper, *Osservatore Romano,* editorialized on the "irrefutable evidence of ritual murder perpetrated by Jews in obedience to the Talmud."

This insinuation was echoed ten years later by a literary organ of the high Anglican Church. In 1911, at the beginning of the Czarist judicial frame-up of the Jew Mendel Beiliss, when the voices of the whole liberal and non-Christian civilized world were raised in protest, the *Oxford and Cambridge Review* called for a ritual trial! The editors were not certain, so they stated, that Jews did not kidnap Christian children and drink their blood at Passover services.

Thus the Church kept the legend of the blood-drinking Jew alive—and ready for the venomous pens of Nazi propagandists, such as Julius Streicher. In his hate-sheet, *Der Stürmer,* Streicher published serial excerpts from Church-inspired ritual murder trials, including the infamous one held at the Italian city of Trent in 1475. Following is one of Streicher's historical gems:

"Also the numerous confessions made by the Jews show that the execution of ritual murders is a law of the Talmud Jew. The former chief rabbi (and later monk) Teofiti declares that the ritual murders take place especially on the Jewish Purim (in memory of the Persian murders) and Passover (in memory of the murder of Christ). The rules are as follows: The blood of the victims is to be tapped by force. On Passover it is to be used in wine and matzos. Thus a small part of the blood is to be poured into the dough of matzos and into the wine. The mixing is done by the head of the Jewish family.

"The procedure is as follows: The family head empties a few drops of the fresh and powdered blood into a glass, wets the fingers of the left hand with it, and sprays (blesses) with it everything on the table. The head of the family then says, 'Thus we ask God to send the ten plagues to all enemies of the Jewish faith.' Then they eat, and at the end the head of the family exclaims, 'May all Gentiles perish, as the child whose blood is contained in the bread and wine.'

"The fresh (or dried and powdered) blood of the slaughtered is further used by young married Jewish couples, by pregnant Jewesses, for circumcision, and so on. Ritual murder is recognized by all Talmud Jews. The Jew believes he absolves himself thus of his sins."

In the early years of Nazism its propagandists at Jewish Easter times, would publish a "warning to the German and Austrian people" to keep their children indoors because of ritual "requirements" of the Jews. (Similar charges that Jews drank the blood of Christian children were re-

180

peated in *The Fascist,* a British paper published prior to World War II.)

Here lies the secret of anti-Semitic brutality, perpetrated directly or indirectly by most of the German Nazis: to the Christian German and Austrian, the Jew was a sinister, vicious killer.

Punishing those "killers," the Christian German considered not a sin but rather his duty. German troops, who might hesitate to brutalize a French or Danish child, would, with the equanimity of their Christian consciences drive a million Jewish children to a ghastly death in the execution chamber.

*

To the astonishment of all, especially the Church, Archbishop Alessandro Gottardi of Trent in Italy acknowledged in October, 1965 the innocence of the Jews in the death of "Little Saint Simon of Trent." In 1475 twelve Jews had been executed for the crime after indescribable tortures to make them all confess.

The research to clear the unfortunate Jewish victims was conducted by the Reverend P. Eckert and appeared in the *Trentine Studies of Historical Science.* Upon publication of this extensive study, the Congregation of Rites forbade the veneration of relics or saying of Masses in Simon's name.

Father Eckert's conclusion after years of examination of the "evidence" in the archives of Trent, Rome and Vienna is that the trial of Trent had ended in judicial murder.

In spite of repeated requests by Jewish and liberal spokesmen, Pope Paul VI refused to open the hundreds of similar assassinations of Jews as vampires to the critical eyes of objective researchers. Thus the monstrous accusations against the Hebrew people will remain enshrined in the history books, chapels, monuments, and hagiography of the Church. The vampire Jew lives on in Catholic Europe to haunt the dreams of Christian children and childish women and men.

181

VATICAN APPOINTEES

Cardinals, Bishops and sundry Prelates within the Nazi domain were far from neutral or silent onlookers of the "Brown Scene."

Already the Concordat of Collaboration of July 20, 1933, entered into by Dr. Pacelli of the Vatican and the Hitler Government (article 30) ordered that on all Sundays and Holidays in all Churches of the Reich the religious services be concluded with a prayer for the "National Socialist Realm." Cardinal Faulhaber of Munich delivered a sermon in 1936 claiming the Pope to be the best, perhaps the only friend of the new "German Reich."

On June 23, 1950, at the "Catholic Day" at Bonn Cardinal Frings, of Cologne, as first German Prelate, demanded the rearmament of Hitler Germany. As late as 1967 Frings was involved in anti-Semitic utterances.

In June 1933 Germany's Catholic bishops published a communal pastoral letter which emphasized: "We German Bishops do not wish to underestimate or even hinder the 'National Resurgence' of the New Reich." Thus, individually and by hand, underwrote all German Cardinals, Archbishops and Bishops in 1933, the year of Hitler's ascension.

On August 1933 Archbishop Gröber, who later joined the Nationalist Socialist Party as a regular member, ordained: "I see no obstacle in placing the Nazi Flag and the Hooked Cross into the sanctuary of every Catholic Church."

On July 10th of the same year Bishop Vogt of Aachen promised by telegram to cooperate with the New Order.

Bishop Berning of Osnabrück declared all German Prelates would support Hitler's State with "warm love and all their power." Bishop Bornewasser of Trier exclaimed: "With head high and strong step will we enter the New Order and serve it with all our strength and soul."

Bishop Burger asserted: "The aims of the Hitler Reich are since long ago the aims of the Catholic Church (sic!)."

Prelate Steinmann of Berlin deliriously yelled: "Our

chancellor was called by God Himself." Cardinal Faulhaber implored the American Cardinals Hayes of New York and Mundelein of Chicago (1934) to stop the libelling of Hitler in the American press. Faulhaber wrote at the same time to the new chancellor: "Your handclasp with the Vatican implies the greatest moral deed of history, a majestic achievement and innumerable blessings."

In June 1936 Bishop Berning inspected the Concentration Camps of Emsland. The good Bishop praised the diligence of Himmler (sic!) and said: "All those who doubt the future of the New Germany should be brought here."

In 1937 Archbishop Gröber published a "Handbook of Religious Problems of the Day," in which widely quoted Catholic theologians emphasize "Hitler's Reich as a State of Law and Order and as a Defense of European Culture."

On March 12, 1938, the Catholic hierarchy of Austria, under the leadership of Cardinal Innitzer, welcomed Hitler's invading troops with ringing of all church bells and placing of Hooked Cross Nazi Flags at the church altars and gates.

Archbishop Weitz of Salzburg published on March 28, 1938, a "Solemn Declaration" that the thousand year long yearning of the Austrian Church had been fulfilled with the advent of Hitler in Austria.

In the same year the Bishops Conference in Fulda sent Hitler a congratulatory telegram on the capitulation of the Czech government at the same time ordering all Church bells to ring the next Sunday.

In every Catholic Diocese Hitler's 50th birthday was celebrated with the Praying of the "Pater Noster," bell ringing and raising of Nazi Flags before the Altar.

Archbishop Jäger of Paderborn called the war against the allies a struggle in defense of Christianity; Bishop Rackl of Eichstätt referred to Hitler's attacks as a holy crusade and Bishop Galen expressed again and again hope for a German victory.

In the war against the allies the Austrian archbishop Ferdinand von Seckau spoke (1944) of Hitler's "heroic deeds," and Archbishop Kolb of Bamberg cried: Behind

183

our army of soldiers stands an army of devotionally praying Germans. (January 31, 1944.) Further Kolb: *"Christ expects that obedient as He was we too willingly take upon us the Cross."*

So wrote a Catholic Bishop in 1944 of the Beast of Berlin, killer of a million Jewish children.

VATICAN LINE

This was the name given a group of Catholic clerics in Rome, led by Bishop Alois Hudal, who in the early years after Hitler's war helped Nazi elite members, among them Eichmann, to escape to Argentina. The Vatican Line ceased functioning in 1949.

Bishop Alois Hudal, Rector of the German Church in Rome during the Hitler era, called the Nuremberg Laws "unavoidable countermeasures" against "alien" elements.

VENGEANCE

"This is a time for vengeance on the Jewish serfs and vagabonds for what they did to our Lord Jesus. Let us stamp out their houses and their brood and burn their synagogues and talmuds."—Martin Luther

"Let us take vengeance on the Jewish beasts for what they did to German folkdom and pitilessly wipe out the foul brood."—General von Reichenau, 1941

VENICE

On December 3, 1943, the Cardinal Patriarch of Venice lodged a complaint with the German Consul General that the Italian authorities had failed to arrest all Jews in their drive to segregate non-Aryans. The cordial wish and desire of the Patriarch was to have all Jews behind ghetto bars to assure their extermination once and for all.

VESPASIAN

The Roman Caesar threw legion after legion into the war against the Jews. He pleaded with them, as did his son Titus, for a token surrender, guaranteeing their freedom except for the minimum of Roman sovereignty and Caesar's bust in the vestry.

The Jews had accepted the rule of their land by foreign despots backed by overwhelming power, but never desecration of their Temple. They would rather see it go up in flames, and they did.

And these were the same Jews who are supposed to have traded cows and sheep in their house of worship! So says the Gospel spread by Roman Bishops to discredit the Jews, who would rather give up their souls than their faith.

The Catholics thus marked the Jews as godless moneychangers. But the only change made by the Jews of Jerusalem was into armor. And so died a half-million men that their God might live.

VICHY FRANCE

The *Semaine Religieuse* of the d'Evreux diocese, at the request of regional propaganda staff officials, agreed to publish a communique justifying the Vichy measures taken against the Jews, using a similar edict of Pope Paul IV as their justification.

VIENNA

On March 12, 1421, Duke Albrecht V of Austria had 210 Jews, men, women and children, burned alive for refusal to accept conversion to Christianity. For decades thereafter, the Jews called Austria "Bloodland." Little did they know that five hundred years later the Austrians would kill and burn a thousand times this many Jews, with Cardinal Innitzer blessing the dominant hooked cross.

In 1610 the medical faculty at the Catholic University

of Vienna announced that every Jewish physician was bound by his faith to kill every tenth Christian patient.

Bishop Kollonitsch of Vienna "inspired" the destruction of the great synagogue in his city. After the expulsion of all the Viennese Jews by Leopold I on July 25, 1670, St. Margaret's Church was erected on the ruins of the Hebrew temple, following the thousand-year-old precedent established by the clergy.

As late as 1760 Empress Maria Theresa of Austria ordered that all Jews wear a yellow badge on their left arm. Hitler's Gauleiter repeated this Catholic order almost two hundred years later.

W

WANDERING JEW

Legendary figure who taunted Christ on the way to Golgotha. As punishment, he was condemned to live without rest or end. He was reported alive in 1227 by no less an authority than an Armenian archbishop. This confirmation was widely hailed by the learned Catholic clergy of the time.

WELL POISONING

by Jews was an accusation given wide credence by Church authorities, especially in the fourteenth century. In 1348 the Jews of Provence were burned as well poisoners. In Germany they were even accused of poisoning the Christian air! The spread of leprosy was attributed to them, and suspects were tortured to provide "verification." In 1679 Abraham a Santa Clara accused the Jews of Venice of having "caused" the pestilence.

WET-NURSING

In 1205 Pope Innocent III, in a letter to the Bishop of Paris, accused the Jews of pouring the milk of Christian women nursing their children into latrines during Easter-

time. Christian women should therefore not enter the service of these hateful disbelievers.

A law prohibiting Christian women from serving as nurses in Jewish homes was promulgated in 1581 by Pope Gregory XIII in his bull *Antiqua Judaeorum*.

WHOSE HOLY CITY?

May, 1967, witnessed one of the most dramatic exhibitions of the persistent Christian gospel prejudice against the children of Israel. When fourteen Arab nations, with a population of over a hundred million bristling under Egyptian incitement, surrounded the little Jewish state with thousands of tanks, planes, cannons and missiles, they threatened the Jewish people in the Middle East not just with war, but with extermination.

"We shall liquidate the Jews," came the voice of Radio Amman; "After this war, there will be no Jewish survivors in Israel," echoed the commander of the Arab "Liberation Front," Achmed Shukairy; "We are prepared to annihilate Israel," exclaimed Jordan's King Hussein; "We shall destroy Israel," responded Nasser.

Yet, with all these public proclamations of impending genocide, in the United States of America not a single Christian clergyman, minister or priest, bishop or cardinal, raised his hand or voice to stop the expected slaughter of a small and ancient people!

The Christian churches maintained silence, the silence of a cemetery. The silence that prevailed when Hitler brutally proclaimed in print and spoken word: "I shall kill all Jews, men, women and children."

Shukairy, like Hitler, was outspoken and sincere in his hate which was amplified by modern communication media into apocalyptic thunder. The hellish intent of both was loud and clear, yet no Christian churchman heard their threat.

Yet, when tiny Israel gathered its forces and swiftly as the Dark Angel smote the war chariots of the Egyptians

187

with man and horse and wagon, *then,* and only then, did our Christian ministers of the Lord regain their hearing and sight—and voice! All over America they trumpeted: The Jews must leave all the occupied lands and especially, very especially so, the Old City of Jerusalem.

It was all right for the Moslem King of Jordan to have been master of the Holy City for twenty years, but no Jew should rule the city of Jerusalem!

These clergymen know that the democratic citizens of Israel will certainly govern the old city with keener judgment than any Arab sheikh, but it seems no Christian clergyman can stand by silently while the anti-Semitic pronouncements of the New Testament, of the eternal banishment of the Jews from the Holy Land, are brought to nought; none can bear to see the city of Jerusalem, where "no stone be left upon the other," reborn and glorified, as never before, by Jewish hands.

To the custodians of the biased books of the New Testament, the land and faith of the Jew is accursed, and must remain thus in eternity as "just" punishment for *the* Jews' guilt of Jesus' crucifixion.

The New Testament demands the Jew to be a pariah forever, and the coming glory of an all-Jewish Jerusalem is a curse and blasphemy to the upholders of this Testament.

Could it be that the hate of the Jew is the core of the New Testament, deeper than the tepid "love of mankind" professed so often, but so selectively?

"The Jew may not rule the Holy City." This fiat, sent out by the Vatican when Israeli soldiers were still at the gate of the old city, was echoed by the Protestant World Council of Churches and the sundry Orthodox Patriarchs and Coptic dignitaries.

One truth they all tremble to face: If Israel holds the Holy City, then the great message of the gospel, the "guilt" of the Jew and his perennial punishment, is rendered patently false and comes back on the heads of the Church fathers, past and present, who have propagated it for 1800 years.

WORMS

The whole Jewish population of this German town was killed by the first Crusader bands, incited by such preachers as Peter the Hermit, a saintly figure in all Catholic history books.

Y

YELLOW BADGE

See *Gelbe Fleck*.

Z

ZENO, SAINT

Bishop of the fourth century, who bewailed the circumstance that when inspired monks invaded Jewish homes and killed the resisting inhabitants, they burned only the corpses. He meant that the Jews still living also should have been given to the flames for the greater glory of Jesus.

Selected Bibliography of Readily Available Documentation

Adler, H. G., *Die Juden in Deutschland: Von der Aufklärung bis zum Nationalsozialismus*
Andics, Hellmut, *Der Ewige Jude: Ursachen und Geschichte des Antisemitismus*
Baum, Gregory, *Is the New Testament Anti-Semitic?*
Berdyaev, Nicolas, *Christianity and Anti-Semitism*
Bernstein, Peretz F., *Jew-Hate As a Sociological Problem*
Blumenkranz, Bernhard, *Le Juif Médiéval au Miroir de l'art Chrétien*
Buchheim, Hans, *Das Dritte Reich*
Celnik, Max and Isaac, *A Bibliography on Judaism and Jewish-Christian Relations*
Cohn, Norman, *Warrant for Genocide*
Corsten, W., *Kölner Aktenstücke zur Lage der katholischen Kirche in Deutschland* 1933-1945
Coudenhove-Kalergi, Count Heinrich, *Anti-Semitism Throughout the Ages*
Daane, James, *The Anatomy of Anti-Semitism and Other Essays on Religion and Race*
De Haas, Jacob, *The Encyclopedia of Jewish Knowledge*
Deschner, Karlheinz, *Das Jahrhundert der Barbarei*
————, *Mitt Gott und den Faschisten*
Duquesne, Jacques, *Les Catholiques français sous l'occupation*
Eckert, Willehad Paul, *Judenhass—Schuld der Christen?*
Esh, Benzion Dinur Shaul, *Yad Washem Studies on the European Jewish Catastrophe and Resistance*
Falconi, Carlo, *Das Schweigen des Papistes*
Flannery, Edward H., *The Anguish of the Jews*
Friedländer, Saul, *Auftakt zum Untergang*

―――, *Pius XII and the Third Reich*
Glock, Charles Y., and Stark, Rodney, *Christian Beliefs and Anti-Semitism*
Hargrove, Katharine T., *The Star and the Cross*
Hay, Malcolm, *Europe and the Jews: The Pressure of Christendom on the People of Israel for 1900 Years*
Heer, Friedrich, *Gottes erste Liebe*
Hegner, H. S., *Die Reichskanzlei 1933-1945*
Hilberg, Raul, *The Destruction of the European Jews*
Huss, Hermann, and Schröder, Andreas, eds., *Antisemitismus zur Pathologie der bürgerlichen Gesellschaft*
Hyamson, Albert M., and Silbermann, A. M., eds., *Vallentine's Jewish Encyclopaedia*
Isaac, Jules, *The Teaching of Contempt: Christian Roots of Anti-Semitism*
Katz, Robert, *Death in Rome*
Knight, George A. F., *Jews and Christians: Preparation for Dialogue*
Kuhner, Hans, *Encyclopedia of the Papacy*
Lebreton, Jules, and Zeiller, Jacques, *The History of the Primitive Church*
Lewy, Guenter, *Die katholische Kirche und das Dritte Reich*
Livingston, Sigmund, *Must Men Hate?*
Marcus, Jacob R., *The Jew in the Medieval World*
Marx, Karl, *A World Without Jews*
Mosse, Werner E., *Entscheidungsjahr 1932*
Müller, Hans, *Katholische Kirche und Nationalsozialismus*
Munck, J., *Christus und Israel*
Noller, Sonja, and von Kotze, Hildegard, *Faksimile— Querschnitt durch den Völkischen Beobachter*
Olson, Bernhard E., *Faith and Prejudice*
Parkes, James, *The Foundations of Judaism and Christianity*
Plaidy, Jean, *The Spanish Inquisition*
Poliakov, Léon, *The History of Anti-Semitism*
Poliakov, Léon and Wulf, Josef, *Das Dritte Reich und die Juden*
Raisin, Jacob S., *Gentile Reactions to Jewish Ideals*

191

Reck-Malleczewen, Friedrich Percyval, *Tagebuch eines Verzweifelten*

Roth, Cecil, *History of the Marranos*

Runes, Dagobert, D., *The Jew and the Cross*

Rynne, Xavier, *The Fourth Session: The Debates and Decrees of Vatican Council II, September 14 to December 8, 1965*

Sachar, Abram Leon, *A History of the Jews*

Samuel, Maurice, *Blood Accusation: The Strange History of the Beiliss Case*

Shirer, William L., *The Rise and Fall of the Third Reich: A History of Nazi Germany*

Silberner, Edmund, *Sozialisten zur Judenfrage: Ein Beitrag zur Geschichte des Sozialismus vom Anfang des 19 Jahrhunderts bis 1914*

Singer, Isidore, ed., *The Jewish Encyclopedia*

Synan, Edward A., *The Popes and the Jews in the Middle Ages*

Tetens, T. H., *The New Germany and the Old Nazis*